D0317997

To Debbie

Get Motivated

Be Wicked

Lots of love

Tributes to Derrick

From My Wife

I am married to a man who is multifaceted and super talented, who is open to what the world has to offer – and what he has to offer the world! His suitcase of life is so packed with experiences, it's a wonder the seams haven't burst!

His is not the typical rags to riches story. His journey, it seems, has just begun. I have had the immense pleasure of journeying with him for the last 25 years.

It has been a roller coaster of fun and happiness.

I gladly share him with many thousands of others, people from all walks of life, from all over the globe, and whose lives have been touched by this man and his enigmatic personality.

Journey with him as he tells his story, then you will know who he really is, and just what lies beneath his psychedelic leotards. This read will certainly open the many sides of my husband and best friend – Derrick.

…Love Palmer

From My Son

I want to tell the world how proud I am of my dad.

He means the world to me.

What is contained in these pages is an amazing story…

Put simply…my dad is the best man I know. He is always there when I need him. Despite being a pain in the backside, he is the most colourful, the strongest, and the most passionate person I know. He is a protector, a comforter, and an eternal optimist.

He's challenging, headstrong, ridiculously in shape, demanding and stubborn, and relentlessly driven.

He teases mercilessly, sleeps only four hours a night, is given to bouts of hunger followed by induced grumpiness, and he is a troublemaker. My dad is never ill, he's frugal, direct, loud and is the definitive show stealer.

My dad is a leader, impossible to ignore, loyal to a fault, nobody's fool, responsible, just, and has a real thing for stealing spoons.

My dad is the best man I know!

The story behind the Lycra
with television's

MR MOTIVATOR

THE
WARM
UP

The price of success is perseverance

DERRICK EVANS

Published by
Filament Publishing Ltd
16, Croydon Road, Waddon, Croydon
Surrey CR0 4PA, United Kingdom
Telephone +44(0)20 8688 2598
www.filamentpublishing.com

© Derrick Evans 2016

ISBN 978-1-910819-57-9

The right of Derrick Evans to be identified as
the author of this work has been asserted by him
in accordance with the Designs and Copyright Act 1988

All rights reserved. No portion of this book may be copied by any
means without the prior written permission of the publisher.

Printed by 4edge Limited

DEDICATION

To my dear wife Palmer,
my children: Abigail, James, Carolyne and Ebony,
and grandchildren: RJ, Daniel Hadassah and Karen.

For the joy that you have brought to my life.

THANKS

Thank you to Janey Burton for editing the book.

Table of Contents

Introduction: 2014

My agent called and wanted me to be in the UK to meet the staff of a development team from the BBC. I had been to many such meetings before and they followed a similar format, especially when to do with reality shows, and not one, in the end, had wanted me to be part of it. *I Am A Celebrity... Get Me Out Of Here!*, *Celebrity Big Brother...* After many interviews, the answer was that putting in the Motivator as part of the mix of celebrities would not work. Jo, the owner of the agency Talent4 Media, and I arrived at the BBC offices and met a group of people involved in what was to become a new prime time Saturday night show, using a mixture of gymnastics and circus skills. A celebrity would be paired with a professional gymnast and a British gymnastic coach, and over a period of eight weeks taught various skills from floor work and hanging from a hoop, to vaulting. It would be called *Tumble*.

We left the meeting to greet lots of people who had recognised Mr Motivator. I said my hellos, shook hands and took some photos, and then Jo and I stopped for a coffee and dissected what we had just heard – it was a great opportunity, and it could be just what we had been waiting for.

Should I take it? It would not be easy; I did have doubts as to whether we could change a body that had been set in its ways for the last 35 years. This body was fitter than most, but to make it into a strong and flexible gymnast? I had some doubts.

A week later, we received an offer. I would need to be in the UK for an extended period, and I had planned our usual timeshare holiday with Palmer and Abigail in Florida, so they would have to go without me. There might have been a possibility for me to take a break from training and then join them for part the week but I thought better of that suggestion when I saw the training schedule: I would fall way behind. Nine other celebrities would be involved and one alternate just in case something happened to any one of us.

I intended to go all the way to the final. This was a new challenge, an opportunity to relaunch myself.

Before any training, the BBC wanted me in the UK to undergo a physical and a medical. I flew up and sailed through a number of different exercises and disciplines from being suspended on a hoop, to a small dance routine. The medical was comprehensive but at the end of it, I was given a green light.

It wasn't long before a provisional training schedule arrived in Jamaica. There was a lot of preparation required, most of it prepared by Neil from BGA, focusing on developing core strength, and flexibility training. I found it tough going. My balance, upper body strength, shoulder and general flexibility were way off.

Echoing in my mind was one of the statements that I have said many times to others. "Listen to your body, don't overdo it, stop and rest often." I found myself in the lounge with a pillow for support trying headstands and handstands. YouTube was my buddy and I watched hours and hours, immersing myself in all that the very talented gymnasts could show and teach me.

Palmer looked on, shaking her head and reminding me how there was a time when she could do each move in a more dignified way. I plodded on; I was learning something new every week.

It reminded me of my early days when I got into fitness. The year was 1981 all over again, the only difference being that I am older now and this body – so accustomed to all that was required for aerobics, interval training, and so on – seemed uncomfortable when being asked to do gymnastics. Four weeks later, I arrived in the UK.

The training for this show was full on and I had a routine each day, with three hours of training. Up at 5 a.m., this was a time for me to have a warm up, a sequence of gentle moves aimed at raising my core temperature. After 30 minutes, I was beginning to sweat, then it was time for the ice pack on my knees and shoulder. It felt good.

Afterwards, the very hot shower was welcoming. I had always maintained that the best part of working out was that moment. But this early shower was for a different reason, more remedial; it was good for reducing the swelling and the aches I was feeling.

Then followed breakfast and into my car to be taken to any one of five different gymnastic venues. They did this to keep all celebrities apart. We all had different training times and various locations. It worked but it was a devil in terms of developing any continuity regarding usage of the same equipment.

Each day, Kerry, my professional gymnastic partner and my GB coach, went through all the elements that I was expected to perform on the live show. One day, it was floor work, from tumbling to lifting my very svelte partner. Once a week, it was the circus space, a place where aerial and circus skills were taught, and I was to be seen hanging from a round hoop suspended ten feet in the air.

I was having difficulty with the balance and the shapes that needed to be done with safety and accuracy in mind. My flexibility was being tested and I was failing abysmally.

These circus skills were challenging, though being suspended up in the air was something I relished, but the flexibility required in the shoulders was proving impossible and the physiotherapists, Karen and Chris, had to tape my shoulder back each day. My visit to the physio became a thrice-weekly attempt to keep my failing body together.

Things were going well and the compliments started to come in. Everyone was amazed, my lines were good and my team's spirits were high, and this filtered through to everyone we met.

The decision and creative folks at the BBC selected and allocated the choice of music costumes and choreography which highlighted the fun side of Motivator.

And so it came to dress rehearsal. Kerry and I had our final fitting for our costumes, and when our turn came for doing our floor work, we felt nervous but quietly confident. I was still aching, but we warmed up the best we could.

We walked into the studio that had been transformed into a giant gymnastic arena with a sprung floor. We had a run through: our timing was a little bit off, the lifts were not bad, but we got the feeling of what would be expected of our performance. We now knew where cameras would be, how to position ourselves for the best angles for applause and also where to stand at the end for a reaction from the judges.

We went for a take. It went well and we felt good knowing that we would still have at least another week to refine and make adjustments before the first live show.

After the take, we went back to the warm up area and did some stretching: we would have a little time until the dreaded vault, which in the event of a tie between the bottom two places, would be used to determine who stayed or left the competition.

I was called, but I did not feel warm. Alberto Cacace, the coach, positioned the trampette and he had a quiet word in my ear: focus on the strike with both feet, the flight pushes off landing. Before I knew it, I was running towards the vault. When landing, I over-rotated, but so as not to do any physical damage, I went into a forward roll, stood up and walked back to do it again.

I did not feel confident. In all previous practise sessions, I had felt better and missing my footing had never happened. Alberto tried to correct the fault in my mind. The atmosphere felt different, the trampette was not like the one I had practised on, but also I felt tight. I did not feel that I would be able to do better.

I hit the trampette with only one foot fully on and I was now taking off at an angle. I tried to correct my body alignment in flight. Both hands hit the box. I was about to land, but I was heading towards the edge of the mat. I landed on one leg and this was not good; I found myself sitting with my right leg bent. There were lots of people all around me; I was telling my right leg to move but it wouldn't. *Kerry, where are you? I am so sorry to have let you down. Forgive me.* I was tearful as the gas mask was being put on; they said it was like having a Gin & Tonic (how the hell would I know?). I was still trying to move my right leg with no joy.

I kept apologising to everyone for letting them down. I heard Karen, the physio, say, "Don't worry, you could still be in the show. Micky said it may not be as bad as it seems." I knew the signs, and the look on everyone's face told the story.

The gas was working as they straightened out my leg. The ambulance came and I joked that the competition had sabotaged me. I was examined and the verdict was a dislocation and a torn patellar tendon. I heard Micky from the BBC on the phone updating those who needed to know. The specialist, Dr Fazal, came to see me and said he would be only too happy to operate the next morning. He assured me that he had done this many times; he had a calming reassuring voice.

Barnet Hospital would have a new visitor as soon as they could sort out a room. I caused some trouble as they wheeled me into the X-ray room; people outside had recognised me and I made comments which made them laugh and made me feel a lot better.

Various technicians came in the next day and talked me through the procedures. In hospital for the next 72 hours, recovery up to 18 months: "not on your life," I heard myself say. Soon I was getting needles in my arm and then it was time to count backwards from 100.

I drifted… and I was receiving a call from *GMTV*; the year was 2009. I had been away from them for years, but the senior producer wanted to discuss my coming back to work on a New Year project.

It was to be a New Year, New You, *GMTV*-produced video showing the state of the nation in respect of obesity, and suggesting that this had all come about because of my being missing from UK television screens. Now there was only one person who could save the nation: Mr Motivator! I agreed on the basis that I would be allowed some say in the content and also that some things would be different this time. The PR department was put into overdrive. The wheel started all over again and I was caught up in the publicity machine of non-stop press interviews and newspaper articles. I announced on air that the Motivation Club had been set up to provide free information on fitness, health and nutrition, and within four weeks 250,000 people joined. Doctor Hilary was part of my team going round the country, dropping in on individuals who had changed their lives.

Did I want to be back? Well, I saw it as an opportunity to revisit the public and it would give me a new and wider audience.

But I knew that you could go back to a past relationship with willingness and the promise that things will be different. But it will not be long before it starts to return to how things were before.

The roadshow around the country was going well and audience figures were up, but was I different, or was it that it all felt the same as what I had wanted to get away from? I was not happy; I was feeling used and what happened next indicated to me that I should be in another place.

With Prime Minister Gordon Brown.

Someone decided that they needed someone else involved with me on-screen, so they brought in a lady who had been in a video that came out some years before, shot in a gym with one man and many scantily clad women thrusting and gyrating to *Call on Me* by Eric Prydz.

So it was that Deanne Berry came to join me on a Mediterranean cruise. We would visit a number of countries taking with us three women with a pear or apple shape, and we would transmit live into the main station information regarding eating habits, exercise and something of the Mediterranean diet.

On the very first morning, Deanne was in tears so she did not appear and I had to do the show on my own.

The cruise went ahead but I stifled my unhappiness. At the end of it, Deanne Berry went back to the career that she was determined to resurrect and I went into the regular morning routine with *GMTV*.

I was in conversation with Universal to do a new DVD. Terms were close to being agreed, and I worked on a format, music content and shooting location.

In the midst of my negotiations, I got a call from the *GMTV* production office asking if I would be interested in doing a new DVD. I said yes and that I did have a format in mind.

In a meeting with the then-editor in his office, he said he was prepared to offer me 12.5% of what they had negotiated with Universal.

I told him no, I wanted 70% and *GMTV* would get 30%. He looked at me blankly; he said that could not work and he would not budge from the offer. I said this DVD would be driven by my name and concept.

He said if I did not accept the offer, then I no longer would be with *GMTV*. I countered that I had proved that I had managed to survive without *GMTV*.

With that all said and done, I was shown the door. I had been right all along: never return to a relationship that has gone wrong.

Sometimes when things don't work out the way they should, I believe that there are deeper reasons afoot. In the same way, I know that every meeting is an opportunity. While I was back in Jamaica, an email came in from JML, the TV shopping channel. They wanted to do a DVD about rebounding, an exercise activity using a mini trampoline which I knew very little about, so before I gave a reply, I did some research.

The internet – what a vehicle! The answer was easy; it was a great exercise with many benefits. I was in and I wanted to do this, but before anything, I needed a bouncer. The day it arrived in Jamaica was an event. Nothing is never easy in JA – clearing it through customs, red tape, pay this person and that one. Eventually it arrived at home and it wasn't long, with my music and watching a few videos, I was bouncing away. It was great, and after a short time, I was sweating, and ten minutes later, I was feeling all the benefits. I longed for more.

They flew me to the UK for the signing of the agreement and filming the DVD that would be sold with the bouncer. They selected, with my approval, three on-screen models. We rehearsed the routine that I had put together, and then filmed it. It was a great day and things went very well.

Next was an infomercial called *Mr Motivator's Bouncefit*. A full team of production staff and models flew to Jamaica, together with a presenter to take part and interview me during the filming. We stayed at one of the most expensive hotels on the island, called The Palmyra, for four days of filming.

With perfect weather and a crew that knew what they were doing, everything went well. But we had one major problem: the bouncers were making noises the more we jumped on them. The legs, which were screwed on, began to splay outwards. We had to use new bouncers to get the job finished. I asked, "Are these bouncers fit for purpose? If they are to be sold, would we have a long-term problem?" I was reassured that would not be the case.

Everyone went back to the UK. A test would be done with some willing participants trying the bouncer and new video for a specific period of time, and their weight loss result would form part of the infomercial.

The New Year of 2011 came and it was launched on the JML channel. The infomercial was popular, but about two weeks later, I had a call saying that the product was being removed from sale: it wasn't selling. I was disappointed as I had been paid a lump sum and a percentage of sales was to come.

I had a meeting with the marketing manager, and around the conference table, he explained: demand was low, they did not want to put any further resources into trying to sell this product, TV time was expensive. So they had no choice but to remove it from sale.

I needed somehow to put in place a rescue plan for this very good concept, and within the week, I came up with an idea: if all the research was correct, if this product was marketed right and put into the right hands, it must sell. Could this be the answer to the obesity issue?

I now lived in Jamaica, so how could I run a business from there? So I mobilised people I knew, starting with my best mate Mercier, who would be CEO, and my friend David French as the sales manager. My older children too – Carolyne would be the Admin Director, James would be Creative and Design, and my accountant Gordon Silver would be a shareholder, as we wanted to avoid paying where we could.

The concept was to set up a new business called Bouncekids Ltd. We would provide bouncers to schools: kids, I believed, would not see this as exercise but play, and I was convinced that if we got them doing this, then we would be on to something. This would be my way of dressing up exercise in a sweet coating, just like parents did to ensure we ate our vegetables; they would dress it up in a pie. It would form part of the PE lesson, and with the help of a nutritionist, we'd also provide lesson plans.

To test the concept and idea, I needed about 100 bouncers from JML, so as to set up some trials in various schools in London with a view to analysing the probability and feasibility of such a business.

I felt that JML had messed up. They should have evaluated likely demand better, but how can you take an item off the market four weeks after going on sale? That is just not enough time. I was convinced they would feel they owed me one. So I contacted them, and with Mercier, we had a chat regarding my upset at what had transpired and that I needed their help, starting with 100 bouncers.

I also showed them my business plan. They liked the figures and this was an implied partnership, so I would keep them informed on how things were developing.

We went back to the office and had a staff meeting to agree on schools to contact. Four schools were nominated and a call made proposing I went to see them. That was easy. There is some benefit in being Mr Motivator; it provides an audience in the most difficult of situations.

After seeing all the different headmasters, it was agreed that I would take an assembly on a prearranged date and demo the bouncers to gauge their reaction.

Having a school, with 200- to 300 students, moving to my music was an experience. They saw Mr Motivator as a cartoon character and the joy on their faces made me feel so good. The bouncers were set up and I got into teaching a class of 30 the principles of bouncing. At the end of the fifteen-minute lesson, there was no way I could get the kids off: they were sweating and still they kept going, and the more the music played, the more they bounced. It was a hit; the headmaster was so pleased, he wanted to be part of the test. We left 31 bouncers with him and promised to be back in four weeks to see how the trial went.

When we returned four weeks later, the kids were sad to see the bouncers go, but the test was over. So what was the result? At one primary school in Harlesden where we had taught the deputy head, she had been doing classes sometimes twice per day and lost 17lbs. The bouncers had been used outside as well so that the kids could workout whenever they liked.

That situation was replicated across all the schools. With that successful trial behind us, we started preparing the next stage of our development. But the bouncers were not fit for purpose: they were collapsing, legs were splaying, rubber feet wearing badly. They made a noise the more that they were used. Now I knew the reason why JML had discontinued selling: not because they were not selling, it was all down to quality. I was ashamed and disappointed in them and the action that they had taken. Selling goods of poor quality with my name on them was against the spirit of the contract that we had signed.

I went back to JML: we now needed to find our market. I wanted to launch Bouncekids to UK schools at The Education Show. JML was pliable and offered to help with a stand and all its expenses, and it was the best one at the show. We had so much attention as we demoed the Bouncekids concept. The uptake was amazing and I had interest from some 650 schools, together with lots in foreign countries, especially in Africa and the Middle East.

We left the show elated. I had been proved right and now we needed to make deliveries. We had three months to get the full package all delivered. Schools sent in deposits, things were going well and we were on the way to making a lot of money.

JML placed orders with their supplier for the new bouncer that they had developed. This was supposed to be the one. Much stronger, better and brighter. It had Mr Motivator's Bouncekids written all over it. Deliveries would have a DVD, nutritional guide and, of course, the bouncer.

Delivery was promised to us in three months, and so we passed on that promise to all the schools, but in the end only enough bouncers for four schools was delivered to us. Just as we were ready to deliver to the schools, I happened to notice bouncers with my name on them being sold online for under $20. I was livid; how did this happen? I got in touch with JML; they denied all knowledge. This was undermining what we were doing – the package for schools was being sold at approximately $149. As schools became aware of the cheaper product, interest in the better bouncer died off. I was not a happy person so I instructed lawyers to issue a writ against them.

I was bluffing them; I did not have the money to go through a full on court battle. Letters went from my lawyer but there was no response from them. The stalemate continued for a few months, and in the end

I dropped everything. JML would not deliver the new bouncer; my supply source was drying up.

I contacted a number of suppliers of a competing rebounder – including a mate of mine, Keith Fowler, a man who knew all there was to know about supplies of fitness products from the Far East – with a view to being able to satisfy the orders we had from schools on time.

We were up against it. Time was not on my side and no matter how I tried, I was not able to get anything organised in time. I had ploughed nearly £100k into Bouncekids and I could see no way of saving us, so I had no alternative but to close the office, which I had taken on against my better judgement.

The company Bounce Fit stayed registered, but not trading. The idea was not dead, only resting, as I firmly believe that the answer to the obesity epidemic is to get everyone, no matter how young or old, bouncing. Play is an important factor in getting children (or adults) to keep something going: once on a trampoline, you can never get kids off it.

To say I was disappointed was not the word. I felt kind of let down by many people, and before I went back to Jamaica, I sat down to evaluate what just happened. I had spent over a year trying to set up a business with my own money. I had listened to others instead of me. It was my concept and I normally have a good eye for things that will work. But, like an orchestra without a conductor, I tried to run the business from afar. I entrusted my dream to someone else. The answer was for me to run things, even from afar. Employ and pay a wage, rather than expect favours. We had been very professional; the office was being well run, all promotional material was brilliantly designed by James, and the coordination of all matters was in good hands. But we did not need the expensive offices we were in, with their overheads. I had wanted to start small, and then we would grow.

For the future, I will listen to my inner voice, and by doing so, I am sure that I will be more successful. The idea is not dead, I will find another way to bring this concept to market: just you wait and see, I told myself.

I could now see a room with lots of people milling round, and through half-closed eyes, I knew that the operation was done. I hear someone in the darkness say something about recovery room and was I feeling OK? I was not feeling any pain but everything was in a fog. I was still asleep, I think, or was I trying to wake up? It seemed little time had passed so I allowed myself to go off into the darkness. And I continued to dream, as clear as if it was happening now. But this all seemed too real, this was no dream. I was seeing my life pass in front of me, recalling so much over so many years.

It had started towards the end of 2009. I noticed that each time I sat at the computer, there was a small area of blurredness in my right eye, and this small, circular area, as the weeks went by, became more blurred. I was getting concerned.

So I made an appointment with my optician in Jamaica. He did a full examination and afterwards set me up with a specialist in Kingston. He did a series of tests and then he delivered the result. "You have a hole in the macula, and you are losing the ability to see small detail." Had I had a trauma, such as hitting my head? I could not recall.

He stated that while there is a condition called macular degeneration, which happens as you get older, mine was a hole in the macula, which is very different, and I would need an operation called a vitrectomy, where a bubble of air and gas would be put in to act as an internal, temporary bandage as the hole healed. Surgery would only need local anaesthesia, but afterwards I had to remain in a face down position for up to two to three weeks, so the bubble would press against the macula and be gradually reabsorbed. This was crucial to success.

I asked him if he would do the operation and when could it be done. He was busy but he could fit me in, although he was not about to provide an accurate date or time. I was not convinced that I could depend on him to perform such a technical operation on my eye, so I flew to the UK in March.

My appointment at Moorfield's happened like clockwork; an X-ray of the hole in my macula, and a date and time fixed immediately for the operation. I would stay overnight, so I went away to get myself prepared. The specialist also told me that any operation on the eye would bring on the need for a repair of cataract earlier than normal; it would not be long before that same eye would need surgery.

I called Palmer; she would need to come over to help in the aftercare. I had sold all my properties in the UK, so there was only one thing for it, and I booked into a hotel in London Victoria for three weeks.

It is kind of strange to see a needle at the back of my eye; it extracted the fluid and then in went the gas. Soon I was in recovery and then moved into the hotel. My son, James, had prepared movies and documentaries that I could watch from my face down position. Everything was set and in place; my world became this room and a view of the floor. How can you see eye to eye with someone, when you are always looking down on them? I had no faces to see from my prone position, but I was able to see the bubble full of air and gas.

I was allowed to be up for ten minutes every hour, but the rest of the time, I had to be on my stomach. The specialist said there was no evidence that it made a difference if it was for two weeks or three weeks, but although difficult, I was going to do this for the max. The operation was in the March of 2010, and in April, I was booked to be in Austria at Snowbombing, a yearly Easter break right at the end of the skiing season where students, mainly from the UK, converge on a small village in Austria called Mayrhofen. It was a week-long party of bands, artists, and DJs, and a must for anyone who wanted to party and drink all day and night. I was to be there to do some warm ups on the piste.

When I saw the specialist, he said it was healing well but the bubble was still there, and if I flew, there was a chance I could lose my eyesight. What to do? London to Austria can be done by train, but it would take about 12 hours.

I had very little choice if I was going to fulfill this PA, so I booked the trains: Eurostar to Brussels, then Frankfurt, then Munich, and then Mayrhofen. I am glad I made the effort; the beauty of the air and scenery aided my recovery, and I met up with James and my nephew, David, who had both flown in, lucky devils.

The week went quickly and at every session, the crowds turned out. I spent most of my time in the hotel as to go anywhere took forever: everyone wanted photos, and I could and would never say no.

Whilst I was doing my crowd-pleasing, Palmer was in Jamaica looking after a group of 21 Baptists who were visiting the island for a week. I missed her and Abigail a lot; it is amazing how your life can feel empty, even though there are many humans around you.

The journey back to the UK seemed longer, but eventually I was back in the hotel. There was another job on, for an agent of Reebok in Singapore; they wanted me over there in ten days' time. But how would I get there, and could I take the risk and fly?

There were lots of benefits to going. Palmer advised against it, and the specialist said it was dangerous with the air/gas bubble still in my eye. But I wanted to know at what stage it was dangerous; has the bubble got to disappear completely or not? The specialist could not be sure, and he knew no one who had flown with a bubble.

I slept on it, and when I woke on 19th April, the bubble looked too small to see without a microscope. But when I closed my eyes, I could see it; it definitely was small, about the size of a pin head, but I could not be sure.

I called the specialist and told him of my decision; I was going. He advised against it. On 24th April, as I boarded the flight to Singapore, I was apprehensive: What if the bubble burst? What if I became sick?

What if I was in pain whilst on the flight? How would I cope with the altitude? What would I do if I needed emergency medical attention? I was wrong to go when so many obvious questions had no answers.

The flight was smooth. I relaxed into my seat not knowing what to expect. I was not having any reaction, no pain, no tightness, but I was nervous and scared at the same time. I was so worried that I started to make plans: if I lost the sight in my right eye, I would have coloured eye patches, just like the singer Gabrielle. I consoled myself that this would make me cool.

It was a long flight. We landed, and it was straight into radio and TV interviews, and appearances at shopping centres. Later that first day when I got back to my hotel room, it was full of all of Reebok's latest products. I was thankful; I could still see the bubble but I had not lost my sight. The next morning when I woke, the bubble had gone. I said a silent prayer, a sigh of relief. I called Palmer, who was ecstatic.

My whole week consisted of being taken from appearances to TV studios and the audiences loved Mr M. Wherever I went, they were out looking at the brightly-coloured tightly-dressed man. On the final night, 500 people turned up to a disco and we danced for hours.

I flew back to the UK, and the next day I was on my way back to Jamaica. I went straight into raising the profile of my business, H'Evans Scent, a tourist attraction featuring ziplining and paintballing. I have learnt over the years that when I am away, the business can be managed day-to-day, but the forward planning side falls away. So I immediately produced a TV advert to raise the profile with the native Jamaican.

Rebonding with Palmer and Abigail was top priority. I did hate being away, but there was a need and I had to ensure that our fridge was always full, and the sacrifice was I had to go where I could earn well in a short period of time.

Soon after we had a great week in Orlando at our timeshare: families needs time together to bond, and reassure each other that life would be empty without the other.

Then I was back in the UK, and one particular PA I enjoyed was the passing out parade at Sandhurst. I was the surprise guest at the officers' early morning workout. They went wild at my appearance; it was a joy to be there. Most would be commissioned to Afghanistan, and I felt honoured to have shared some time with these young men, especially as many would not be back on these shores again.

I continued to do my PAs in the UK, attending many conferences and working with companies on the promotion of their product - this is an area that I enjoy to the fullest. Meeting people who grew up with me, and were now the decision makers out there, filled me with a warm feeling. No matter where I went, all folks had to say was that they were there when I woke them in the mornings – many had been made late for school whilst waiting for me to come on their screens.

I worked in Dublin for Electric Ireland, London for a Wall's campaign, and many others. Some wanted me to just be the face, others wanted a motivational talk on my life. Each gave me pleasure, and that is how I now make a living. Throughout this book, I've put in some pieces of advice, things I've learnt through my eventful life, under the heading 'Mr Motivator Says'.

I was now fully awake from the operation on my knee, and in a room allocated for my overnight stay. I had hoped to go home the next day, but that seemed unlikely. I was slightly woozy and had very little feeling in the elevated leg. Over the next 48 hours, I had lots of visitors and friends, some bringing me food which would stave off the hunger I was feeling.

Hospital food is not that good at the best of times, especially if you are careful with what you put into your body. I was sad that I was out of the competition but in some ways glad, as I would now have time to reflect on what is important in my life. I made a number of life-changing decisions. And I have started to put them in place.

I was determined to be at the first episode of *Tumble*. Palmer and Abigail flew over, as I needed help with so many things. I felt so helpless but I was determined to be on my feet in the shortest period: I gave myself three months, even though the specialist said 9 to 18 months.

I found using a crutch and stairs difficult so a physio showed me the trick, and I set myself a target of making my way to the bathroom, up and down stairs. Abigail and Ebony decorated my crutches with bright paint and tape. I was ready to get out.

My first engagement, a week later, was the first show for *Tumble*. I arrived to loud applause from the crew and participants, as I manoeuvred past them. The effort was worth it; everyone cheered when I got in the studio and the audience showed that they cared.

Four weeks later, I was out of my leg brace and exercising regularly. I was also able to attend some of my PAs. I am not back to normal yet, the leg swells especially whenever I exercise or drive. It will take a while before I return to full fitness, but I am grateful for all that has happened. I learnt that someone who is disabled is more able than us who are not. I now appreciate so many things that I might have taken for granted in the past: the limbs that I have, being able to talk and move when I like, and so on.

I am now back in Jamaica at the Yellow House, four months have elapsed since my surgery. I have to train every day, although I do rest when I feel like it. I have no pain, just discomfort.

The Yellow House is the realisation of a dream, the place where I would retire, the place where I would enjoy the pleasures of life, and starting at age 50, it is mission accomplished!

I can remember arriving in Jamaica in the seventies and eighties to see my folks, on this same hillside. It is still a vivid picture of Auntie T (my adopted mum) sitting on the veranda looking down the hill. My childhood home was a simple and humble abode, a place of cherished memories. As I walked up the hill, I would see her before she saw me. Only when I was right in front of her, would she peer at me quizzically and say, "What a boy look like Derrick!" As I drew closer, the hands would go up in the air and she would exclaim, "Oh my God, it is him!" The hugs and kisses would follow as she smothered me in her huge breasts and that feeling of being wanted would encompass me and make me feel safe – at home.

How I wish that these two special people were alive today to see the Yellow House. It took four years to build, and in my greater plans, the house was also to have become their family home, where they were to have lived out their final years. Alas, I was not able to afford construction before my parents died. But I know that their spirits are still here with me celebrating and saying, "Well done, my son'."

It will not be long before I start to take classes again, so in the meantime, let me tell you about my past.

"The Price of Success is Perseverance"

How did I get here? Where did it all begin? And how is it that I now feel so wise, so sure and contented about the future?

My journey into the past will provide the answers. Life has taught me the importance of knowing who you are, where you came from, where you are, and where you are going.

Chapter 1: Born to Live

1952 was a good year.

But 15th November of that year was exceptionally great, because that's when I came into this world, the firstborn of Enid Richards. She was just seventeen years old, a chambermaid at the Villa Bella Hotel located in Christiana, Manchester, Jamaica. It is still standing today, looking a little bit worse for wear, but new owners are in place.

Enid had befriended a man who was not one for staying around. As it usually happens, passion overcame sense and reasoning, and I was conceived.

I am not sure whether there was any real regret about my conception and birth, as there is little information about how my birth mother's family felt about my imminent arrival and presence. You see, I always wanted to know how people and family members felt about me, but nothing has ever been forthcoming. But the following incident will perhaps provide an answer.

When I was three months old, Enid was going about her business, with me in tow. An older woman approached us. The conversation was quite normal and this is quite close to how it happened:

"Good day, ma'am."

"Well, hello."

"What a pretty baby you got there."

"I know, he is lovely, isn't he?"

"Boy, he is so lovely. Give me him, nuh?"

"Are you sure you want him?"

"If you want to give me him, I will take him."

"Well then, if you want him, take him now."

I was given away at three months old. I was given to another family, the Rose family, just like that.

I cannot remember much of those early years and having no photographs or letters, I have tried to piece together bits of information that I have picked up over the years. I can only assume that I was a well-behaved and well-looked-after child.

Our house was on a hill about 50 yards from the road. It had a veranda, a lounge and three bedrooms. The kitchen was outside, as was the toilet, and a bath pan constituted our bathing and washing facilities. If you got caught out in the night, you just aimed 'it' out the window or you used the chamber pot, or the chimmy, as it was sometimes called.

My family comprised of Popa and Auntie, stepsister Cherry and brother Earl. They each had their own rooms, but I shared with Auntie and Popa. We also had a helper at home called Lynn.

Lynn was the source of what seemed an endless stream of old Jamaican fables that she would reel off at every opportunity. We learned about curious characters, such as Bra Monkey, the clever little monkey that seemed to get away with every prank. Then there were the scary 'Duppy' stories – those quickly became my favourites. These were purposeful stories about ghosts, many of which formed the very basis of our religious upbringing.

But they left us so scared each evening that if we got caught short, there was no going to the outside toilet, even if we wanted to. Some of those stories remain with me to this day.

One such story was the story of a young man who went out partying every night and came home late time and time again. He would not heed the warnings and beseeching of his parents to come home early.

One particular night, he had been out and, as usual, he returned home late. As he walked home in the dark, he could hear the loud beat of music in the distance. He walked towards the sound of the music. He walked for what seemed like ages, but at no time did he get close to its location. After what seemed like miles of walking, he looked into a gully and saw bright lights. He could hear the sound of people partying. The music was now whipping up into a frenzy, and this quickened his steps towards the location of the party.

Now running, he hollered at the top of his voice, cupping his hands around his mouth, "Hello! Wait for me, I am coming!" He had barely finished his statement, when all of a sudden, the music stopped. Everything went pitch black and there was a deathly silence. He could not see his way in the dark and it took him three days to get out of the bushes. After that night, he never stayed out until dark ever again.

While at infant school, I do remember clearly that I had to start my mornings with home chores. This was not unique; it was the norm for all kids, no matter their age. In fact, as soon as they could walk, they were given small tasks to perform, such as gathering firewood, and later would be expected to travel down to the river to fetch water. Every morning, you had to feed corn to the chickens, and then get yourself washed and tidied for school, and this was all to happen before six o'clock – yes, in the morning.

Then it was a walk to school. I was lucky as Pike PA School was only about half a mile away, so I walked barefoot until I reached school and then I put my shoes on. They were off again when school was dismissed, and, after walking back home, I repeated my chores from the morning, and anything else I was asked to do.

Never once can I remember complaining about what chores had to be done – how very different things are now. Maybe it is because if you ever refused, the alternative was the belt. You see, beatings were a part of life; it was the way in which you were corrected; when words failed, then the 'strap would talk'.

Everyone in the community took part in your upbringing. If you did wrong outside of your home and a grown-up caught you, they would spank you. Ha! You would not dare go home and tell your parents, because they would spank you too. Young and old, community policing made you a better behaved person. Today, in some areas of Jamaica, this practice is still in place; neighbours looking out for each other and keeping the peace.

One of the few times that I recall being disciplined was when I decided that the young girl across the road deserved to be kissed in the banana walk. This I duly did, the sort of a kiss where the initial passion outweighed the result. I felt nothing other than the large fingers of someone's hand on my ears, twisting and pulling, and someone shouting, "What yuh doin' wid' mi daughter?" I had nothing to say, except, "Ow, that hurt!"

I was dragged screaming to Auntie, who listened to the report and rather than dismissing my action as that of a young but randy eight-year-old, used my bottom as the target practise for a hand that was much larger than my backside.

It is funny how Jamaican parents never ever took us on their laps and held us, and told us how much they loved us. They assumed that we as children naturally knew that they did, and I suppose I knew that they did, just by the very fact that they were there for us. There were always so many children at the house; as soon as someone could not manage to look after their own children, Auntie and Popa took them in.

The roles of husband and wife were never spelled out. Once you got married, the assumption was that the man was the breadwinner and, of course, he went to work. In Popa's case, he was a policeman and a farmer at the same time. Holding two jobs was the norm, and probably the only way to make ends meet.

Popa was a big, wide man, and when he was annoyed, you knew it before he spoke. His stature seemed to change. He became more upright and he grew from his 5ft 11in frame to a size that seemed more like 6ft 6in. He was very strict in all things, a very deeply religious man and, for as long as I can remember, he prayed day and night – when he could not be found, all I had to do was to check the church.

Though a highly spiritual man, he was quite extreme in handing out punishment, showing intolerance for perpetrators of the law. He was known to have little mercy, especially on thieves, who if caught, would be beaten almost to death. That was the norm at that time for any thief.

This unwritten law exists even today in small pockets of the island. If you steal anything, in particular another man's cow, goat, or means of living, you are subjecting that person or family to extreme poverty, and even death, and that should also be the fate for any would-be thief.

This discipline and attitude towards any wrongdoing spread throughout our family as well. Popa's word was always law, and, as such he ruled his family accordingly. If he said move, you moved, and if he said stay, you stayed.

On one occasion, Earl was sent to the shop to buy some bulla. These are flat cakes made with flour and sugar, a little bit like large, hard soda biscuits. When baked, they are linked together, then they are broken apart and sold in singles. Popa, upon receiving his bulla, accused Earl of picking at the ends where they were joined. Earl, of course, denied this, but to no avail. According to Popa, he had picked at it, therefore he should be chastised. Out came the cow cod. This was the same belt used to beat thieves. It was made of strips of leather plaited together to make a whip about 4ft in length. Earl now knew what to expect, so when Popa grabbed him by the collar, he made a dash for it. He was quick – it is amazing how self-preservation makes the legs move! So there he was running down the streets faster than Popa could move.

Yet, he was a lovely man and he had a heart of gold. His huge foreboding stature belied his many acts of kindness and gentleness. He wanted the very best for us, and to that end, he worked very hard. But despite that, there were many days when our meals were without meat. If there was only sufficient food and meat for Popa, he would share his little, his last, with all of us, or if someone came in, he would immediately offer to share with them.

And yet, to reinforce his authority and power, he was very stern in the way he reprimanded us. There was one particular day that he asked me to go to Mass (Mr) Joseph to borrow a hammer. I was only five, but

I set out in the direction that Popa pointed to. After about five minutes, I got lost in the woods. So, instead of turning back and admitting failure and taking my punishment, I sat by the roadside which was more like the jungle, and simply wept with a morbid anticipation.

At some stage, it occurred to Popa that I had not returned with the hammer, and as a concerned and caring parent, he came in search of his missing son. I saw him coming, and from a distance I was sure he was going to say, "Derrick, never mind, let's go together," and reassure me that if he was to show me the way once, in the future I would know. As he drew closer, I realised that this was not the face of a father about to guide and show love to his son. I knew I was in for it. I was to learn later in my life that Popa never waited for an answer.

He asked, "Where is the hammer that I sent you for?" and, immediately, without my replying, he broke lots of twigs, put them together and set about, initially, drawing on my bottom the directions to Mass Joseph. When he ran out of space on my bottom, he started demonstrating on the rest of my body, showing the main roads and the back streets.

I cried as each stroke came down with the words, "When I send you to get anything, you go and get it and bring it back immediately." To him, I was wrong to have delayed coming back to a waiting parent, but in my eyes, I was lost, and when you are lost, you sit and cry.

Though still in a temper, he took me home to Auntie, who was there to administer the hot water with drops of Dettol to my bruises. She cursed quietly when Popa was not in the room, and whispered, "Never mind, it will get better soon."

Auntie was always there and never argued with Popa. Yes, she complained, and under her breath you would hear her say, "De old fool, why him have to behave like dat?" She certainly disapproved of some of Popa's methods and she would willingly mop up our tears with a quiet grumble.

So I remember him as a man who not only ruled us with a rod of iron, but one who also gave us the will and ammunition to survive. If only he used the words, "I love you," to us or Auntie, it would have made all the difference, but this was just the way things were. As I grew up, I began to realise the importance of using those same words to my children and anyone whom I cared for deeply.

That incident was my last recollection of Popa in Jamaica. He soon left for England. After that, I would be sent to collect the mail from the post office in Pike. There was always a registered letter addressed to Auntie, and when it arrived, there was always a celebration, because we knew that Popa had sent money from England.

There were many other children carrying registered letters, the contents of which were well known. In 1948, many Jamaican men had answered the call of Winston Churchill to go to England and help rebuild their mother country. Popa was one of these, but he left much later in 1958, when I was six years old.

Everyone in Jamaica was into farming – from bananas to sugar cane, yams and Irish potatoes. The life was hard, but what choices did they have? Not many. Historically, our forefathers left very little to each child. My folks were given some education, a machete and the belief that with God's help, all things are possible.

Pike, a small village in Manchester, consisted of one dusty street, on which the local Baptist church was located and on whose grounds several generations were buried. Next door to that was Pike Primary and Secondary School, an old building made of wood that had deteriorated with the years.

On the other side was the local shop, which sold everything from bread to soft drinks. Behind the shop, and quite a walk into the woods, was the local abattoir, where once a week, usually very early on a Friday morning, the final and shattering squeal of a pig or cow would be heard.

Back to the main road next to the local shop was the bar. This was the town centre for entertainment and gossip. All who had a story to tell, or who felt that they could out drink every man in the neighbourhood, found their way to this bar.

The Jamaican drink for 'real' men was White Overproof Rum, so strong it could be substituted for paint stripper. White rum was the drink for the brave. The fainthearted chased it with milk or water. Down from the bar was the post office and other shops selling a bit of everything. This was a dirty, dusty little village, almost like an American Wild West town waiting to be invaded by Indians and cowboys.

Christianity played a really important part from very early in life. The whole family went to church, not just on a Sunday but during the week as well. Popa led the prayers every night, and every day began with a blessing.

He was not a man of few words, and many times the food was almost cold after he had finished praying. After he left for England, Auntie was responsible for continuing our religious upbringing, but she did things with a more liberal attitude, which was to our benefit. She was truly a kind-hearted soul and we received much comfort and love in her ample bosom. She cared greatly and while she did not always express it, we knew that she had our best interest at heart.

Auntie took me everywhere with her. One night in particular, we held hands and walked to choir practise at the main church in Pike a few miles away. My usual habit was to sit quietly in one of the pews and irreligiously fall asleep as I listened to the choir. On one occasion, the choristers, seemingly 'drunk' in the love of the Lord at the end of the practise, left for home hardly noticing the sleeping six-year-old on the pews.

Sometime later, I awoke to the dead quiet of the church. It was totally dark and all I could think about was the burial ground outside the church, visible from the window nearby. I was scared, especially when I heard the clanging of keys and disembodied voices! I hid under the pew, wide-eyed and shivering.

I heard the door creak open and the voices came nearer and nearer, and all of a sudden, a hand reached down and touched me! I felt myself being lifted up, but my eyes were tightly shut, and then I picked up a whiff of a familiar smell, one that I had grown so used to, and all of a sudden, I felt safe.

Auntie had arrived home and only then did she miss me. She ran all the way back to the church. What a spectacle she must have made – this ample, robust woman running a two-mile journey to get her beloved child!

A typical Sunday consisted of getting up early to prepare Sunday dinner. The meat, which was often chicken, would have been seasoned the night before, and the gungo (Congo) peas would also have been soaking overnight. Early on Sunday morning, we would fry the chicken, and the peas would be boiled until tender. Our traditional Sunday meal consisted of chicken, rice and peas, and coleslaw. We would always prepare dinner early, because it was impossible to predict what time church would be over, and at least the dinner would be ready to eat when we returned home.

After doing all the chores, it was time to put on our 'Sunday best.' No matter how poor a person you were, there was usually a suit of clothing reserved for the Sunday fashion show. And a show it was, as folks paraded their finery of dresses and suits, topped off with fabulous hats and ties, gloves and even flowers (for the ladies), a colourful family affair.

The service was always too long, lasting no less than two hours, but I felt fortunate because as children, we did not have to endure the full service. Halfway through, we were excused to hear Bible stories under the apple tree on the grounds.

When church was finished, it was off to home for Sunday dinner, and we shared this meal at the table. We barely had time to finish our food before we had to be back for Sunday school. When we came home, it was our parents' turn to go back to church for the evening session. The whole of Sunday was set aside for worship, and we were not even allowed to listen to a radio.

As part of my household chores, I had to clean the floor in all the rooms. Most floors were either wooden or concrete; either way, they were red in colour because of the dye that was used. I would then spread on the polish with a cloth and then I would be down on all fours to buff. Using a coconut brush made by horizontally cutting a dry coconut in two, I would push, slide, and pull all in an attempt to bring about a sparkling shine to the floor. When it was finished, I would stand back covered in red dye to admire my handy work, and to await the approval of Popa and Auntie when they returned from market. I needed approval to avoid the whip.

My housekeeping duties took a spin one day. I was left at home with Lynn, our helper, to do the housework. I was in the lounge polishing away when I heard Lynn calling me from the bedroom. As I approached the room, I could see her lying on the edge of the bed with her feet hanging over the side. She told me to come closer, and as I did so, I could see that she had her dress up to her waist, and she had no panties on. As I stood in front of her, she drew me to her and took down my pants.

This kind of abuse is commonplace in Jamaica. At the time, I am not sure how I saw this; I know it happened repeatedly. I cannot have been any more than six. As a young child, I don't know how I felt. I am pretty sure that I knew it was wrong, but I was in the care of an adult who should have known better.

Mr Motivator Says: *Parents need to be always on the lookout as we do not know who we can trust, and the very person we put into the position of carer can be the abuser. Childrens' exposure to matters of sex too early in life can have a long-term effect on how they respond to affection and relationships in later life. We must at all times be vigilant to ensure that the innocence of a minor is protected until the moment and time is right. There are enough secret monitoring devices available on the market to give each parent peace of mind, to know that their child is being looked after properly at all times.*

Regarding abuse, teach your child to recognise inappropriate touching and conversation that is unacceptable. Don't just tell it once, but show them over and over again. Practise role play with your child, and that will prepare them for something that might not happen but if it does, they will be properly equipped to handle it. One final note on this matter: make them understand that if they tell you, they will not get into any trouble and as long as they are telling the truth, then you will always believe them first.

Chapter 2: Migration

1962 was the year of Jamaica's Independence from Britain.

At Pike School and all other schools, the children had been practising the National Anthem for months, as Independence was imminent. There was a full agenda of celebrations across the island, marked by street parties of music, dancing and revelry. The real significance of being an independent nation meant nothing to me, but I was certainly excited taking part in the festivities.

Unfortunately, Popa, who had been in the UK for a number of years, wanted us to join him there. Auntie did not want to go. I wasn't sure about it either.

Independence Day was on 6th August, and we were to leave four days earlier. I really didn't want to go, as I was going to miss all the celebrations, but Popa had spoken and I had no choice but to follow the directive. All the plans were in place for us to leave.

Arrival in the UK

Most Jamaicans had heard, and many believed the statement, 'the streets of England are paved with gold'. So they made the journey in the hope of better times. The good ship *Windrush* set sail for England in 1948, carrying the first of many such migrants, mostly the menfolk. Popa waited another ten years before setting sail.

He had set up home in Leicester, and was working as a labourer; initially for the railway and then for a local factory. Things went well enough in that he was able to save enough to send for us.

Cherry, my sister, was already in the UK living with Popa, and she worked as a nurse. On 2nd August 1962, we boarded the BOAC plane to England. I was truly disappointed at missing my performance, and, even more, missing my Independence gifts and goodies.

I don't remember very much about the flight, other than we seemed to have been herded into an area after landing. For some reason, we were all kept waiting, and I began to feel quite ill. In fact, I was boiling up, and feeling very faint. My throat was dry. I recalled seeing one of those water dispensers at the end of a very long room, and in a daze, I struggled to get to the water. On arriving in Leicester, I was told by Auntie that I had picked up germs on the journey.

Here I was, nine years old in Leicester. Everything seemed strange. It was not warm, at least not as warm as I was used to. In Jamaica, at this time of year, the temperature would have been at least 90°F.

I expected everyone in England to be white, as I was told. But, as I looked on, I realised people were a mixture of colours, and from many different cultures. There were West Indians, East Indians, Pakistanis, but not, surprisingly, one white person in sight.

Popa had found some rented accommodation for all of us. It was a very small terrace house, with three bedrooms. We would be using two of those rooms and share the kitchen. I shared a room with Tony, my nephew, Cherry's son.

School

The first school that I went to in Leicester was an infant school called St Peter's. I remember a large, imposing building like one of those from the days of David Copperfield; high towers and gables, large classrooms, all unheated with an eight foot wall surrounding the school grounds. I seem to have forgotten or hidden away the memories of those early school days. It may be because I did not truly like school. This probably explains why I do not recall the whole of my school life; instead, it is just certain incidents and events that spring to mind. I was rather surprised about that, because most West Indian children are almost forced into realising the importance of a good education.

During my time at St. Peter's, Auntie decided to go home to Jamaica. Although she only spent one year there, she hated living in England. It was too cold for Auntie, and she missed her way of life at home. Cherry's sons, Tony and David, went with her. I was devastated. Auntie was my only source of warmth, my anchor in a bewilderingly strange sea. When she said her goodbyes, I shed some bitter tears and clung to her, not wanting her to leave me behind. But the decision was for me to stay with Popa. I made the best of it and got along as best I could.

I remembered nothing about my lessons, but I do remember being bullied by a boy called Marvin, and he was to follow me into Moat Boys Secondary. Originally from one of the other West Indian islands, he was average sized, but physically stronger than everyone else, and he used that strength to devastating effect. He featured in the lives of many of the kids at school – he hardly took a break from making everyone's lives hell. His bullying went on for four more years at school.

There were many characters at school: Cordell Heskey, born of West Indian parents, whose son or nephew was to later become the Liverpool striker Emile Heskey. Sartorelle, the largest and biggest person at school, was the brunt of many jokes and endured serious bullying from everyone. Each class had specific days when they took swimming lessons at the local baths. One day, coming back from swimming, Heskey beat Sartorelle all the way back to school. Now, as I look back, I realise the humiliation he must have felt, and the whole indignity of it all.

I remember I loved music and art, and at the time of my report, I was given A+ for both subjects. However, before I had a chance to take my report card home, this was reduced drastically – by the same teacher. Why?

At age 13, I already had early sexual experiences. My hormones were running wild! So when this lovely creature sat at her desk in front of me wearing the fashion of the sixties, I saw, and heard, nothing of the lesson, because my eyes were fixed only on her lovely, crossed legs. Skirts were very short in those days, as dictated by Mary Quant.

I had difficulty concentrating on the lesson. How could I? I couldn't contain myself, so I touched her leg. After all, beautiful legs, crossed, with a mini skirt so short it was hardly hiding anything – it deserved to be touched.

It was like a drug and I felt out of control; I could not fight the urge any longer. All reason went out of the window and I found myself drawn like a magnet to her thighs. Everything around me became a blur as my hand took on a life of its own. I could not hear anything; there was a heavy mist, and through it, all I could hear was Miss shrieking, "Derrick Evans! How dare you do that! Report to the corner of the room!" I am not sure if my past was part of the reason for my doing what I did; I see this as just a young school boy prank, hormones are running around at this time, urges are in place, and we do what we do.

Needless to say, I never attempted that again with any teacher, but I got such extreme pleasure from that incident that any punishment would have been worth it – except that one; my report card was changed from A+ to C- in both of her lessons.

Then there were sports. I knew about swimming. In later life, I was to learn why there were no black Olympic swimmers. Apparently, black people have greater muscle density, so if a Caucasian and a black person, each weighing 12 stones, were asked to float in water, there would be more of the white person's body above the level of the water.

If only I had known that fact, I could have avoided the many years I spent trying to learn to swim. No matter how I tried, I could not manage to do more than a short distance. That fear of water remains with me still.

I did do physical education and I got good reports, but my love of the physical was minimal; I was just ordinary at sports, and never qualified to represent the school at anything.

Me and two mates.

I did enjoy certain parts of school, and hated others. I couldn't quite grasp the logic of winter sports. What purpose was served in the dead of winter, with snow and mud on the ground, when one would put on shorts that left very little to the imagination, and go outside and freeze your nuts off?

I tried rugby, but why should I, feeling like a frozen block of chocolate ice cream, run through mud, get hit by a guy built like a steam roller, only to cry out in pain? No way! On my island, all we ever played was cricket, and the weather was never a point of concern.

I later tried hockey, which meant running with a large stick, chasing a small, very hard ball, and attempting to hit the ball with a stick in a general direction of someone else's goal, whilst trying to keep your shins intact. This was not my idea of sport.

A boy with dark skin was often faded by the cold, always trying to keep warm. I couldn't understand how some white folks could go out in the dead of winter, in shirtsleeves alone, and not feel the cold. I developed short-sightedness very early at age 12, and that meant no more contact sports for me. Thank God!

Indoor sports made better sense. Badminton became my focus and I would find any excuse to practise this sport. Basketball was a love that was not just confined to the very tall; I was now about five feet five, not as tall as most of my friends but tall enough to be able to shoot well and this got me on the school team.

Bullying existed in Moat Boys and this was the primary occupation of Marvin. He was to be the bane of my existence for many years. He beat me most days.

I dried my tears before I got home though, because if I was to go in crying, Popa would not ask for a reason, and if he did, before I could explain, he would clout me and send me back to face my foe. This was viewed as good groundwork for character building and developing independence. You had to learn to cope with it.

West Indian parents were like that. They expected you to defend yourself, no matter your age or your circumstances. If your teacher told you off, you didn't go home with a tale, because you would most certainly be beaten, the reason being that during the day your teacher was like God.

There were times when I felt alone, because I had to learn on the hop, and with no information or help on hand, it meant that I suffered for quite a while until I figured it out for myself.

I started wearing glasses when I was 12. This was to give Marvin the task of finding a name that he thought befit me – one was 'Dog Face'. Why? I don't know, but for a few years I was to suffer his taunts. Marvin was something else; he was relentless. Everyone was eligible to be at the receiving end of his verbal bullying. This was only hurtful when he had all his mates and the rest of the class in attendance, because they laughed at what he said. Funny thing is most of them eventually became the recipients of this same treatment.

By the time I was 14, I began to realise that I had a voice. I began to get back at him, firstly by using certain choice words. He did not like my verbal insults and I was to pay dearly for this with the other part of his repertoire of bullying, the physical abuse.

He started to call me the Professor; he said that I always had an answer for every problem. I had tried threatening him with, "If you beat me, make sure that you do it well, because if I can't get revenge, my kids will and if they fail, their kids will get back at you!" This didn't stop him, it just made him even madder and I was beaten even more.

But there is a saying, 'Every dog has his day,' and mine was to come when I was 15. It was September 1967, the start of the new term, when I took a seat at the front of the class, the first desk as you walked in. Marvin came in and insisted that I should move from his seat. I ignored him, which made most classmates smile, and me laugh.

Marvin got mad and pushed me. I still ignored him. He tried to pull me out of the seat, and for the next few moments, a fog descended over me. I remember getting up. I was shorter than him but this did not matter.

I recall landing on top of him, thumping, scratching, pulling, kicking, and arms still flailing as the teacher pulled me off him. When I got up, I saw the damage I had caused to Marvin's face. What had come over me? All the other kids were smiling and, all of a sudden, were acknowledging me. I was sent to sit at the back of the class, but did I mind? Did I heck!

I sat there trying to analyse what had just happened; I had fought back, without even considering the consequences. I had summoned enough courage to fight back. That surprised everyone, including Marvin. Inside I felt good, but I had to prepare for his inevitable revenge, revenge that must take place, but in what form? I did not have long to wait. It was break time and for some reason my legs would not work very well. I was glued to my seat, as everyone left the classroom, except Marvin and four of his mates.

I prayed that the teacher would not leave the room, but she did. I was hoping that the ground would open up and swallow me, but it wouldn't. Marvin didn't keep me waiting for long. He got up and slowly sidled over. I thought I saw smoke coming out of his head; it could have been his eyes, but I was not prepared to look into his eyes. What was I to do? I was caught in a corner, and escape by running was out the question.

His face was in my face, "Eggbands [my new name]," he said, "I am going to give you such a beating, you just wait 'till you come downstairs!" He left the room with his mates patting him on the shoulders and egging him on.

I had caught a glimpse of his face; it was bruised all over and I came to the conclusion that he was not as convincing as he had been in the past. His voice did not put fear into me anymore and I was beginning to feel very confident, but I was not going to test him, so for three days, lunch and all breaks came and went, but I would not venture out into the playground. By Thursday, I thought whatever he was going to do, he would have to do it, because I could no longer stay indoors.

Gingerly, I started the short, but seemingly long walk down the stairs. As I got to the bottom, his mates were waiting for me. They gleefully called out to Marvin and he came running. Goaded on by his followers, he rushed at me, but I was prepared for him and we fought. He wasn't able to get the better of me; instead we rolled into a crate of free milk and sent the bottles flying. In my desperation, I was equal to him and, that day, we were to see the beginnings of mutual respect. A friendship emerged. I believe Marvin was humbled by the experience; he became a quieter, calmer person, as if all his deep seated rage had seeped away.

After that incident, we socialised for a while, but, after leaving school, I never met with him again. I have since been made aware that he is now a devout Pastor.

Mr Motivator says: *If you are being bullied, do not suffer in silence. Talk to a grown-up, and if your parents will not hear or listen to you, then try and speak to someone at school in a position of authority, who seems willing to help.*

I often played the fool in music class, and I was to receive punishment from the teacher for some misdemeanour that I was not aware of.

Mr Green was a bit of a buffoon really, with a face that looked as if he had failed to develop since birth. Dressed in an ill-fitting grey suit, white shirt and tie, he proceeded to try and administer his punishment.

He opted to use the very slim, thin cane, which stung like crazy. I protested my innocence, but Mr Green was going to give me three of his best across the hand.

As I stood in front of him, defiantly, with my hand outstretched, he raised his hand and down came the cane with a swishing whistle. Very carefully, without him realising, I pulled my hand away to the sound of my agonised, "Ow!" This was repeated twice more, and each time, I did the same thing. My performance deserved an Oscar, and, as I turned and left the room with a "Serves you right!" from Mr Green, I was grinning like a Cheshire Cat.

Another occasion when I was punished was after a particularly pointless game of football. All the boys were in the changing room, some waiting to have a shower, and I was showing off my penknife. The supervising teacher gruffly told me to put my penknife away and head for the shower. I got up to oblige, but as the teacher turned to walk off, he overheard one of my schoolmates swearing. Thinking it was me, he promptly aimed a backhander across my ears. I raised my hand in defence, but unfortunately, it was the one that still had the penknife in it! Naturally, this was taken as a threat and made him mad, so I was marched off to see the headmaster.

The punishment for swearing and threatening with a knife was an automatic six of the cane that hurt the most (did I say the canes were graded? The thicker ones hurt, but the thin ones really hurt and stung for ages after.) On the way to the headmaster's office, I tried to remember what all my mates had told me. First lesson: avoid getting the cane when you are wearing shorts. Second lesson: if caught in shorts, then get something between your butt and the shorts as quick as possible. Some used an old T-shirt, others put in an exercise book. I quickly grabbed an old T-shirt and smoothed it around my backside, then cautiously approached the head's office. He was not in a mood for explanations and, as I bent over his desk, I heard the swish of the slim cane – the padding worked, I made all the right noises, and left his office, beaming, with his parting words, "That will teach you!"

I think that caning was a good deterrent. Things were different 45 years ago, punishment was different, but it happened and the measure of the effectiveness of this form of punishment is, did I learn from this? And I would have to say yes, I did. I was never to be punished again.

Church and Boys' Brigade

Popa worshipped at the Melbourne Hall Church in Highfields, Leicester. I think he had become a member of this church because it was convenient – it was close to the house – and also because the services encouraged a chorus of agreement from the congregation, from "Amen," to "Praise the Lord!" This Evangelical church was in the heart of the community, and as such, it became my focus and lifeblood when not at school. This is where I could be found.

This church had much going on; from Boys' Brigade, (B.B.) to visiting pastors and other well-meaning individuals. Thank God for the family that existed at Boys' Brigade and outside, otherwise I had little to share at home. I very much lived on my own and I saw little of Popa. While he worked, I was schooled, went to B.B. and then the Hungry Eye in town, which served up the most amazing pancakes with maple syrup and ice cream, followed by a Knickerbocker Glory, which the menu stated "baffles description".

At the back of the church was The Walker Hall. This was used for many activities, from five-a-side football to B.B. display nights. This hall was the central meeting place for everyone. The ancient room, with its wooden floor and balcony, hosted many gymnastic displays, and the crowds that came to watch were very close to the action; you heard them and could just about feel them breathing down your neck.

These displays became an important part of our time in Boys' Brigade, and we developed a wide circle of friends in the church. The B.B. (the 8th Leicester), led by Ted Baker, became the guiding light for many a young man growing up in Leicester – with its motto, "Sure and Steadfast", it provided youngsters with a meeting place run on Christian principles.

There was a full range of daily and weekly activities that most of us took part in. We would practise drill marching, singing, or playing an instrument. In my case, it was the guitar. We met every Friday night and apart from the formal stuff of the B.B., we would play table tennis, football, basketball or gymnastics.

Gospel group.

Once a year, there would be a general parade that featured many of the other battalions from the surrounding areas - by now, I was drum major, and that meant marching in front of the whole company twirling my mace. I took this honour very seriously and it gave me a great sense of achievement. The drum major before me carried the mace with immense style. He was a really nice guy called Nick Sercombe; I learnt a lot from watching him and perfected my own style.

We also went camping each summer to various seaside towns in North and South Wales, Cornwall, and the Dawlish Coast, usually for a week each time.

Bullying reared its ugly head again with two guys about three to five years older than me; one bullied while the other supported. The bully was called the General; his short cropped hairstyle together with a low-toned voice earned him this title. He had muscles everywhere, even his face was a bank of muscles. He made my lack of muscles a problem. He was verbally supported by a boy called Graham, who was over 6ft tall and, from my short height, seemed to go on forever. The proverbial dim giant, he followed the General around like a puppy.

The General frequently reminded us all of how strong he was and no one argued with him; he went around enforcing his will upon everyone. He was only five feet tall, but when he pushed his chest out, his flares and large collared shirts only highlighted the power packed in this midget of a bully. I hated to be bullied – well, who wouldn't? I was never very good at fighting back physically, and whilst I would usually verbally destroy my opponents, when these two were about, I suffered in silence. I was often physically abused by these two and it came in the form of being pushed and knocked about whenever they went by. It is an odd thing; when you are being bullied, you don't ever talk about it with anyone – the victims don't seem to get together and plan a joint attack. I don't think personal fear is the only issue – most don't want to admit the fact that they are being bullied.

The bullying went unnoticed by others, and I felt that I was the only recipient, but I am sure there were others; they kept it quiet and perhaps self-preservation made them disappear as fast as they could when the two were around.

Stealing

Despite this closeness and all the religious guidance I received, one summer holiday I was to prove that we can all get influenced by the company we keep. One Sunday, I left Sunday school with one of my mates, Reginald Johnson. Whilst walking home, we ran into two guys from school who I knew fairly well. A conversation developed and all of a sudden, we were going to rob a factory right in front of Leicester Prison. We didn't know why and how these guys knew there was money there, but we were tempted to find it.

We began the long walk into town. En route, we planned what we were each going to do with our share of the haul. Mine was to get a new bike and lots of sweets, the others varied from a holiday to a new stereo.

We arrived at the building and all was quiet as was expected. Each window was meshed and every way in was barred, but Reg was into car mechanics and, as he was also the biggest and strongest of the bunch, we nominated him to forcibly remove the mesh. He did so with ease; the window was pried open and in we went.

This was a garment factory and all around us were sewing machines and finished articles, but little evidence of money or a safe. Horace, the guiding light, suggested that it was all upstairs in the office; to get up there, you had to climb up a chute that was used to send the products downstairs – this was filled with bagged clothing, which we removed.

All four of us went up the chute. By the time we had climbed to the top, I was so hot I took off my fashionable overcoat – you know, the one with three buttons up the front and that fur collar - and I threw it back down the chute. We started looking around for the haul. Well, we found lots of pens and about £2.00 in small change from all the desks. We left our first 'job' quite disappointed.

Reg and I went off home thinking how stupid we had been to listen to those guys, and thanked our lucky stars that we had not been caught. We decided to avoid meeting Horace and his friend, at least until the new term began.

The next Tuesday evening, there was a knock at the door. We lived upstairs in a house that had four bedrooms; Popa and I shared one, and another family shared the other rooms. I was upstairs when the door was answered, and I could hear a voice asking for Mr Evans. Popa's surname was Rose, so the person who answered the door said, "No sir, no Evans live here." I ran down shouting out that I was Evans, and as I came to the bottom of the stairs, I was met by two men in blue uniforms.

As I led them into the lounge, Popa's face turned almost beetroot and I was wetting my pants. I tried to avoid Popa's stare; he knew something was wrong, and I knew what it was.

One officer began. "Mr Evans, where were you on Sunday?"

"I was in church, sir," I replied, sweating.

"How many pairs of glasses do you own, young man?"

"Two pairs, sir," I wondered where this was leading to.

"Can you show them to me please?"

"Hold on. I will just go and get them." And off I scuttled.

I could find the case to my regular pair but as for the second one, it was nowhere to be found. After seeing this, the officer said, "Is this what you are looking for?" and promptly produced my specs case containing my spare pair. I thanked him and was just about to leave the room, when he said, "Mr Evans, those were found at the scene of a crime that happened over the weekend."

I said that I did not have a clue how it got there. He said it was found at the base of a chute in a local factory that was broken into.

Any denial was pointless, but my mind ran over the sequence of events on that Sunday, and of course, the specs were in my pocket of my coat; when I threw my coat down the chute, they must have fallen out. I was caught, and there was no escape. Popa gave me the look that said, "Come clean and you will feel better for it." The police officers were convinced that I was not the mastermind behind what was a stupid crime and he asked for the names of the others.

I came clean, but I only mentioned Horace. They left, saying that I would be hearing from them.

I couldn't face Popa, so I went up to my room. The stairs were difficult to climb, as if my legs had turned to lead. With each step, I felt sick to the bone. There was no hiding place; Popa would surely let me have it that night, and so I sat in my room and waited. He never came in.

I was due in court two weeks later and Popa came along with me. Reg got shopped by the others and we both got two years' probation. The others, due to their previous records, were sent to Borstal.

I was banned from ever seeing Reg again, by his father, even though I did not tell on him. That had nothing to do with it; we had committed a crime. Reg and I met in private as we saw out the probation period, and we were never to sin in that way again.

The last occasion that I recall any real contact with Popa was at the house on the corner of East Park Road and Everton Road. We had two rooms upstairs, and we were directly across the road from the local cinema, which showed Saturday morning matinees, *Lassie* included, and thrillers which always ended with *To be continued...* . You had to go back the following week.

I was now sweet 16 and Popa's curfew for me was 10.00 p.m. I always obeyed, and got back at the right time, but one night I was met on the stairs by a lady lodger who asked me to go down the road to the corner shop and buy her some stockings that she needed for the next day. Ever helpful, and totally unthinking, I did as she asked, but I had failed to ask Popa's permission. When I got back, it was 10.30 p.m. and the door was locked.

I knocked but got no answer. I threw stones at the window and although the lights were all on, I couldn't get in. Eventually, the lady on the top floor opened her window and said she was unable to open the door as Popa had locked it, but if I could throw up the stockings, at least she could go to bed!

Astounded, I told her where to go and knocked even louder. Popa opened the door, and let me in with that serious look. I tried to explain, but he wasn't hearing any of it; I had made a mistake and he was going to let me have it.

I went to my room, and thought I had better not take my overcoat off. I sat on the edge of my bed, waiting for the sound of his steps on the creaking floorboards and the inevitable beating that would result. This part was often worse than the beatings; the mental torture that was conjured up by the anticipation of what was to come and what would be used to execute the punishment. I waited for almost an hour to hear the creaks, and then Popa walked into my room carrying an old piece of dirty garden hose. Before he could grab me by the collar, which was the usual move, I darted under my single bed, my backside just missing the bare bed springs, and clung to the frame. I was being yanked by the legs, but I held on for dear life, and I wasn't letting go.

Something happened, I don't know what, and Popa let go of my legs. I seized the opportunity and shot out of the room, down and through the front door, and ran, not knowing where to go. Lungs heaving, legs pumping, I made a vow right then that I was never, ever, going to be beaten again.

I slept rough for a couple of days but I still managed to go to school. Around the third day, Popa waited outside the school and asked me if I was going to come home. I said I wouldn't if he was going to keep on hitting me. He said that it would not happen again.

Chapter 3: The Work World

One day, Popa just retired, upped, and left for Jamaica. I was now on my own, with rent to pay. What was I to do? The mock exams came and went, and I knew that I was going to take approximately six CSEs. I could not wait for school days to come to an end and get out into the big wide world. I knew I was never going to be an academic. I met with the careers officer, and all he told me was that, based on my potential, I would end up in an office as a clerk. That was all. After hearing this, I didn't bother with taking the exams. So I left school, and went into my first of many office jobs.

My first job was with the gas board. I spent (or was it wasted?) the very first two years of my working life, in an office of 500 people, all facing in the same direction. I was a 'customer complaints' clerk. This meant that if you had a problem with the gas board, equipment or supply, you initially came to see me, often with the faulty meter in hand.

I remember clearly the computer department that controlled the gas board's business; there was the gigantic old IBM machine that took up an area of about 200 yards, the total space below the office of 500 people.

Every transaction had to be logged and typed, and each customer's information was held on an oblong card with small oblong holes punched into it. The computer read this information and produced, overnight, a report on reams and reams of paper for us to examine the next day. How things have changed! This same information can now be held on a device the size of a pinhead.

This place with the very long corridors and row upon row of desks became my prison. I did not enjoy or care to remember much of it. It led me to quickly try and get out, and make a better future.

It was a very unsociable set-up and forging friendships was difficult. I cannot even remember who the prime minister of the day was. If you were to ask about what plague and pestilence, what wars or threat of wars were around, I would not be able to say.

I suppose we all had differing levels of awareness in those early days. I was just getting on the road to life and there were other important matters that concerned me. Needless to say, I jumped at the earliest opportunity to move on, but that took nearly two years. I was then 18 and full of life – girlfriends came and went. My friends and I passed girls around just like you would a bag of sweets. You chose one, liked her for a while, and then you passed the bag to someone else.

Each time, I thought I was in love, but the pain of parting did not last long, except from one redhead called Elaine, who lived opposite the park. She came to Sunday school and belonged to the Girls' Brigade. She was taller than most, and she was beautiful!

And so began a round robin of coffee bars, church and the Hungry Eye. We saw each other frequently and our romance consisted of holding hands and kissing – and holding hands and kissing. But the time came for her to move on, and she gave me the elbow. This did not sink in, and many a time I could be found outside her house crying and asking why? Her parents did not heed my tears but, instead, threw a bucket of water from the third floor window and drenched me.

It wasn't love. It was just that, as men, we were the ones who were supposed to call off the date, and not get dumped by the female. Real macho men timed the break-up perfectly, and real men called it off first. I had timed it wrongly and if word got out that I was dumped, ridicule and micky-taking would follow. So my emotional pleading was geared towards getting her back before word got out, then I could dump her, thereby saving face. My plans failed miserably.

The guys got a bellyful of laughs and I moved on to Jayne. She had wide, luscious lips, a figure to die for, and we could not keep our hands off each other. She was memorable, but eventually she went the way of all the others.

Mercier Mainwaring, the eldest of my friends from B.B., was responsible for introducing me to merchandising and stock control, and it was with no regrets that I moved to Easiephit as a stock controller. I spent two years working for Greenlees/Easiephit Shoes, a company which was part of the larger group called the British Shoe Corporation. Greenlees sold inexpensive shoes to the masses, and at that time had at least 400 shops. While at Easiephit, I knuckled down and learned a craft that was to take me far and wide. This was a small, intimate office, and Mercier and I were the only two black people employed there. My responsibility at work was to allocate a range of shoes to the many shops around the country. Each morning, we would look at the stock and sales report, and we would look at each individual shop's position and replenish stock to its proper stockholding position. There were various warehouses around the country that reacted to our stock allocation directive, and stock would move daily to each shop. This form of stock control was how things were done in those early years. Later, centralised warehousing was to become the norm.

Dissatisfaction with the job set in soon after I had mastered all the skills it offered and I started to look around. It was to no avail.

Mercier was going out with Doreen Harper, a young, ebony-coloured girl with lovely white teeth. Their dating was coming to an end, and, as was the norm, I was waiting in the wings. We soon started a relationship. This was to become my first full-blown sexual relationship.

We were young and in love, and had eyes only for each other. Everything else went by the wayside, as we spent every conceivable moment of time together. Her mother did not approve, but how do you stop young love? We were with each other every moment and, soon enough, Doreen became pregnant.

Now here I was, barely out of nappies, earning about seven pounds ten shillings per week. I had rent to pay, food, light, etc. - oh, and going out with the boys. No one even mentioned abortion, I am not sure we even knew what it meant. But Doreen's mum had to know about the pregnancy. She was told and, naturally, my name became even dirtier than before. Church folk began to see her expanding waistline and we knew something had to be done. But what? Now, this is where the rest becomes blurred. Someone must have suggested marriage. This did not come from me or Doreen, but it made some kind of sense. After all, 18 and 20 year olds do get married, don't they?

So, we got married in the church before the birth. With Popa gone, I had no one to stand by me, but all my friends were there. Doreen and I had a white wedding. We took the inevitable photographs on the steps of Melbourne Hall and, as for our reception, I'm not sure if we had or could afford one. But I was a young man with a wife whose name would be changed from Harper to Evans. We were about to have a 'great' start to married life - living in one room with a baby almost due. How were we going to manage?

I thought about running away so many times. I knew I could manage if I just left and avoided what was inevitably going to be heartache. But my upbringing would not allow me to shaft my responsibilities. Popa and Auntie always taught me to remain steadfast and to never cop out. Ringing through my ears was the motto of the Boys' Brigade: 'Sure and Steadfast.'

Mr Motivator says: *You know, it is at times like this you need someone around you who has the sense to say, "Come on, babies, do the sensible thing, rather than the right thing." If I had someone like that, maybe I wouldn't have continued along the road that was doomed to failure. Yes, we should always try to do what is right; however, when you are young, you need to converse with someone who is older and hopefully wiser. If you don't have the luxury of a family close by, then take time to seek out others, organisations who can offer free advice. Being well-armed and prepared will pay dividends in the end. Don't travel life's road alone; with help and companionship, the journey can be so much easier. Seek always the counsel, of others.*

Carolyne's Birth

The months went by, and Doreen got bigger and bigger. Carolyne Angela Evans came along on 23rd August 1972.

She was lovely. She looked like me, but it's hard to recall all the fatherly feelings that I know I had, because, with an unplanned child, and us so young and inexperienced and pressured by new responsibilities, how were we supposed to feel? All I knew was that I now had to work even harder than before.

The mornings were early and the nights were late, and I had to make ends meet, but I seemed to have lost my way – what was I to do? I kept on thinking that something must come up, that God would provide. But is it not stated that 'God helps those who help themselves'?

Each day, I got up and went to work at Easiephit. The days were tough; we were just scraping by on my wages and I knew something had to be done before long. I set about trying to find work further afield that could offer me more and, at least, give us the chance to leave poverty behind.

London Green Shield - 1974

In what little way that Doreen and I talked, it was suggested that maybe I should try looking for work in London, so I started to apply for any job that needed stock control or merchandising experience. Most came back with the standard reply: "Sorry, you do not possess the right qualifications for the job that we have to offer." I kept my spirits up.

I saw a job from an agency called Bull Homes. They were looking for a stock controller. I applied, got a favourable response and I was invited to go to London for an interview. I actually got the job! I was going to work for Green Shield Stamps, a company started by Richard Tompkins, who had set up a system whereby customers got trading stamps every time they bought petrol or goods. These stamps were saved in a book, and when the required numbers of books were completed, they could be redeemed for luxury items at designated centres. Green Shield had a number of these centres up and down the UK, and these shops held stock of anything from pens to fridges, every item having its own redeemable value.

I would be working at their office in Colindale, North West London. This was a big jump forward and an opportunity not to be missed. But there were some drawbacks. It would mean going to live in London. I went home and told Doreen of my decision. I would stay in London during the week, and come home on weekends. She was not happy, but I had decided and that was how it would be. It was not up for discussion.

The problem was where to stay. I knew no one in London, but Doreen managed to persuade her aunt to take me in. She lived in Stamford Hill with her husband and two children, and I was faced with quite a journey from North London to North West London every day. Undaunted, I packed my clothes, kissed my wife and baby, and left for London. As luck would have it, Green Shield introduced a coach that brought staff daily to and from work.

I was kind of glad to get away, but for how long?

It was cold when I arrived in London and it would get even colder. Living in Stamford Hill had lots of problems. It is never very easy living with another family. Yes, the Howses were a very close-knit family, and they treated me very well indeed, taking me into their warmth and security. But I felt this was not where I should be, and I soon felt that I was overstaying my welcome.

The early morning travel was also getting to me. The traffic across to Colindale was unbearable, and I said to myself that as soon as I felt settled into the job, I would try and move to somewhere better suited for me and the family. It is amazing how time away can either 'make the heart grow fonder,' or it becomes, 'out of sight, out of mind'.

Green Shield offered me new challenges. My role was to allocate a range of gift items to the many redeeming centres that they had. In the office, there were quite a few other stock controllers, each with their own product range to look after. We all reported to the merchandise manager, who reported to the overall manager; we all had dotted line responsibilities to the assistant or buyer. As they brought in goods, we took over.

My horizons were being broadened and I learned some new disciplines and principles of stock control. Whilst there, I developed a friendship with Loel Tuitt, who lived over in Hackney. He served as a good distraction from many of my problems, and the one area that needed to be filled was the void created by being away from all my mates, especially the ones from Melbourne Hall and the Boys' Brigade. I missed the gang badly.

I did go back to see the family each weekend, but it felt hurried, not just in getting down there but also in respect of my mind and attitude. I was growing up and moving on.

I felt as if I was in a huge river, rapids racing by, and me without a paddle. Unfortunately, I was in it. I wanted to go forward, but there was heavy baggage to tow. If I had stayed on my £8 per week and not moved for £40 per week, I would have been protected from all the temptations and distractions of this very alluring world.

Boys' Brigade was my anchor and I was vulnerable in London, with no religious help or moral guidance. I made up every reason for going home every other weekend, instead of a weekly trip. It didn't take long for me to be in London for three weeks before I would set foot in Leicester. Then things suddenly took a change.

I had thought that my wife and new baby were tidily looked after. I was shocked one day when I came home from work to find Doreen, Carolyne and suitcases deposited at her aunt's.

We argued about her returning to Leicester, but I was told, "No way!" She felt that, the more uncomfortable and difficult we made our circumstances, the more likely we would get considered for a council place. Although I was against this reasoning, we decided to move into another lady's front room, and then all three of us went to see Social

Services. They told us that we should go back to Leicester, but that was not in the equation. We packed our bags and went to the final place of help, the Homeless Family unit. The queue was very long, and Carolyne was fretful, but we waited outside, sitting on the one suitcase that held all that we owned. I saw my family suffering and with only me to depend on, and, so it seemed, only me to give any sensible answers.

I dwelt on being away from the closeness of all my mates in the church and the Boys' Brigade – I was now on my own, with a family. I knew I would have to learn to cope. I never felt so lonely.

We had made our choices for good or bad. We spent what seemed like ages sitting on our suitcase outside the Homeless Family unit, and by the end of the day, they offered us a bed for the night. We moved into a bed and breakfast in Holloway Road, North London, our first test of survival – up the river without a paddle in big London.

The B&B was a large, three-storey Victorian building, situated on one of London's busiest roads. Our room was on the second floor and we shared the bathroom with two other families. Conditions were sparse and not clean. There was a bed at the far end of the room, with a dirty bay window on the right as you entered. The carpet was threadbare, and, due to lack of space, Carolyne had to share our bed.

In my heart, I cried, knowing that even if we could, we wouldn't stay there for long. Every day, I made the long journey to work at Green Shield. I gained a lot of knowledge and my experience in stock control was increasing, but I was feeling very restless, and I was on the lookout for advancement and new challenges.

Argos

I spent more and more time away from home and, at the end of the day, I saw few reasons to rush back. Things were going very well at work for me, and it was announced at the end of 1974 that Mr Tompkins was setting up a new catalogue showroom called Argos Distributors and they wanted me to go across as part of the merchandise team. I grabbed the chance, and my first task was to get the merchandise ready for the very first shop opening in the UK, in Colindale.

It was while working for Argos that a number of people came into my life. Some left a lasting impression, while others had little impact.

One that was to become a very useful association was with Connie Worsley, an English lady some ten years older than me, very posh and sophisticated, and still living with her parents in Mill Hill. She worked for Green Shield Stamps as their Charity Coordinator. Her job, as the title suggested, was to organise charity events for the company, the beneficiaries being disabled children and the disadvantaged. Connie's pet project was to raise funds for the Across Trust. This charity took disabled kids to Lourdes in France, and she was heavily involved in other fundraising activities. I cannot remember how we met, but this was a relationship that was going somewhere, she hoped.

Other things were not great. Doreen had a few problems with the other tenants and we had to move to another room near Finsbury Park, then finally one in Endymion Road. These places were no better. We found everything wrong and our tolerance was tested. We squabbled over most things and, from this very early stage, I realised that we had made a mistake, but we needed to try and make things work, if only for the benefit of Carolyne.

Then things took a dramatic turn. We spent considerable time trying to convince the council of our need to have a place of our own and, finally, they offered us a council flat in the same locale. Ennis Road provided us with our first real home; a bedroom, lounge, and our own kitchen and bathroom.

"Heaven!" we thought, until we realised the house backed onto a derelict dumping site that bred rats. The house was full of them! We set about furnishing and making things comfortable; we had to prop up the bed on books, in an attempt to stop the rats from jumping near Carolyne. It seemed to work, but many an, evening they could be seen running around the room. Needless to say, I was not happy. I hated going home, and I started to do so later and later.

I was also being distracted by my work associations. Green Shield had a country club for its staff, and I could regularly be found there playing squash or going to the late night disco. Doreen got more annoyed at my absence and I blamed it on my workload. Little did she realise that this was just one of my many concocted reasons.

I loved my daughter, but unfortunately that was not reason enough to stay. I wanted to be free of commitment and I wanted to enjoy my youth. After all, I had just come out of school and here I was with a family. It had all happened so quickly and responsibility had come about before I was ready.

But we men are such cowards. In my circle, most men behaved this way: don't forget when you do not have a father figure to guide you through matters of a personal nature, you just fumble in the dark. I was never told the facts of life, we never discussed feelings. We see things that are wrong, especially in a relationship, and we know what is required to make it right, but we never, ever grab it by the horns and deal with it. We give hints and show that we have made a decision, but we wait for our partners to make the first move. I did not have to wait long - a plant that is not watered withers and dies, and one day I came home to see someone else watering mine.

I decided to try and get some accommodation nearer work, so I looked through the local paper and saw an advertisement of a B&B for £1.50 per night, so I called the lady up. I told her that I needed something initially by the day and I wasn't too sure for how long but it would help me if I could be as varied as that. She agreed and I packed a small bag and went to see the room after work.

I arrived in a road at the back of Edgware, and the door was answered by a little Jewish lady.

From the look on her face, I could see that she was frightened by my appearance. After all, it was after nine o'clock in the evening, and although she was expecting me, she wasn't expecting what was in front of her.

She said gruffly, "Yes, what do you want?" I said I was Mr Evans with whom she had spoken with earlier that day. She said, "I suppose that you had better come in. The room is upstairs and you have to book for a minimum of three days and you will be sharing. Take your shoes off." When we got upstairs, I was about to put my coat down on the bed. "No coats on the bed! And can I have the money in full upfront?" All of this was said in one breath! I obliged to all her requests and she ran out of the room closing the door quickly behind her.

How strange, I thought, but I could not return home, not now. I also felt that I had to show her that I knew what her game was and I was not prepared to let her continue with her ignorance.

The next day, I went downstairs and waited for breakfast. She rushed into the dining room, threw something on a plate, shoved it at me, and then scuttled out. It became clear to me that she was all alone with me in the house and that must have been her worry. By the end of three days, I was ready to leave, but she was now a little bit slower at going through the door.

She turned after depositing my breakfast on the table.

"Mr Evans, you do know that the other evening I was trying to put you off staying?"

"Yes."

She continued, "Well, why didn't you just go?"

"I felt that I had something to prove."

"Well", she said, "my son always said that one day a black man would arrive on my doorstep and I wouldn't know how to handle it! I mean, all you read in the newspaper is bad things and that black people cause so much trouble, but," and this is the comment that was to be repeated time and time again over the years to come, "you are different to all the rest. Mr Evans, you are welcome to stay with me anytime in the future."

Well, I smiled and left, and I have never seen this lady again.

Chapter 4: Single Parenthood

Doreen Gives Carolyne Up

I called Doreen and we discussed what had been happening and explored a number of avenues, especially getting back together. We talked for a long time and I talked about seeing her later on in the week. I asked about Carolyne, and she said she was fine. Later that week, I thought I'd surprise her. I didn't realise how much of a surprise it would be.

I arrived home early and the door was locked and before it opened, I heard voices and the sound of people scuttling about. Something was afoot. It would seem my timing was off, and, after the door opened, I went in. You know when you catch a child doing something that they shouldn't? Well, it was just like that. An 'old friend' was sheepishly sitting on the bed. Doreen proceeded to explain how he had just arrived to pay a visit and would be leaving later that day. I almost believed them but I decided there and then that the time had come to move on. Doreen deserved to get some comfort and peace in her life, and I had a different agenda.

Carolyne

Time passed, and eventually I got a call to say that Doreen was back in Leicester, living with her mother in a council flat. She wanted to see me about Carolyne.

The next available weekend, I went on the coach from Golders Green to meet up with her. I was looking forward to seeing Carolyne because I had not seen her for a while now. I wondered what she would be like.

I arrived on the Friday evening at about 8 p.m. and went straight to Doreen's mother Frances' flat. They were in, and the door opened, rather cautiously. I got the distinct feeling that I was not truly welcome but, coming from a reluctant mother-in-law, this was quite normal.

Carolyne was all over me. She was young, but children forgive and move on so easily. We grown-ups have such a lot to learn! The tension in the air was heavy and difficult, but I was so immersed in seeing Carolyne that I went to a place I thought no one could possibly invade, but then it was invaded.

Doreen opened with a statement that I never would have thought possible. She said, "I am having problems looking after Carolyne. Could you look after her for a while?"

I was shocked; I did not want to argue about a mother's responsibility, just in case she started to think and change her mind. I immediately said I would go away until the Saturday evening and, if she was serious, to have Carolyne ready by 6 p.m. Saturday.

On the way out the door, Frances gave me a disapproving look and said if I took Carolyne with me, she would lie to the courts to ensure that Carolyne came back home to her mother.

Saturday was a strange day as I wandered around the shops in the Haymarket Centre. I went to see some of my mates and I did everything to allow the time to pass quickly.

I could not wait to get back to see Carolyne. I was so excited about taking her home, the anticipation was killing me. I arrived very early and waited outside. At six on the dot, I rang the doorbell. Doreen opened it and, when I got inside, Carolyne's things were ready. Not many words passed between us, just goodbyes, and with Carolyne in my arms and a bag across my shoulder, I went quickly for the door.

Frances was in the way. "Why don't you let me look after her?" she said. "You will never be able to manage. You are a young man who wants to go out and be free. Give her to me!" I remembered that I had been given away and I knew there and then that I could and would be a better daddy than most. I was going to be there for my daughter.

With Carolyne.

On the coach back to London, I wondered how on earth I was going to manage. I was now living in one room in a house in Edgware. Three other guys shared the rest of the bedrooms, but we all shared the lounge and bathroom. I had to get to work every day. I needed a childminder and I needed some plans. I had no idea what they would be, but some proper planning was necessary.

I needed more than the two hours back to Golders Green to focus on how we were ever going to manage. It was also a time for me to enjoy what I felt were to be my last moments of freedom. Carolyne was asleep and, as I gazed down at her, I knew that nothing was to ever be the same again. The path of my life was set. It is said that the moment of decision is what shapes your life forever. My moment was here. There was no turning back.

I would have to change. I would need to be a father, mother, breadwinner, and a stable and caring person for a young, impressionable person. My daughter would need me in a way that I had never been needed before. I had little ammunition other than the will to survive; I would need to prove to myself that I could do this, and that would silence the detractors.

Carrying a sleeping child can be quite a task, with bags in hand and a long walk ahead. I quickly covered the two miles to our home, but when I arrived outside the house, I stopped and, for a moment, I took a deep breath. For a moment, my breathing synchronised with Carolyne's and we stepped inside. Unsure of what to expect, I looked around the room. The guys all said hello, and as I took the sleeping Carolyne upstairs, I paused, and told them that I had a problem, that I needed some time to sort things out, to bear with me and I would keep her out of their way as much as possible. They all smiled approvingly.

Sunday was a day that I wanted to last and last, just so I didn't have to face my future travelling arrangements. I had to get from Edgware to Harlesden, with a choice of the tube into town and then out, or a 260 or 266 bus from Mill Hill Broadway. I decided that what would make everything possible was to get a childminder near Edgware, or even better, Harlesden. I made some calls to people that I knew and it wasn't long before I was told about a woman in Harlesden who took in three year olds. I called her and, luckily, she had space. It was now evening so I set about combing and plaiting Carolyne's hair – for a first attempt, I didn't do badly. I bathed her, and after dinner it was off to bed. Although she was more settled than on Saturday night, I did not sleep very well.

I had taken on a tough one and very quickly I was seeing why such responsibility sent so many men AWOL, but I was determined and, though I did not know it at the time, I was to realise how much of a blessing it would be.

I awoke at 6 a.m., allowing myself enough time to get everything done and to get to work by 9 a.m. I estimated that, as long as I left the house by 7 a.m., the walk to the bus station should take no more than 20 minutes, then four to five minutes on the bus and, because I was ahead of the school's traffic, I should be in Harlesden by 8:15 a.m. A short walk around the corner to the minder, back on the buses and I should be casually walking up the driveway to my new job.

Everything went like clockwork. I arrived with 15 minutes to spare, but leaving Carolyne was not easy. She was reluctant to go to this lady, a stranger, and although all the other kids gave her some attention, I had to leave her crying for me. I was tearful too, although I knew she would settle in. I promised her a surprise, and this principle of achievement and reward was applied throughout the early years of all my children. I have used this method to spur them on very successfully. This was only the start.

As the days went by, I got more and more accustomed to my daily routine, and surprisingly, I enjoyed looking after her. Her arrival put certain restrictions on what I was able to do and, one thing for sure, I did not want to leave her any more than I already had to; my nights were mainly spent with her and we did most things together.

Already, I was planning and trying to work out how I was going to get enough money together to be able to get a place that we could call home. At some stage, Carolyne's mother would want her back and when she came knocking, I knew I would not be willing to give up my child. I was convinced that, though the days may run into months and even years, surely when she saw her daughter growing up, she would want her back. How would I convince a judge to leave her with me?

These thoughts haunted me, so I continued to formulate my plans. I had left Argos, and so left many friends. I had also moved from Colindale and was now working much further away, but the challenge was great and I found that RHM offered me so much more. I was employed for my Stock Control and merchandising experience. I revelled in the knowledge that I had and was using this to the fullest. RHM produced Saxa Salt, Cerebos Salt, Paxo Stuffing, Bero Flour, McDougal Flour and Sharwoods products. These were huge brands that made RHM a multinational company; there were not many homes that did not use one or more of these products. RHM was very proactive, and interested in getting the best from each employee, and because of its policy of sending all staff on management courses, I gained invaluable insight into all aspects of business. I also spent time working at a Tesco branch learning the principles of stores stock control and merchandising of products when they arrived from manufacturers.

I now saw Connie Worsley very often, and she became a useful person to be around in those early stages. In short order, I was to realise how important 'who you knew' was in relation to 'what you knew.'

Connie seemed to have all the contacts in the world. She met a huge number through the Across Trust, of which there were many celebrities and I was fortunate to be on her arm whenever there was a function. We met mostly on the weekend and she visited me where I lived with Carolyne in West Way Edgware. She became a good friend to Carolyne and, because of her personality, she was a very calming influence in our lives. I had been out with very few ladies and I found Connie intriguing. She had such great qualities and a wonderful nature.

I was drawn to Connie's kindness and attention. I started to want a deeper relationship with her, so much so that we became inseparable. I recognised that Carolyne was going through a time of real instability and she needed me to be there almost a hundred per cent. There were many nights when she would wake up crying, and I knew that it was because of all the moving around and being in a strange house with new and different faces. I was aware that, no matter what, I had to ensure that she was happy, and to achieve this, there was nothing else to do but be there for her.

But I had my own needs for adult attention and Connie's friendship was important to me.

As expected, our relationship developed, and we became intimate. Connie also started to take a real interest in Carolyne. She was caring and responsible and provided a comfort zone for Carolyne whenever she had her for the weekend, but she didn't try to become a replacement mother to her. Whenever I felt that it was possible, we would meet, but away from where I lived. Carolyne was still having some sleepless nights, and there were many a time when I had to stay up just reading her stories and reminding her how much she was loved.

Mill Hill was, and still is, a very strong Jewish community in North West London, and although this area became my home, I was desperate for a better place to live. I knew that we could not carry on living in one room for much longer and, though I got a reasonable wage from RHM, I needed much more before I could ever hope to get on the property ladder.

Doreen met Carolyne under my supervision and, as human nature would have it, especially mothers, she hinted at wanting Carolyne back. I knew that living where I was would not bode well in the eyes of the law. She would be able to offer what could be perceived as better surroundings and a better environment for Carolyne's upbringing. She would be able to show that while she had agreed for me to look after Carolyne for a while, she had a better framework in place to look after her. So what was I to do? I had now altered my way of life so much to be with Carolyne that I was not willing to give her up. But then, wouldn't I be relieved to have the freedom of being no longer married and also not having the responsibility of being a one-parent family?

The thought ran through my head. I could have freedom on the one hand, or restrictions on the other. Was this a decision similar to what my mother had faced? I had many sleepless nights as the day of decision drew closer. A plan came to mind, but I did not want to discuss this with Connie. I knew she cared deeply about me, although, in the eyes of her parents, I was an outsider from a different class, and – stating the obvious – I was black, had a child to look after, and was still married. I was definitely not the ideal candidate for their pride and joy. I also knew that Connie was willing to go against the wishes of her parents and I knew that she was quite prepared to do as I wanted.

But guilt became my obstacle and I was not sure if I could suggest what I was thinking about, and so I debated internally; it would mean commitment. It would mean my intimating undying love. I cared, but I was not in love. I still carried all the scars of my previous relationship and I was not in the frame of mind to jump into another alliance. This much I admitted to her.

So we talked about my needs and her desires, especially to have a place of her own. We talked about the interracial problem that we would have; after all, 1976 was a time when a white and black person being seen in public together was not well received. Connie had the wherewithal and she was prepared to move in with me.

As we went shopping in The Broadway, all eyes were on us; everyone was looking and I felt the first wave of disapproving glances. I was never sure if she noticed or even cared, but I did. I waved at each person, which made them do a quick about face. At the time, it was a big laugh but I did wonder if we would always be able to turn the other cheek. I began to realise that if you are a black person in a white society, you are always reminded of what you are. I never needed that though; from the moment I got up and looked in the mirror, I knew who I was.

Oh, it was so different if you were Jewish or of Irish extraction; you could get away from prejudices and fit in, and, for the most part, get away with it. Yes, I know that when you open up your mouth, you do give yourself away, but a black person doesn't ever get that opportunity. Oh, how I wished things could be different.

I knew moving in and living with Connie was only a temporary position for me, because I did not see myself being involved permanently with a white person. Prejudices come from ignorance; people live in their own little world and whilst we Jamaicans were prepared to leave our homeland and come over to the UK and perform all kinds of manual jobs, we were not welcome. I was here to stay, but I was constantly made to feel that I did not belong. This was a feeling that would remain with me for many years.

I made a vow then, that no matter what, I would never carry a visible chip on my shoulder, that I would do what I had to do to succeed, then make sure that I earned enough to return to my Jamaica. I knew that I needed to do what was necessary and, if it meant exploiting any situation for my family's benefit, it had to be done. Conscience was no restriction.

Connie was prepared to find a flat and live with me, and she was doing this hoping I would eventually come round and want to be with her. I was doing it because I needed to have stability so that my daughter would have what she needed. We found a two-bedroom flat in Millway, Mill Hill and the Jewish lady in question was prepared to rent this firstly to Connie and eventually to me. We settled into our new home and, from there, I was ready to plan the next stage of my battle to win custody of Carolyne.

Back in the Office

I was not a very faithful person; I had the loyalty of the girl I was living with, but I hated the commitment that was required. I started a casual relationship with a Caucasian woman who lived somewhere in Harlesden. This was only a gap filler and I could not even tell you now how long I was seeing her, but somewhere along the line my colleague Mike took a liking to her. Initially, he was not aware of my association with her, so I encouraged it mainly because I was about to move to other pastures.

Mike started this relationship and he went out most lunchtimes for his rendezvous. He was continually late back from lunch and work was beginning to suffer. Someone had to fill in for him. This I did willingly, with the proviso that he paid me for 'overtime'. I prepared most of his distribution reports and I got extra funds for doing extra work that did not take much time.

Deception

It was during this time in 1976 that I met Jewel Poulis. This was just a meeting between two people with a particular need. She worked in the typing pool. We flirted constantly and all my free time found me hovering around her. She was a beautiful young woman, with a slim waist, small but noticeable breasts, long flowing hair, and a chocolate brown complexion. She had the most wonderful, perfect teeth that helped to form a sweet and lovely smile.

Her parentage was Guyanese and she made a pretty picture, with her long hair swishing down the back of the pretty floral dresses she liked to wear. I liked being around her, but she was in a relationship and I was living with someone else. I also needed to ensure that Carolyne was not confused, so I could not let her realise that someone else was in the picture. We went for lunches and occasionally for dinner. It was not long before we were a secret item and Chapter Road, where she lived, became a meeting place for many a rendezvous.

Part two of my plan needed to be put in place because Doreen was on the 'I want my baby back' path and I knew that I had to get to a position of owning a place. I could now not decide whether to continue with my relationship with Connie, or move on. I gained a lot by being with her – was I ready to let her go?

A flat became available in Mill Hill. On my own, I would not be able to afford it, so Connie and I discussed it and we decided to buy it. It would be a joint purchase. Imagine, me, a property owner! This was not how I had imagined it, but I needed to have what could be considered a permanent and homely situation if I was ever to hope to get custody of Carolyne.

Promotion

In the meantime, while the relevant paperwork flew between the solicitors, I continued to work hard at RHM, and things were looking up. They were about to launch a new range of low-calorie drinks called Energen One-Cal. The production would be outside the group factories and most of the organisational set-up would be handled by the marketing department. The marketing manager, Nigel Kingston, advertised for a production controller; someone with the experience of RHM's core products and also the distribution network. This person would visit canning factories and advise marketing on capacities and set-up production plans.

I went for the interview. After all, I had received glowing reports and appraisals from Mike Tait, and his boss Alan West saw no reason not to endorse what Mike had to say. Before the interview, Alan West called me in to tell me that he'd had conversations with Nigel and there were a number of other applicants, many with appropriate degrees; it was a university run department but it was worth going to the interview, if only for the experience – but I should not hold my breath as it was unlikely that I would get the post.

Alan West's little chat was intended to get me fired up, but I had learned that I would never be handed anything on a plate; I had to go out there and take it for myself. I walked into the first floor offices, full of suited individuals hard at work. I shook Nigel's outstretched hand and he invited me to sit down.

He seemed ill at ease, as if he had something negative to say before we had even started. We sat in silence for a while and so to break the ice, I started to tell him about the time I had spent in the distribution department, that it had been enjoyable, that I had attended a number of management courses and felt able to handle whatever responsibility he could throw at me. He listened without comment; I wondered if I should keep speaking rather than stop and give him time to ask a question that would throw me.

I told him that I needed the job, and the extra money would come in handy as I had a daughter to look after; that one important quality that I would bring to the table was loyalty and consistency, which I believed the job required. Nigel made a motion to speak and I saw that I was about to hear what I had seen on his face.

He questioned whether I realised that only graduates were ever employed in the marketing department and, in all the time that he had been there, he has never seen a black man employed in any office department in the company. For a moment, I digested what he said. Only then did I realise that he was right; there wasn't another black person in any office position – I was the only one.

Then he said something else that made me look up and realise that here was a genuine person. He said that he did not care where I came from, that as far as he was concerned, I brought to the table a level of experience that he believed the position required, and that things could get rough, but he was sure that I could handle it.

I thanked him and I also assured him that I would not be letting him or myself down. I left his office floating on cloud nine – at last, I was being judged on ability. I called Connie, and she was pleased for me, but out of the corner of my eye, I saw Jewel and I thought, "Time to celebrate." Connie was going to be late, so that lunchtime, I went home with Jewel. She looked great in this flowery dress. We didn't wait to be upstairs before her dress was on the floor.

Homeowner

We moved into 68 The Fairway, Mill Hill on a beautiful day in October 1976. Connie's folks came over to help us carry our belongings into a first floor purpose-built maisonette. We had use of part of the garden and we looked out at the local primary school.

Carolyne in Day Care

I had been advised by my solicitor, John Harte, to get Carolyne registered at the local school, as this would impact positively on the impending court case. My problem was that I left for work too early in the mornings to take her to school; what I needed was a childminder closer to where we were living. There seemed no way to change things, as we did not know many people locally. I searched for answers, but all the time it was staring me in the face.

One day, Carolyne and I were just walking down to the local park, and we passed a building next to the local primary school – The Fairway. We had walked by this building several times, but I never before noticed the sign, which said 'Orphanage'. My mind ticked over, and I wondered if they looked after children during the day. I saw a woman's face looking out of the window and she smiled warmly, so we went down the drive.

She continued to smile as she opened the door. She introduced herself as Debbie and she asked how she could be of help.

I was desperate to think of a story that would break down any objections, so I asked if we could look around. There were lots of rooms with play things, toys, etc; all the kids were outside playing, but there were not many around; apparently, most had gone to see relatives. We got into a deep conversation and I learned that the orphanage was run by the local council for homeless kids, or families who just could not manage. Most of the kids went to The Fairway Primary School during the day, which meant the orphanage was used as a day nursery for the under-fives. To qualify for a place, one needed to make representation at the local town hall on any working day.

I bombarded Debbie with my problems; single parent, working hours, regular minder was sick, no immediate family in London; and as I pleaded, I realised I was breaking through. "I shouldn't and I can't – there are rules and regulations about admittances," she said. Then, relenting, she said she might be able to do something. I should return in the morning at about 7.30 a.m. and if it were possible, Carolyne could attend the day care for a few days, but I needed to get onto the town hall. She wasn't sure how favourably they would look upon my circumstances.

I thanked her and took Carolyne home, forgetting about the park. She was excited about going to the nursery and she couldn't wait until the morning. I was not able to prepare her for any possible disappointment. Carolyne got up earlier than usual, and I got her ready for the short walk across the road. I wasn't nervous about it; I felt positive things were about to start, and the lady we had met liked us and seemed prepared to help.

We said goodbye to Connie and went across the road, where there were lots of kids milling around, arriving after a weekend away. We walked down the drive to meet Debbie, and her outstretched hand made me realise she had arrived at a favourable decision. As she took Carolyne's hand, I left feeling that, at last, we were on firmer ground, something new and wonderful. I was so happy for Carolyne and I now needed to make this a permanent phase in her life.

I had no need to worry. I never needed to go to the town hall; our lady did it all for me. I did not ask what she did or what she said, but I have been forever thankful for what she did for me and Carolyne. Later, I was able to enrol Carolyne into The Fairway Primary School. I dropped her off each morning at the orphanage at 7.30 a.m. and they would make the short walk up to the school with her at 8.30 a.m.; they would then collect her at 2.30 p.m. and look after her until I got home. Some evenings, I would be home late, but as long as I telephoned the nursery, they would make all the arrangements.

Life could not be better.

It was great watching Carolyne growing up. She was definitely more settled, and I saw her as an essential part of my life and my well-being. But was I going to be able to keep her when her mother wanted her back?

On top of all this, I had made my life a little bit complicated. Connie loved me dearly and she saw her life with just me. She wanted me to be divorced so that we could get married, but I was not in a hurry to get divorced. I did not have to make a decision about Jewel because she was to leave for Jamaica to meet up with a policeman that she had befriended a few years before.

RHM was great. I felt good with my working environment and I could see the potential of all that I was doing. I was being paid good wages and I also had usage of a pool company car almost as required.

In my personal life, there were many other things that needed my attention. When the letter arrived, saying that Doreen wanted custody of Carolyne, my heart sank. The hearing would be in Leicester, so I had contacted my solicitor, John Harte. I had hoped that the use of a solicitor would not be necessary, but I wanted Carolyne to stay with me. I felt she was better off staying with me and I was willing to fight for her.

Mr Harte felt I had a good chance of winning. Carolyne was in a nursery, I was in a flat, and she was settled in a stable environment. The courts would loathe disturbing her, and although they would normally act in favour of the mother, there were these and other things stacked in my favour. Due to a requirement for a health visitor's report, the hearing date was cancelled and we applied for it to be heard in London.

I was prepared for the day at court. The hearing was to be held at Willesden Court House in a closed court. I arrived early. Carolyne was at nursery; she was not aware of what was about to happen and all my hope was pinned on Doreen not turning up. Running through my mind was what her mother had said on the day I arrived to collect her. I now expected a confrontation in court with the prospect of her grandmother lying through her teeth. I kept my fingers crossed and I looked up at every footstep, half expecting that it would be them.

We waited and waited; the appointed time came and went, and the usher kept saying to give her more time.

Doreen did the right thing; she did not arrive at court. It was Carolyne's day on 16th June 1978; it was ordered that, 'Carolyne Angela Evans to remain in the custody of the Petitioner Derrick Evans'.

The only item of my planning that had truly worked was getting Carolyne into school and getting her settled; I did not need to mislead Connie. Now I had custody, it was time to set Connie free. The cloud that had been over me lifted and I felt good. Everything worked for me; I was to receive my decree absolute, and with all this, I was officially a free person, but a single parent.

I've said before, men are cowards; I could have sat Connie down and talked it over. I could have done the grown-up thing and told her the truth – that I cared for her, but never loved her and that I wanted us to part. Instead, I began to show her less respect. I went out often and left her holding the baby.

Mr Motivator Says: *When we go through a lot, it is quite normal that in amongst all that hurt and disappointment, we long for some freedom, but using someone without their permission is not right. If I had sat Connie down and fully explained my feelings, at least she would have gone into things with eyes wide open; she would not have been used, and the outcome would have been the same: I would have got custody without the need to hurt someone. I became an obnoxious individual, who was selfish, unloving, and an unpleasant person to be with. This was all engineered to ensure that she became unhappy, and would take the hint and decide to move on.*

Connie was older than I and she did the mature thing; she confronted me. She knew things were not great. She did not deserve the kind of treatment that was being dished out. She felt that there was someone more deserving out there, and she was going to find him. She wanted out of our arrangement and if I couldn't buy her out, the place would have to be sold. I just nodded my head in agreement.

Over the next few weeks, I explored many avenues to a solution. It would have been easy if I had a legacy or close family, but there was no one around who could help. I was on my own. I went to see my bank manager, at Lloyd's of London in Mill Hill, who ushered me into his office. He knew a lot about me from the stack of customer cards, and he also knew that I was in front of him wanting to borrow money, with no security, which was to be used as a deposit on a flat costing £13,000.

He said he couldn't help. I was not prepared to give up so easily; I needed this place to be all mine. Carolyne's stable conditions had to continue. I was not sure how long Connie would be prepared to wait until I sorted out my funds, as she had already begun to withdraw from me, but more importantly from Carolyne. I tried to avoid the obviously tense atmosphere at home, but it became increasingly difficult to keep up appearances.

Connie was away more often without explanation and I had no right to ask. I cared, but as she had taken the decision, I just did not want a change of heart. So I said to the bank manager, "How about you loaning me the 10% deposit and as soon as the mortgage offer is received, I will give you security on the property for the £13,000?" He looked at me, surprised and puzzled, then replied, "I have never heard of that approach before, but if your mortgage is forthcoming, why not?"

We smiled at each other, I thanked him and left. This was to be the last time I saw an old-fashioned bank manager doing a real job, one who made decisions based on his confidence in me as an individual. That changed in the nineties and all decisions had to be referred to the head office. I left his office elated, I could now have my own property; Connie was free to leave. I watched her pack. I did not fight over any material things; whatever she wanted, she took. Her parents came to help her, and as she walked down the drive, Carolyne and I stood by the open window and waved goodbye.

There were no tears from me, just sadness that something so right could be so wrong and to this day, I sometimes wonder how she is. Life settled down and felt good; I spent most of my time with Carolyne and we did most things together. I rarely went out, and if I had been asked if I missed doing all the things that one did in their twenties, I would have had to say, "No".

I was watching a little girl growing up and, in spite of our rough, unstable beginning, she was carefree and happy, and life could not be better. I was not seeing anyone in particular, so I submerged myself in my work. I enjoyed the security that RHM offered me, but I felt I had done my time. Although I occasionally had use of a pool car, and I went out visiting all the production outlets, there were not enough challenges and very little variety. As I became more mature, job satisfaction was becoming even more important. The money was fine and I was able to pay all of my bills. I purchased a large number of suits from Burtons, the popular tailors then.

Life became more organised. I could easily find babysitters, and going out was never a problem. I was not a clubbing person, although Mike Tait did drag me along to many a disco night at the New Penny and Baileys, in Watford. There we met loads of girls who liked my moves. I was not the greatest dancer, but when I did my thing, everyone wanted to dance with me. A typical evening would start with us having a drink and as we were not into strong drinks, a St. Clements was our order (orange and lemon).

As we drank, we observed the great divide on the dance floor. Girls danced in groups with other girls, and boys just looked on. We wasted no time before heading to the dance floor. Now, Tatum, as I always called Mike, was no mover. He needed help badly, but no matter how much I spun and bounced, he would do it all to a rhythm of his own. I became very conscious of this and sometimes held off a bit. This cramped my style and I decided to put lots of space between me and him. He did get a lot of attention though, and managed to make me do all the work, then moved in on the women that I pulled. We usually danced the night away, and left dripping wet, with a conquest, or none at all.

There was a friend, Ian, who worked for RHM, that I played badminton with every Tuesday night. I would pick him up from his bedsit; this was my normal Tuesday night excursion. From the moment we met, we had a great friendship, but, apart from occasionally going out for a meal, badminton was the main thing that we shared. He was a young man of 24, very quiet and quite the opposite of me, but he was a thoughtful and gentle person, with whom I shared many interesting and diverse conversations. But one particular Tuesday, I failed to meet him because of work commitments. He was not at work the next day, and, in fact, not for the whole week. The following Tuesday, I went to collect him as was customary, only to be told by the landlady that he had committed suicide.

This was an important point in my life. Life is precious but loneliness can make you not want to keep it. My friend was lonely and he longed to be home in the Midlands. He lived in one room and did not socialise much with anyone, except possibly myself, and as I look back, I became convinced that he had been crying out for help, but no one was truly listening. Although we shared a few laughs, I had missed the warning signs. I faced a significant reality check and concluded that we all should place great value on ourselves and focus on how we will be remembered in the great jigsaw of life. We should never be the missing piece.

Mr Motivator Says: *There are so many times when we feel unloved, lonely, have difficulties and can't go on; times when it all can seem pointless. At times like these, you need to give some kind of sign to someone you know cares: talk, be vocal even though it is difficult. If those close to you don't seem to have the time or are missing your signals, then go outside, make a phone call – there are lots of organisations out there. You can always try some self-help, and that means getting away. Removing yourself from the things which make you feel low is the first step. So change your routine, find new things to do, take up new hobbies, do something for others. When you do something social, when you administer care, it rewards you and makes you feel so much better about yourself. Above all, tell yourself in the mirror that you are important, and then treat yourself.*

Jewel

I was driving one of the pool cars, and, as usual, I was playing my music and feeling very jolly; life was great and organised, I felt in control, and I had few worries. Money was there and I was not concerned; yes I could be earning more, and yes, I needed new challenges, but isn't it funny that just when you feel everything is going well, something happens to change it all?

I didn't have anyone special in my life at that moment. It was easy to get female attention, but I had made a decision to just play everything cool. It would be great to have someone in my life, but whoever it was to be would have to love me and my daughter. But there is always a price to be paid for such commitments; it was only a few years before, around 1979, that I gave up on exactly that situation.

Knowing what I know now, I most certainly would have carried on my merry way and ignored seeing someone I recognised.

I thank the Lord for my wonderful son that came out of this decision, but I could have done without all the other things that were to mar my life, my abilities, my personality, my faith in human nature.

Where is this all leading? Stay with me.

Chapter 5: Second Marriage

It was a lovely day. As I drove my way through Harlesden, just by the police station, I saw someone familiar waiting at the bus stop. The smart dress and that poise, it looked like Jewel, but I couldn't be sure, so I turned the car round and, sure enough, it was her.

We were both surprised. I leaned across and opened the car door so she got could get in. Jewel had gone to Jamaica to meet a policeman that she was friendly with, and in that short space of time, they'd had a baby called Ebony. Jewel decided that it wasn't for them to remain together and returned to the UK with the baby in search of a new life.

Timing, being in the right place at the right time, can be one of the most important things. We met again at a time when we both had no commitments. Things were different; originally we were both in relationships and what we had was an affair; we were not able to commit to each other. So the passion started again and we got closer, physically and emotionally. I genuinely wanted all that she had to offer. Jewel had so many qualities that seemed to be all the right ones, and I could and would benefit from it all. She was a complete package. The saying goes, 'Good things come in small packages, but so does dynamite!' She was to become my nemesis!

There were a few rough edges. She had a temper that could erupt at a moment's notice, but the next minute, she would be caring and loving.

I gave her a lot of space, and, as the months rolled by, the inevitable happened and the question was asked: "Where are we going?" I was not ready to face up to this degree of interrogation, I was having a good time and I did not need to commit to any more than us seeing each other occasionally, going out, eating at her home, and me going back to my place.

Jewel had some dubious friends, who lived on Stonebridge Estate, people that I did not feel very comfortable around. They smoked all sorts of things and drank way too much booze. Jewel did none of these things, but I did not like her friends and did not want to be in their company, although sometimes in order to see her, I had to go where they were on the estate.

I made the second major mistake. Jewel had said she wanted to call things off if I was not willing to go to the next level, so, as we walked into one of her dubious friends' flat, she asked, "Where are we going?" and I flippantly said, "Why don't we move in together and then get married?"

I was so insincere, but she was not willing to hear my insincerity. She had heard what she wanted, and before I knew it, she was in my two-bedroom flat in Mill Hill. This was extreme weakness and it was my heart ruling my head. There were so many things wrong here, but I refused to listen to my inner voice.

Mr Motivator says: *When making life-changing decisions, you need to sit calmly and write the advantages and disadvantages down on a piece of paper. Think long and hard; weigh up all elements. Never make a decision on the spot: take time out to be able to evaluate with a clear head. As always, seek counsel in others. Percy Sledge wrote a song called* Take Time To Know Her: *essentially, everyone knew what the girl in the song was like, and they told him to take time to know her; it is not an overnight plan. Take time to know her, please don't rush into this thing.*

There must have been some good times before we got married. I know that I am no saint; I have done my fair share of wrongs and made errors. It would have been wiser on those occasions to apologise, rather than to defend my position. Looking back, I feel that a number of issues existed; I was ambitious and set in my ways. I was a single parent and I had all the scars of years gone by. We were young, not necessarily ready for all that marriage entailed, and maybe we had not given ourselves enough time to grow to love one another.

I showed no interest in all the arrangements that were being made for our eventful day. I was no longer sure that marriage was what I wanted, so instead I went about my work and left most of the arrangements to my wife-to-be.

Jewel was a well-organised person, and, I have to say, I saw a side of her that I really liked. She looked after our home well, and as for her cooking, that was second to none. She was very house-proud and her creativity made our home special. She changed the rather masculine feel that existed prior to her arrival and I approved of this, and I felt comfortable in releasing some of the reins I held on Carolyne. My confidence in her as a mother for my daughter grew, and I knew that with all these obvious qualities, she would treat her as well as she treated her own daughter, or so I thought. I was prepared to give her the chance to bring up my daughter, and at the time she approved of us sharing responsibility for Ebony.

Clothes Parties – First Business

In my quest to find more interesting work, I started selling kids clothes to earn extra funds. I saw that there were a number of people who wanted to earn extra cash and were also prepared to hold clothes parties in their homes. So, putting the two things together, I went down to Petticoat Lane, purchased a variety of kids' clothing as samples, and set up these parties. I had to be assured that each item would be available when I returned with orders.

I tried to purchase items that would give me the biggest margins; bibs, two-piece suits, socks. I spent many hours on a Sunday morning going into the warehouses to find good items to sell. This was an area of East London that was totally dominated by the Indians who owned, operated (and still do to this day) wholesale warehouses that sold direct to individuals, people who retailed in markets or small shop holdings.

There was always a similarity in the stocks. However, this did not make my job easy. I still had to find the unusual so that my customers would not be able to say they saw the same item cheaper down the road. But if they did, at least it would still be better buying from me because they would have saved on the bus fare.

All this was the beginning of my first real business. I was using all the experience that I had acquired from my many jobs and the training sessions I received at RHM.

I always arrived home sometime in the afternoon after leaving at 6.00 a.m. each morning. Oh, how I wished that the warehouses opened on a Saturday, but there seemed to exist a strict code of practice that I believe may have been a holdover from the original Jewish shopkeepers, and so the area surrounding Whitechapel and Commercial Street was a ghost town on Saturdays. On Sundays, it came alive, with the noise of vendors calling out their deals and the heady aroma of a variety of cultural cooking.

So Sundays became my business days. After arriving home and eating Sunday dinner, I would go into the attic, and list, code and price all my items. Once recorded, I packed the selected samples into suitcases in readiness for the house parties to be held on evenings in the coming weeks.

At each party, I had little problem persuading the ladies to part with their money. I invariably took sizable orders from them as they purchased for resale at their own parties. At the end of each week, the orders were totalled, and a final list prepared of the required quantity of each item. Then, on the next Sunday, I was off, buying the ordered stock and selecting new items. Goods were delivered to each hostess and money collected, and it was their job to ensure that all monies were collected from the end customer.

I made a profit margin of some 40% with the hostess getting at least 10%. The money kept coming in, and each week I was able to supplement my basic income to take care of my now larger family.

This was a real training ground. Not only was I making money, but I also learned about dealing with the public and how to get them to part with money that for many people was in short supply. But, more important than that, I was gaining valuable experience of the fashion business; not high fashion, but geared towards the council estate, where disposable income was tight, but luckily, every mother wanted their child to look great and 'with it'.

Shop-Within-Shops

I needed more challenges, and, before I knew it, I talked my way into a new job, working for a company called Baggage and General (B&G). This was a company built by a Mr Tony Macilwaine, who started his business from his living room. His wife, a very creative, well-to-do English woman, was instrumental in forging the first of what was to be a trend in retailing business, called concessions. They negotiated with store groups or individual shops to put a modular unit within the stores.

All these items followed the fashion trend at the time, so if red, yellow and blue were the fashion colours, then accessories would be used accordingly to complement the overall look.

B&G had well over 400 such shop-within-shops around the UK.

The buying team was led by Mrs Macilwaine, and Tony designed accessory items that were sent to the Far East for sample design and eventual production. Their operation was quite complicated, in that sales of larger items were recorded with visa sales tickets, but jewellery could not be ticketed; technology at the time meant that recording sales on small items required a ticket larger that the item being sold. So sales of jewellery were a problem, and therefore repeat orders from suppliers were often inaccurate because the buyers would rely on stock counts to ascertain possible sales. Sales records never matched with income, because the stock loss element was always a part of the count. This whole area was full of inaccuracies, and as a result, there were missed sales.

I was employed to put in a system that would control stocks and regularise the buying pattern. Although it was a tall order, and I knew what to do, there was already a system in place, and we all know what it is like to try and use a new broom to sweep clean and change a pattern of existing behaviour. So, quietly, in the corner of the office/warehouse in Avonmore Road, Kensington, I set about trying to fully understand how they managed to get everything to work.

The year in, year out figures shown on the balance sheet showed that a very high value had been placed against stock that had been put into shops, had not sold and subsequently warehoused. This was quite worrying, because the value placed on this stock was being used to further the borrowing needed to keep the company buying. I was in a dilemma. If the true value was to become known, it could have the effect of restricting the buying potential of the company, because it would expose to the bank that what they thought was valuable stock would be shown to be virtually worthless.

So a decision was made to mount a sale of all the old stock to try and realise as much funds as possible. All the shop-within-shops took part, and we did sell some, but in the end, it was impossible to fill the counters with so much out of date, out of fashion stock. Sales were buoyant initially, but as the weeks went by, it started to wane.

The buying power of B&G was frozen, and the company was forced to close.

During this same time, I had been noticing a long blond haired, hippy-looking young man standing in a phone box outside the trading estate, not once, but many times. I did not know who he was, but I remember his face fairly well. I learned later that this man became the billionaire Sir Richard Branson.

Marriage to Jewel

At home, I was being cajoled into a marriage that I knew I did not want. The appointment with the registrar was set for 11.15 a.m. on Saturday 11th July 1981, at Hendon District Registry Office. There was no going back; invitations were sent out and the reception would be at a local hall.

The day came, and before it ended, we'd had a disagreement over the amount that I tipped the taxi that took us to the reception. The result was we sat in silence at the head table for a while.

It was still a nice day; the food and company was good, and a number of my friends from Leicester even made the journey.

We went back to Mill Hill, and a while after, we made the journey to Jamaica to spend our honeymoon. We visited a number of places and we stayed in my parents' humble home. This made me see a different side to my new wife. She refused to use the outside toilet, which meant I had to help her with the commode or chimmy (potty). Her not being prepared to help around the home was another thing. Auntie was not impressed, and on the quiet she said that I had made a big mistake. Two weeks later, we were back in the UK.

Out of Work

So now I was faced with bills to pay, and an unhappy wife nagging me. I had to do something, but what?

Although I hoped that something would happen, or someone would call me with an offer, the phone never rang. I loathed the idea, but I had to go to the dole office. For the first time in my life, I walked through the door and joined the queue. I hated the feeling; it smacked of the desperation I felt the first time I was dependent on social services.

After waiting nearly two hours, I approached the lady at the desk. Her attitude made me feel like a criminal: the curt questions fired at me, about my family, why I was out of work, and whether I was trying to do something about my position, made me feel very small.

I was a very impatient man, so I looked her in the face and said, "You'll never, ever get the opportunity to see me in here again. I don't need your handouts! I won't be back."

I smiled, turned, and left. I felt good but knew I was being stupid. I needed some funds, and I was entitled to the handout, but pride got in the way; was I going to let my family starve because I was not prepared to eat humble pie? I hesitated at the door; why not go back in? I thought of that smug look on her face and I said, "No, never."

I walked out and went back to my armchair. This was one of my lowest points and when you don't have any support, it is a lonely place. There were so many bills to be paid, but I was confident something would break. I believed in divine help; I also believed that God does help those who help themselves.

Mr Motivator Says: *Never let pride get in the way of your entitlement. It worked for me. Walking out of the Job Centre, I knew I could make it; I was convinced that I had the experience and the gift of the gab to talk my way out and into a new situation that would be better. But if you don't have that strength yet, to walk away when you are being treated badly, bite your lip and take what is your due and then go away and work hard in trying to improve your situation. Hard work does pay off, but sometimes you have to go down to pick yourself back up.*

Destiny

Then it came to me; what I knew about was stock control, the fashion business, and running a business! So I called up the offices of an independent fashion company called Jane Norman. This company had about eight shops in various locations but there were three that I was interested in, all on Oxford Street.

As usual, I bluffed my way in (don't wait for your ship to come in, swim out to it!). I asked the receptionist who the MD was and asked to be put through to his office. Strangely, the MD, Mr Freed, answered the phone himself. I explained that I had a business proposition I wanted to put to him, and he agreed to meet me. I was surprised he said yes so easily, but that probably explained why he was so successful.

I had begun to formulate plans for my own business. I would specialise in old stocks of diamanté; black, gold, and as many colours as possible.

I knew where I wanted to be, and what lines I wanted to sell. I just needed the shop space and the opportunity.

I needed samples of stock for Mr Norman Freed to see, so I rushed down to Oxford Street and bought a selection of items from most of the accessory stands, and laid them out in a tray.

Dressed in a suit, I was now ready for my meeting, and feeling as nervous as I ever remember being, I went to his head office above his shop on Oxford Street.

Mr Freed greeted me warmly; a portly, happy-faced Jewish man. I felt positive vibes when I looked into his face. I explained about my role in B&G, and he was aware that they had gone under for a lot of money. I told him that I needed to start somewhere to be able to get my own business going, and also feed my family.

He took me for a walk down to the shop floor. The front was small, but he explained how valuable the space at the front of a shop was. I made him understand that I knew how important this was and I would not let him down. I was hungry, and I had a choice of staying away from crime and working, or being faced with no other choice but to commit larceny to feed my offspring.

I left his shop with his words ringing in my ears: "I haven't got a clue how you can bring this off, but if you make it work, I will give you the other two shops, 388 and 262, to trade from." I had assured him that I would make it work, and we parted; me with a smile of trepidation and he with the smile of someone who has just done a good deed.

But how was I going to bring it off? I knew it would take dedication and time, but I could do it, and do it I must.

I got some money together, and went to Berwick Street in the West End. This street was famous for supplying most of the imported costume jewellery items, so I searched many of the warehouses and basements there in a quest to find the unusual. I bought far more than I needed, but if a line looked sufficiently different from what others were doing, I bought it.

Not much could be purchased for £2,000, but my face was well known to many of these suppliers, and I went home laden down with diamanté and all the current fashion colours.

I could not wait to get home, and when I did, I went straight into the attic and began to number and label all the items, recording purchases in a ledger; item number, description, quantity, cost price, retail price, gross profit, etc.

I was now almost ready to open; I just needed staff. I called Lola White, a friend of mine, and she agreed to work for me. The shop front of the head office store was smaller than most, and although I had over-calculated how many units I needed, and bought too much stock, I felt great and was ready to get going. I bought some of the display units previously owned by B&G.

Lola was willing to do sales so I did what I thought was staff training, and over the weekend, the unit was set up, ready for trading on Monday.

I opened and everything flew out of the shop! It surprised me, but by the Wednesday, I had to go back to my suppliers around the corner and purchase more stock.

Mr Freed was happy, I was ecstatic, and my suppliers were glad because I was shifting dead stock that they had put away in boxes. I'd had the foresight to go for what was different, and it was paying dividends.

The good news was that at the end of the first week, I had taken £1,800 from this small stand and I had to hold my breath when Mr Freed came in to the shop and said that if business continued in the same way, he would have no problem in recommending that I set up in the other units.

The flagship Jane Norman store was almost next door to Selfridges, and I felt that if I was able to take this kind of money from what was considered the rough end of Oxford Street, then I would fly at number 388. One month later, I opened there and the sales went through the roof! I was up and down between Berwick Street daily just replenishing the stock. We were taking far more than anticipated, but as was my habit, I never had a budget, just the belief that whatever I was to embark on would work and would at least lead to other things.

Mr Freed was proved right, and he was now insistent that the look at the front of these two stores should be replicated in all branches that had the space. I was uneasy; I was making a good living in two shops and doing all the buying. The more stores I had, the more responsibilities and greater pressures, but I was caught between a rock and a hard place. More stores would mean greater buying power and I would have greater influence; it would give me greater strength with Jane Norman, reducing the likelihood of another operator coming in the back door.

TopShop was also knocking as they were in the market for a jewellery operation. A new shopping centre was about to be opened in Brent Cross, North West London, and I felt that due to its close proximity to my home in Mill Hill and its newness, it should be a place worth trading in. Having my units in a store group other than Jane Norman would give me a pillow, just in case anything went wrong with my arrangements. After all, I had no contractual set-up with Jane Norman.

I did not have to negotiate hard with TopShop. They had seen my operation and were only too glad to have my business in their new store. They were very particular about the look of my units and wanted architectural designs showing how the allocated space would be accommodated. This I did, although it meant spending nearly £7,000 just on a display unit. Stocking the unit was not a problem; their sales profile was a bit younger than Jane Norman, but whilst some of my lines could be in all shops, TopShop needed a stronger allocation of the current fashion lines.

I had to take on new staff because the opening hours in Brent Cross were longer than the other stores, and due to its location, staff could not be easily moved from Oxford Street for cover. Overall, it was a costly set-up. But once opened, it very quickly settled into the usual pattern of better than expected sales and more than enough work for me.

I was not enjoying anymore what had started as a means of getting food on my table. I was making more money than I ever expected to make, and Jewel made greater demands on me for material things. I still travelled on the buses to buy, sell and make deliveries to the shops, and many times I just moved between supplier and shops with stock held in plastic bags. I did not have the time to take stock home for pricing, I just sat on the floor in the shops, pricing and labelling.

By the end of 1981, I had expanded my concessions and I was now trading in another Jane Norman shop in Knightsbridge.

On the home front, this period in my life was a little vague. I knew we were settling into home life, but I wanted to live in a bigger place: with four of us sharing a two-bedroom flat, we did need more room.

That winter, we sold the Fairway. I was sad to see the flat go to someone else. This was a place that had brought me lots of joy and very fond memories; of overlooking the Fairway playing fields, with its central mock well in the garden at the back, where there was never very much room for the kids to play, but at least the view was great, and all they had to do was wander across the road to the local park.

How times have changed. In those days, you never worried about where your child was and what they were doing; they would occasionally drop back home for a drink, have something to eat and then they would be off again, playing safely. Very rarely would you have to mention being careful who they spoke to. Nowadays, you cannot take the chance of letting them out of your sight.

So I bought a house just up the road in Southdene. This was a three-bedroom house with lounge, dining room and a very large garden. I had bought the Fairway for £13,000 and sold it for £26,000; this house had cost me £43,500, and Jewel settled in to making it a home and stamped her character on it. I had bought it in both our names, and with shared ownership, she became even more difficult.

Jewel had a flat in Kensal Rise that she rented, and which was making good money, though it should not be sub-let. I turned a blind eye.

She bought herself a car; once again, this was hers, and not ours to share.

At this stage in my life, I did everything that I could; there was not an opportunity that went by, and as long as I could find the space, I tried it. You see, although I was making money, it was not my driving force. Job satisfaction was paramount, and chasing money did not keep me going. I always looked for more challenges; therefore, I tried a number of different things.

Pop Mobility

I enjoyed physical activity, and when I played badminton or basketball, I found the camaraderie and the socialising amongst the players a great stress reliever. But with running a business, time did not allow me the luxury to keep them going. The result was that I started to put on weight – frankly, this was a state that I never want to revisit – so I looked for another activity, which depended on me, and me alone. The guys at basketball got impatient with me constantly letting them down, so I joined the Harrow Leisure Centre and took up karate, Wado-Ryu.

These sessions were to prove invaluable in getting and keeping me at a level of fitness that I needed, so I went along two or three times a week with my mate, Ted; he was married and also had problems at home. We also played squash.

It was one of those evenings as I arrived to play squash that I ran into a large group of women dressed in long stretch leggings, ankle warmers, head and wristbands, and trainers; the sheer numbers queuing out the door and around the corner. I hovered at the reception area, more to observe all the different shapes and sizes; there were some good lookers amongst them.

I followed them as they went into a very large hall at the back of Harrow Leisure Centre. There must have been 200 women, with a sprinkling of men. I was no longer interested in squash; transfixed, I watched a lady get up on the stage, put on some pop music and start to move. Everyone seemed to know the moves, and they all followed her lead. At the end of each track, they clapped; they all perspired copiously as the leader took them through their paces for track after track, and at the end, I found myself clapping too. I needed to know more.

This is where I was first exposed to Pop Mobility. I was hooked and I did not fully know why, but the next week, I was back, in my shorts and trainers. I too was being taken along with the whole energy and ambience of this new phenomenon. I learned the steps, but I was not so confident about teaching it.

I happened to be driving in Neasden when I noticed a new building going up at the bottom of the lane, before the roundabout. This was to be a church hall, with a few other rooms off to the side, a kitchen and a sizeable car parking area next to it. Here I was, trying to get away from Jewel's friends on the Stonebridge Estate, looking at the only available hall that's backing on to the very same estate.

I went to see the vicar, negotiated terms, and booked each and every Tuesday evening for one and a half hours, from when the hall was finished.

I went back to the Harrow Leisure Centre where I had noticed two young girls who moved well and seemed to be happy in being in the class. They showed good rhythm, so I approached them and asked whether they would be interested in teaching for me. They were 16 years old and lived near Stanmore, but were willing to make the journey if I organised transport, so I spoke with their mother who agreed.

Everything was now in place, except getting people to come in.

Neasden Church Hall. This is where it all began.

As usual, I had taken on a number of different things, all to do at the same time, but this is how I am – always of the opinion that in life, you need more than one iron in the fire, and that you should run your life as if it's a department store, with a variety of different things, so that when one particular thing is not selling, sure enough, something else would be in demand. Bill Gates would disagree with that principle, because for him, specialisation worked a treat, but Richard Branson will tell you different.

It is interesting mentioning successful people here, because as I look back, I cannot see who would have been my greatest influence. I know that my religious background set the rules that govern me, and Popa and Auntie gave me standards with which to live by. I also know that I hold true and dear all the friends that I have grown up with – I mention Mercier here and Reg.

I was desperate to put bread on the table, and if the truth be told, there were many times that crime seemed a great and easy alternative, but I am so scared of the look of prison bars from outside that the very thought of looking at the bars from the inside made me decide that the only sure way of getting whatever I needed was to work for it.

First exercise photo.

There was no one to share my joy with at home. Jewel and I just drifted through each day, none any more special than another, and my success made no impression at all. Yes, we did talk, but we just existed. Marriage requires skills, and when you are young, you think you are sailing along, but you are actually paddling in different directions. We were married, but there was no 'us'. The only real happiness that I got was going home and seeing the kids.

Jewel had miscarried several times at about three or four months, and each time it was a boy. To be honest, these were not planned pregnancies, and I was definitely not ready for more babies. Carolyne had been enough for me and the very thought of more children was too much to contemplate. Mother Nature sometimes does have a way of controlling situations, and just maybe, with the stresses within our marriage, another child would have been too much for the family to bear at that time.

Life With Jewel

Jewel wanted a mink coat, and although I protested, it was not long before I found myself walking with her into the furs department in Selfridges, where the furs of various animals were held in cool storage. I don't particularly have any views about people wearing furs, but while women wanted this body covering, I suppose one had to accept that the demand was there.

We got strange looks as Jewel chose and walked out of the store with her American mountain fox jacket, and my pocket thousands of pounds lighter. In a way, I minded, but not that much; I was the official breadwinner and my family had no need of anything. We were able to go away almost whenever we wanted, buying material things was easier, and for a while I had bought the full attention of my wife. That was the thing; when things were good, they were very, very good, but when they were bad, things were 'badder'.

I needed a car, and a good car as well. I hadn't had the money to buy my own and I didn't like loans, so I waited until the time was right. I saw the one that I wanted. They were new on the market and many a time I had just wandered past the Ford showrooms and looked in, dribbling at the mouth.

My pocket had the cash and it was burning a hole. Once, I stepped inside the showroom and I chose my car, but the salesman said delivery would be three months. I couldn't wait. I told him that I was paying cash, and I wanted it within the week, or I would go elsewhere. He spoke to the manager and it so happened that a delivery would be made of another one that same week.

I paid £7,000 and later that week, I drove down the road in my brand spanking new black XR3I.

Derrick Evans had arrived!

Getting around was now much easier with this new baby.

I also found it really difficult to manage and run Dee's Accessories properly from the home. It dominated the living room, stock was everywhere, the garage was like a warehouse, and what with the extra phone lines and people constantly in and out of the house, I felt that maybe this arrangement was adding to the pressures that were affecting our marriage.

The alternative was to look for somewhere to set up my operation base, and very quickly I found a place on Cricklewood Broadway in North West London. These premises proved invaluable for everything I had to do. I had two floors above a carpet shop; on the first floor, the front room became my office, and the room behind was the reception, with toilets and kitchen following on. The second floor housed all the stock on metal shelving.

I moved in immediately, on a five-year lease for reasonable rent, and the freedom was worth every penny. This place gave me the means to grow and expand. It also gave me a reason to stay away from home for longer periods.

As a family, we went to lots of places together, but we could not afford a holiday abroad, so our lives worked around weekend barbecues with family and friends, and general socialising. It's funny looking back now, but there wasn't any substance to these activities; yes, it was nice to meet up and get together, but if we did not play host, no one else seemed to want to do it, so it became the norm for friends to come round and we would provide for everyone.

I did the party host thing, but I longed for people to just go, and, paradoxically, I wanted them to be around as this served to fill the gap between me and Jewel.

We shared nothing except the fact that we lived together, but, occasionally we had physical relations and, because I thought she could not get pregnant, we did not use protection. Someone, I am not sure who, thought that having a baby would be good for us, and advised Jewel that to go full term would require stitches to her cervix and as long as she remained calm throughout the term, she would be able to have a child. I did not know about this, so when Jewel told me she was expecting and how, I was not very happy about it.

I felt that with our marriage in such disarray, we should wait a while, but whatever she wanted, she got – and to much joy, James Earl Ray Alexander Benjamin Evans was born on 3rd December 1983, at 3.15 a.m., three months premature, weighing 3lbs 3oz. He stayed in hospital for a while because his lungs were underdeveloped, but he was a fighter. After great improvement, he came home, weighing almost as much as a newborn. For a while, we had to dress him in dolls' clothing. Seeing him now, it makes you wonder how someone so small could get so big; at age 20 his chest was bigger than mine, but he has a smaller ego.

He was tiny and cuddly, and so fragile all I could do when holding him was to marvel at the vulnerable life that we had brought into the world. It is amazing that someone born so small could grow into the man he is today.

We put aside our differences, and things seemed to improve. We really came together as a family, focused as we were on the new arrival.

For a while, I started to come home much earlier and I did not want to be away from the family. Everything seemed fine but the saying that 'a leopard cannot change its spots' proved true, and, it wasn't long before we were back to the same old scenario, ignoring each other and not talking.

This was so childish, but with each new incident, all we did was jockey for our positions. We wanted to win at every confrontation, so much so that we forgot about giving and taking.

My joy was short-lived. It was great going out with the kids, but the missus was not happy, and neither was I. OK, James was giving us a lot of 'together with James time' but the longer we were alone in each other's company, the more I realised that I had made a terrible mistake.

Being the coward I was, I found it impossible to just sit down and discuss how I truly felt. I was unable to voice my fears, and yet I knew that unless it was discussed openly, she wouldn't know what was on my mind. Instead, I chose to suffer in silence; I engulfed myself in my work, fitness classes and the kids, and I began to be neglectful about the house and home. Jewel wanted a breadwinner and a husband, I maintained that she could not have both; I was a breadwinner and a good father, but I wasn't into the go home and do the 'husband-putting-up-the-wallpaper' thing.

If the tiling needed doing, I would rather pay a tiler to do it; the wall that would take me a week to do is one hour of application for the professional tiler. Why do I need to do something that God definitely invented someone else to do? If not, then why does it take the professional so little time to do something that takes me so long to complete? This was my argument, which Jewel did not like; she wanted me to be this kind of husband, so we argued about my lack of interest in doing such things which, she maintained, showed a lack of interest in doing anything around the house. We argued about things that truly did not matter, and every little thing that in the past was of no consequence, became the focus or the reason for our dissatisfaction.

I had found my solace, and what I was doing gave me real peace of mind. I knew that I needed to succeed, so I persevered with all that I was doing, but at home I was only happiest when I saw Carolyne, James and Ebony. Jewel, though, did not want me to share in anything to do with the upbringing of Ebony, and made a point of reminding me that I was not her father at every opportunity, especially if it was a way of getting back at me after an argument. When it came time for Ebony to go to school, Jewel insisted it was her responsibility to take her child; I was not to be party to any decision concerning her. The result of all this was that I showered all my attention on Carolyne and James. This caused Jewel to become extremely jealous of Carolyne; her way of handling the situation was to try to come between Carolyne and me.

The way I flirted around people who came to my classes became a problem; although I saw this as harmless fun, she did not. And one thing after another started to push us over the edge.

I stayed away more and I started to neglect some of my responsibilities at home, but I honestly did not know what else to do. My presence only seemed to make things worse, but there were definitely times when I should have been more careful and paid more attention, in respect of Carolyne.

During all this time, I did not see Carolyne's unhappiness. Every time I saw her being 'naughty', I thought she was just rebelling against me sharing my life with another woman. That may have been part of it, but little did I know, until much later on, how much physical and mental abuse went unnoticed by me, and behind my back.

Carolyne is now married and has given me the pleasure of four grandchildren. She has moved to Antigua, where her husband is from.

When I was a male single parent, I found getting female attention easy; most women noticed Carolyne first, then looked at me, and then must have automatically felt that I was a really domesticated type of person; a good catch.

We men, on the other hand, are very protective of our offspring, but we want a woman that figures permanently in our lives, and therefore we look out for someone with what we think has the ideal qualities. But there are times that we totally throw caution to the wind and go into a relationship with the hope that things will work out. We do have difficulty in sharing the closeness that we have with our daughter or son with someone else. I tried my best to give space between me, Carolyne and Jewel, and it is this space that allowed me to overlook what was going on.

I only now have become aware of some of the things that transpired, and it saddens me to see that I neglected so many things that went on under the same roof.

I did not, and would not ever condone what Carolyne now tells me was the trauma that she was subjected to.

To help me understand what went on, I have asked Carolyne to put things down in her own words.

Carolyne's Story

I remember my first meeting with Jewel outside the house at Allington Road, and I could see that this woman was more to my dad than just a friend. You know how a lioness has its territory and an invading lioness tries to take over or be a part of the pride? Well this was how I felt. Dad was all mine. I had not shared him and wasn't really prepared for what was to come. I think I was about nine years old, and I remember enjoying Ebony's company as my little buddy to play with. The visits became more regular, and sometimes Dad would leave me there, sometimes overnight. I never liked to hear trains as they thundered by, especially when I was trying to watch TV, a little black and white one where the picture went every time. Sometimes, I found Jewel was watching me, almost, I believe, trying to work me out, but I was wary and wondered what part this lady was to have in my life...

My next major recollection was the engagement and then I realised that I was to share my dad. I was going to get a new sister, who I loved dearly, and I needed to get used to the idea. Dad threw a surprise party at the flat in the Fairway and I wondered, why, oh why. You see, by this point, I had a taste of Jewel's temper and was scared of what could come. I know, I was a typical spoilt child, raised by her dad and you know what dads and daughters are like together, and Dad and I were very close. Jewel did not like this, and did everything she could to break up this bond. On one occasion, I remember that Ebony was doing something to annoy me and I spitefully pushed her onto a heater giving her three stripes across her tummy. I tried to stifle her cries as Jewel came down the short hallway, where I got some serious smacks before I could say or explain what happened. Now, by this age, Dad had already given me my share of beatings (which is what Jamaicans called smacks). It was rare, though sometimes necessary when I was naughty, but with Jewel, the degree was always that much worse.

There was a rule that I had to come home from school, set the table, and then I could go back out to play. Well, children will be children. We lived directly across the road from my school, so I looked out, saw neither Dad's nor Jewel's car, and decided to go to the park before they came in. A couple of hours later, I strolled in thinking everything was OK and as I walked up the stairs, I heard someone in the bathroom. My heart was pounding so loud, I thought I was going to explode, as I peeped into the bathroom.

There was Dad sitting on the bath edge, tiling the bathroom walls. I totally forgot that he was going to be home. He just looked at me and told me to take off my skirt, as he was going to lay me across his knee and give me six of the best! Of course, he took his time to clean up and come out of the bathroom. By this time, I'm pacing my bedroom, wondering how I can get out of getting these licks! I knew what to do! I got three of my Enid Blyton hardback books and put them down my P.E shorts, as though he wouldn't notice. Haha, who was I kidding? Dad was not amused, and I still took my licks and cried like a baby, which meant I got less.

Over time, Jewel wasn't so compassionate. I did the same thing a few days later, and this was the first recollection I have of being terrified. I was beaten with a belt until my skin was cut and bled, and then I had to run a hot bath, around six inches high, with no cold water and two cups of salt, and I had to sit in it. The pain was excruciating. I was confused; was I so bad? Only now, as an adult, do I know that the salt was to reduce the swelling and help the wounds to heal quicker, but at the time, the pain was almost unbearable. Dad came home later that evening and I decided that he must know what happened. I was naughty, I was punished, but obviously he must know the person he is living with. Only now I know how wrong I was to think that.

Carolyne's early recollections of those days are truly dark to me. Although I had noticed and had spoken to Jewel about certain levels of reprimand, I had a talk on avoiding any physical punishment for the future as I did not like or condone the level it had reached. I did not want to see any more usage of implements to administer punishments. We would, for the future, have to discuss things. Although I also knew that she exhibited jealousy towards Carolyne, I did not know that the situation had gone so far. I am saddened that I could have been so neglectful, and I am so sorry for all the pain that young girl endured; hopefully, in her heart she will realise that I was in no way involved. I am concerned that, in trying to give them the room to get to know each other, Carolyne was submitted to a whole catalogue of abuse.

Jewel, as I said before, had miscarried three times, and she was convinced that Carolyne was to blame for these because, she maintained, Carolyne had put her under undue pressure. Needless to say, things deteriorated badly after James' birth.

I was now making some serious money from my concessions and Jane Norman wanted the same format in all their stores. I just wanted to be in the ones in Oxford Street, but they wanted me to go to areas such as Bromley. I saw this as a logistical nightmare. Control would be a problem and providing staff for such an out-of-town unit would not be easy. They offered to employ any staff that I required in exchange for an increase in the percentage I would pay.

I was not happy with this arrangement, but I was caught between keeping my business, and giving it up to another company who was better able to cope with the development into all the Jane Norman branches.

In exchange, I was given 262 Oxford Street as my next trading location, so now that I had three stores on the same street, and I was taking a lot of money, it seemed as if I could do no wrong.

Staffing arrangements were good. I had nearly ten people working for me in-store, I still did most of the buying, and I was in control of the day-to-day running of the operation.

Business had grown to ten locations across a number of different companies. My accountants, Hamilton's, were recording a sizeable turnover; financially, things could not have been better. I was now in the new offices, the move had gone well, and I was able to watch James grow up.

I showered all the kids with my love, even though Jewel and I were heading for a disaster. I was certainly glad to get away from home and to be out of sight; this saved me from having to face up to the shambles that was developing around us. But, most of what I did was the cause of the rift between us getting wider, and this divide got to the point that there was no way of it being repaired. If only I were man enough to grab the whole situation and sort it out.

Mr Motivator Says: *Happiness cannot be bought by money; happiness comes from striking a balance between health, wealth and mental fitness, but if your emotions are in disarray, you can't work, eat or play. So striving for emotional happiness is the pillar that will give you the foundation for greater things. If you are not happy with where you are, then move on.*

Takeover Neasden Lane

I was so submerged in everything I was doing, I became shielded from the bad energy at home, but I knew that if I was to continue at the pace I was going, then something had to give. My classes had grown at Neasden Hall to include Thursdays, and there were so many new people joining up. I was making money and having a great time as well. It wasn't long before I was doing other classes at a local squash club using one of the courts. I put together a circuit class especially for squash players who wanted to improve their game, and once again the class was a hit. I was fully involved in all classes and running a business that was also growing.

I had sales people looking after all the units, but I did most of the buying, occasionally getting some managerial help from an Irish woman called Lucy, whom I employed to look after the shops. She was great at keeping all the staff in check and most importantly, she was willing to work all hours. I wonder sometimes where she is now.

When I look back at those times in my life, everything was so muddled and confused. I knew that good times were close by; I did not know whether they were to be financial, physical, emotional, all, or just some.

Expansion

By 1985, I had a number of concessions; five Jane Norman shops, four TopShops, two Lady at Lord John, and one Snob. They were demanding but I was doing well; some months, I registered gross takings in excess of £35,000.

I still bought from Berwick Street, but now my buying power was greater and I was able to command better discounts.

I decided to look at buying from abroad, even if only a small range, because I would increase my margin. To do this, I needed to travel abroad, and I started by visiting the Prêt-à-Porter in France, an exhibition that predicted fashion trends and gave me access to many buyers from across the world.

It would take a while to fully interpret the evidence that would emanate from these shows. I did not have the time; I needed to respond as soon as possible to any information. Everything on my units had to tell a story, mainly in the colours, but these choices needed to complement whatever Jane Norman decided that they would sell. To help me arrive at a decision, I needed more help, so I ended up at the Fashion Forecasters. What they did was to look at all the trends in Paris and Milan, and for something like a thousand pounds, you could get what was considered a bible; it would say what type of fabrics, colours, and how the clothes fashion would dictate the overall look for the coming season.

In running my business, I had relied on my instincts alone. I would go in and clean out warehouses of any particular lines that took my fancy, and most of my time was spent with the older people who traded in Berwick Street and any that existed in the surrounding areas. I also spent many hours in places like Ropers in Shoreditch and Cha Cha Dum Dum, which is now located on Western Avenue.

I took all these items and sprinkled them around all the proposed new fashion colours. What sold by the bucketload were not so much the fashion colours, but the unusual. I was no more trusting of my instincts that ever before. But trouble was on the horizon.

Liquidation

I was in Holland ordering belts of every military description. The Fashion Forecast bible had predicted khaki and tan would be the next season's colours; they had to be right because I had seen the very same thing in Paris. I came away with my plan of how the stands were going to look, and I spent thousands to replicate this look across all branches.

I ordered £20,000 worth of belts, £10,000 worth of brooches, combs, earrings, necklaces and socks, plus all the other non-fashion colours. We decorated the units, and whilst they looked great, the colours were wrong; we were a full year ahead of ourselves! What was I to do? Sales were not there; no one wanted this new look. How could I have got it so wrong? Answer – I had not followed my golden rule of listening and depending on myself first. I had gone all sophisticated, and in doing so, I had lost my way. I had to liquidate the company later that year, and once again, I was at home wondering what to do next. My exercise classes became an outlet for my anxiety. Things were going well there and I was on a roll, but I needed to make some real money.

In the mid-eighties, school teachers were continually on strike, and Carolyne was not happy at home, so I thought that I should find a way of ensuring that her education did not suffer. I looked around for a private school, and after much searching, I found a boarding school in Beaconsfield. Although the fees were crippling, I knew that I had few other choices. Oakdene had a lot of good qualities and I felt this was what she needed. She boarded during the week and had the choice of coming home at weekends. Initially she did come home, but as time went on, she preferred to stay at school. I hardly saw her at home; instead, I had to go and see her, or wait for the holiday breaks.

I made ends meet from my exercise classes, but only just; the pressure that I had put myself under was beginning to bite.

David

In February 1982, I brought my nephew David Thompson to the UK from Jamaica. He was my sister Cherry's son, and I was happy for him to stay with us, but this was not for long. Jewel was not happy about the arrangement, and so as soon as her council flat became available, David moved into it.

I still kept in close contact with David, and as he was in his teens, I knew what it was like to be a young person in a strange country. I put him through further education courses, and became very much his mentor and confidant. Together, with my mate Eddy, who I had met at Willesden Library sometime before, we would go off each Friday evening to meet up with his mates in South London.

Eddy Clarke

I had found a friend in Eddy, who came from Barbados, and whilst he was an academic – he had got his doctorate and was now a qualified psychologist – he was also very down to earth.

South London would see me riding shotgun in a yellow beaten-up mini – Eddy with his trademark afro and I still holding on to lots of hair.

Most Fridays the police would harass Eddy - after all, he did look like a male version of Angela Davis, the civil rights freedom fighter. No matter how he looked, he was targeted. I was not; I wasn't driving.

We took it in turns to meet at each other's homes; it was never too warm at mine, so I travelled.

Nigeria

Eddy was searching for something to do. I had become aware that Nigeria, having so much oil and a population of 90 million, consumed a lot of goods, so Eddy and I visited the London Chamber of Commerce to investigate Nigerian companies' purchasing needs. We found they needed spectacle frames, and I had met a company in Holland called Silhouette, who was a major manufacturer of spectacle frames.

We got catalogues together, and customers' telex information and full contact details. We also had our own trading name, Overseas Commodity Services, or OCS. So we went off to Nigeria to sell spectacles. On the way to the Federal Palace Hotel in Lagos, we were subjected to our first rip-off. The taxi charged us double; we found out later.

The next day, we wandered around the markets and saw what was being sold. After meeting a number of customers, we left Nigeria with a lot of orders for products.

We arrived back in the UK and started to put together a good business. OCS was a venture that could go places. Eddy was doing his bit to become the business man, and we started to send out the orders together.

Nigeria being Nigeria was great on demand, but terrible on honesty.

Eddy and I were able to supply a few orders for spectacles and we did make some money, but all the promises made by the Nigerians led to very little; it was all extremely disappointing. We spent a lot of money going to Nigeria and we had returned with what I had thought was a lot of orders. This was just the beginning of our problems; we waited for Letters of Credit from Nigeria but when our bank checked their authenticity through the BCCI, a bank that eventually went broke, we found that they were worthless.

This was a time when incidences of illegal LCs were cropping up everywhere. Needless to say, this was the most unsuccessful period of my life.

So, here I was. Behind me were a failed jewellery business, a failed export business, one failed marriage, and another now unsteady marriage. How was I going to make ends meet? My fitness classes were doing well, but not enough to keep the family in the lifestyle that we had grown accustomed to.

I knew something would come up; as usual, something would happen to make everything all right.

Mr Motivator Says: *You know, it is amazing how blessed I have been. Ever since those early days of being hungry, I have found that whenever it seemed that things were difficult and everything was tight, God always provided; it is as if He is watching over me. He never lets me suffer for any period of time, and things always seem to work out in the end.*

British Heart Foundation

I had bills to pay, school fees to pay, and I needed a break. I didn't have to wait long for an opportunity to knock.

The British Heart Foundation decided that they wanted to run a campaign, 'Exercise for Life', and they wanted me to be featured on all their literature and posters.

They had heard that I was making waves across London. It was true; my classes were going from strength to strength, and I was on a roll, but here was a chance to put my name across the UK. At this stage, I was still just Derrick Evans.

It was decided that I would go to a number of leisure centres in various cities across the UK. At each centre, I would give a talk on the benefits of exercise and then take the attendees for a 45-minute gentle exercise class.

I had no qualifications, and the only knowledge I had of exercises had been gained from books I had immersed myself in, and also a lot of time going to other teachers' classes.

I was getting physically fitter by the minute and I became very well known; everyone talked about Derrick's classes. I started to do classes at Heathfield Squash and Racquet Club, and this became a very popular class, but not as popular as Pop Mobility. It was more of a circuit class, that I defined as one way to improve the game of squash. Again, the class filled up, and I was able to play squash at the same time for free.

Every teacher should do the same; recommend that your participants go elsewhere and visit other classes. If you are good, then your participants will come back to you. If they find a better teaching format for them, then you have done them a service.

Center Parcs

Center Parcs are groups of holiday villages located in various forested areas around the UK, and have been the custodians of my Fitness Motivation Weekends since 1990. It all began with a phone call I received from a lady called Heather Ewing, their Entertainment Coordinator. She had heard about me, and also that I had gained a good reputation for some fitness weekends that I had set up in the Norwich Sports Village.

These events had started some years earlier. On most weekends, I would take in excess of 50 people, which meant hiring a coach to take us there.

We would leave by lunchtime on the Friday, pick-up at the Brent Cross Shopping Centre, and the coach would drop us off in Norwich, and then return for the home trip on Sunday.

Over the weekend, I woke everyone early, dragged them out for a run, then back for breakfast. After breakfast, a whole series of classes would begin from bench stepping, to circuit.

I arranged a dinner for the Saturday and then off to the disco until early morning. Early on Sunday morning, the sequence of classes would start again.

As I said, the format of these weekends worked, and I was about ready to expand the operation when Heather came to see me.

She was looking to introduce the same sort of concept into Center Parcs, and, after discussion, we set up the first branch in 1990. The very first advert simply showed a picture of me wearing a black lycra unitard and a cap. The caption said, 'This man wants your body for the weekend.' It worked; we had over 100 people attending, and I employed a number of teachers with other class disciplines.

This first weekend went off with a bang, and as a result, we expanded to include all Center Parcs locations. We had over 250 each weekend, and the busiest location was Elveden, which in one September weekend got at least 400. It become very much a part of my calendar, and also for many of my friends and teachers, who attended every chance they got. Elveden always was my favourite location.

Needless to say, Heather and I have developed a friendship, and to this day there has never existed a contract between us - each year in September, we sat down and decided class dates and the format for the following year.

And so it was that I needed to do more. I was becoming more and more successful with my fitness classes, but I could not, for the life of me, see where and how far I would be able to go with it. Could I truly make money? I was not sure.

I remember Carolyne as a child, asking me what I did for a living, and I thought long and hard about what my occupation was. I was not able to focus on any specific job. I proceeded to tell her about all the different things I was doing, from the building business I ran, to the exercise instructor I was. Carolyne listened and went away slightly less confused, because some time later, she was heard to say in response to the same question, "Oh, he is an odd job man." I was pleasantly surprised at the honest and clear way in which she saw things. She was right; in her eyes, I did bits of everything.

Things were not great at home and I could not face up to the fact that we were now not just drifting, but miles apart. I was on an ambitious trail, and work was my diversion. Jewel was not wrong to make certain demands of me, but she needed someone else, not me.

I was unable to change the very essence of the person I am. Yet how could I make things right? I felt this was not up to me alone; it had to be a sacrifice on both sides, but neither of us would budge.

If you stretch an elastic band and keep on stretching it, it is bound to snap, and snap we did, when we least expected it. We didn't sort our problems out, we did not sit down and discuss situations and try to arrive at a conclusion, we did not set rules that would control behaviour, and so something was bound to give. We started to have arguments that were not just verbal but were close to being physical. We began to push back the boundaries of decent human behaviour.

Once you are on a treadmill of arguing, making up, arguing, and making up, it is difficult to see the way off it. Of course, the making up made you feel better for a moment, but then the cycle would start again.

We had married in 1981, but were ill prepared. I had gone into marriage for all the wrong reasons; I needed a mother for Carolyne, and not a lover for Derrick. I was always able to get that part, but I do not remember ever asking Jewel what she wanted.

When things began to go wrong, we tried to patch up our relationship but we had no experience of what we should do to make things better, and we should have had counselling, but we were each too proud to make that move.

To show how bad things were, if either of us wanted to do something we just did it – blow the consequences or the problem it could cause – because we were too individualistic.

A good example is when I decided I wanted some puppies. A then-friend called Winston kept Rottweiler dogs and as I wanted dogs of the same breed, he introduced me to a breeder in Kent. I bought two of them and they were installed as part of the family. They brought a welcome distraction, and each morning I enjoyed running across the fields with them.

Jewel hated this and did not offer to help with the care of the puppies. I sometimes felt that it was a mistake to have them, as they placed similar demands as a young child would, and the extra responsibility caused extra conflicts.

I focused most of my attention on the kids. Jewel went to college and we continued to drift apart. We found little to share; even going into the same bed became a problem. I found peace falling asleep in the armchair in the lounge, and I would eventually get up and creep into bed, lying with my back to her, feigning sleep if she was to wake or stir.

I needed out but how was this to happen, unless I made a decision or we talked about it?

Eddy, my Overseas Commodity Brokers friend, had gone to Lesotho, a little independent state in South Africa, to lecture at a university. I wanted his counselling. Eddy is eight years older than me and our friendship was based on mutual trust. He provided good guidance, but he too had a strange relationship with his wife, one that I did not admire, so I often did the opposite of what he would suggest. I used the guise of selling goods to South Africa as my reason to go there. He was there to meet me as I landed in Johannesburg, and it was great to see him. Eddy had a large circle of friends for me to meet, and, although I missed the kids, I thought being away was necessary therapy. Apartheid was rife in South Africa and I have never before felt what it was like to be so oppressed because of your colour. Yes, I have been discriminated against in England, but that was minimal in comparison. Signs were everywhere that restricted access to blacks, and there was always an element of fear felt by blacks. I saw first-hand the inhumane treatment of anyone not white – the taunts, the beatings. Things were not good for the blacks living in Johannesburg or Soweto, and we didn't stay too long there; the one saving grace was that in Lesotho, things were different.

We picked up a couple of Eddy's friends, who were going in the same direction. I did not know them but they shared conversation with Eddy while I dozed and looked out the window. There was a lot to take in as we drove towards the border; SA is a very large country and it was not advisable to be driving on your own. After many hours, we arrived at the border checkpoint. There was a long queue of blacks that stretched for hundreds of yards; we heard the crack of a bull whip, we saw men straightening up, we noticed the quietness, then we were ushered to the front of this mile-long queue of bodies.

We were able to pass because we had British passports and this gave us protection.

We were questioned, but I was in a daze. When Eddy suggested I come out, I did not know what to expect, but this form of inhumanity, those in authority detaining anyone who was black, was totally against what I was used to in the UK, and made me want to turn right back. But I persevered and we were allowed into this land, totally surrounded by SA, and though considered independent, it was totally dependent on SA for what it needed.

Lesotho had become the playground for wealthy South Africans who fancied a bit of black and were unable to get it in SA. It was against the law to cohabit, or to be seen, or to be intimate, much less seen in public with a black person, so with their black lover in the back seat, they went to Lesotho for a weekend of freedom.

I met a lot of Eddy's friends and we went partying. Lesotho is considered by many to be the healthiest place on earth; the air is fresh and clear, and the people suffer from very few Western illnesses. My stay seemed short; I had made a few contacts, but Eddy felt that I could gain more by going to Johannesburg and meeting some cash and carry people that he knew. He was desperate to supplement his rather low salary from the university, and so trying to expand our overseas market was the target.

We picked up the two ladies we had come across the border with and made our way to the checkpoint. We got through the Lesotho checkpoint easily enough, but it was the South African one that caused the delay. We waited and eventually my patience ran out. I went to see the captain and asked about the delay, and he promptly told me that we must wait until he saw fit to let us go. I held up my British passport, which he almost spat at.

I went back to the others, then some time later Eddy was called to see the captain. He came back a while later with a puzzled look, and told us that the captain wanted him to inform on the two ladies we were travelling with. They wanted locations that we stopped at, information on who they met, and where they were eventually dropped off. If we agreed, we would be free to go, so Eddy had come to talk it over before giving him an answer.

We all agreed to comply, but when we got in the car, we were both rather quizzical about our passengers. We asked who they were and what was the 'state secret' that they must be carrying. Then we learnt of the value that they were to the police force... their father was incarcerated at the same time as Nelson Mandela.

On the way back to SA, we were repeatedly stopped by the police. For no visible reason, we were being harassed. We were so glad when at last we got to our hotel.

I spent the remaining days of my trip observing how blacks lived in such a depressed state, and I have to say that I am lucky; freedom to think, speak, and act is a God-given right to us all. However, when this is removed, there is no peace of mind. How the people managed to smile throughout all this oppression is beyond me.

I went to Soweto, and this was the only place that I felt at home. However, each day I was reminded by the police, and the crack of their bull whip on the back of a slightly disobedient individual, of the oppression that they lived with.

I left SA feeling so sorry for what I had witnessed, and glad that I am afforded the comforts that I enjoy without question.

My commodity business did not benefit much from my trip. There were a few orders for hair products that needed fulfilling, but this was not going to pay any bills immediately. It had been great meeting up with Eddy and family. I had made some friends and nourished a number of business contacts, but for many reasons, I could not see myself trying to do business with this country.

I did visit there a number of times after the first trip, but I did not make any real headway and so I walked away. I had also learned from a number of individuals how easy it was for banned SA companies to beat the embargoes against supplying UK companies. Many companies who were not allowed to import from SA did so by using a trade-free zone, which allowed them to re-package and re-label goods with new countries of manufacture, goods which then found its way onto the shop floor of many outlets in the UK.

When I came back home, picking up the pieces was difficult; I had gone away confused and I returned even more tormented. What was I going to do for the future? I needed a new direction and I felt that this did not include Jewel, but how was I going to get away and still be able to see the kids who were so important to me?

Our arguments became fiercer, and more and more physical. I felt as if I was trapped in quicksand and I was being drawn down and down, and the more I tried to flounder out, the more I became submerged. We had started our courtship with so much fire, but now the flames had sputtered out and to rekindle it required specialist help.

I was not in that frame of mind; I just wanted out, but I did not know how to do it, how to say it. Carolyne was away at private school; Ebony, as I had been reminded many times, was not my daughter, although we shared James. Leaving him behind would break my heart, but at the same time, we could not continue with the incessant squabbling and fighting.

I did not have to wait long before the tension between us pushed everything over the edge. We now fought over so many things; everything we did annoyed the other, so we continually set about causing the most hurt.

Before the end of 1984, we were in court, fighting. It was eventually resolved, but this was to become the pattern for many years to come.

Misunderstanding on both fronts made us argue and then fight physically. When I look back, time makes me realise how stupid we both were. We aimed to create the maximum hurt, and if it meant Jewel throwing and smashing a valuable antique clock across the room, she did. I retaliated in the same vein many times, but I see this now as a weakness, and I should have avoided the confrontations.

We would argue about intervening between visiting friends who were quarrelling. When I suggested she stay out of their problems because we had our own, she would let fly a kitchen knife, only to be restrained by our visitors.

I was so ill-equipped to stop the arguments, and by physically and verbally fighting back, I became the weaker person. I had various painful encounters, from a poker in my face, to an iron which has deadened part of my left leg, and much more.

When I say that our relationship became physical, this was totally one-sided. I can remember hitting her once, but most of the time I was on the receiving end of so much physical hurt. I was pushed to the edge so many times, but fighting back was not in my DNA.

We were in a state of turmoil and parting should have been the final answer. Jealousy on Jewel's part reared its ugly head many times, and, sadly, I have to admit sometimes I created the situation just to get her riled, and when she did, I silently laughed.

As I would find out later, courts do not believe when men say that they are being abused. They look at the size of the woman and, consequently, as in my case, the judges say that they could not be expected to believe that a woman of such small size and stature could inflict the pain that I said she had.

If I came home and did not acknowledge that she had ironed all my shirts and that they were hanging up in the wardrobe, she could be seen moments later, cutting off all the buttons, or throwing them in a bath full of water. Then the next day, without me ever saying anything about it, she would be re-ironing or sewing back the buttons. Incidents like these happened all the time.

And so it was that after one of our fights, she took me to court and tried to get me barred from the home. She told her side and I told mine; the wise judge saw it as tit-for-tat and suggested that we agree not to molest each other.

After another one of our arguments, I cannot remember what about, I was upstairs in bed with James, and everything seemed too quiet. I came quietly downstairs to see what she was doing and I peered from halfway down the stairs into the kitchen. I could see her over the stove, heating a pot full of cooking oil, and rocking back and forth, talking to herself. I suspected that once again, an argument, that I was just as much to blame for, was going to result in one or both of us doing harm to each other.

Back upstairs, I knew that time was short before the inevitable violent confrontation. But was I being melodramatic? What was she going to do with it? Was it as I suspected, or was it for some cooking?

I decided prevention was the better course of action. As James slept, I now waited anxiously. I paced up and down and wondered how to defuse the situation, and if not, how to protect James in bed. I thought that maybe if I stood by the window where she could clearly see me, I would be able to put the wardrobe door between me and the hot oil. I did not have to wait too long. She came in and as she moved towards me with the hot oil in the pan, she said, "This is to remind you never to argue and hit me again." With that, she raised the oil and threw it at me I simultaneously pushed the wardrobe door in the way, then quickly moved towards her and restrained her. The police were called and I needed medical treatment to my burnt hand.

We made efforts to make up, but it wasn't long after that we were at each other again.

Mr Motivator says: *Hitting back can never be right and if you find yourself in a situation where frustrations are boiling over, and when all seems to have failed, then you need to seek counselling and help. Start with talking to your friends, but remember that they will always agree with you; close friends find it difficult to be objective in their assessment of your situation and they will not necessarily offer the best option. If that is your only close outlet, then seek professional help. If you can persuade your better half to go with you, it is a great step but if they see little point in sitting in front of an independent person, then don't force them but you go anyway, because someone needs to be strong and having an impartial person assess the situation could offer you the strength you need to make a decision about what to do next.*

In 1984, Jewel signed a petition seeking a divorce. We remained living together during 1984 and early 1985, but relations had deteriorated badly and the violence between us just continued to increase.

After the hot oil incident, I felt that I couldn't continue to live in Mill Hill any longer, and I moved into the office at Cricklewood Broadway.

Carolyne, although still at boarding school, shared the top floor of these offices with me when she came home and everything was fairly well organised. We had two rooms and a bathroom, with a kitchen on the first floor.

I was lonely. I missed being with the kids, I missed the house in Mill Hill, and I also missed, for what it was worth, the comforts and companionship of family. There was many a night that I cried, especially when Carolyne went back to school after a weekend with me.

There was a point at which I was given access to James and I had him for weekends. However, these were short-lived. Soon after, Jewel started a round of court appearances designed to make it difficult for me to enjoy my time with the kids.

This was the start of what became over a decade of litigation and costly expense, the only real winners being the large number of different lawyers I had to employ to fight for my rights.

From Cricklewood Broadway, I was to orchestrate my future, with no plan or direction.

Mr Motivator Says: *In spite of all these traumas, I have come out very well, and before I continue about my past life, it is important to note that if you have arrived at a position in life in which you are happy, then don't start looking back with regret at things that did not, at the time, work out.*

I had made choices, and although there was a lot of sadness, I believe that was all part of the learning process, and if I was to go forward, it was unavoidable. I now enjoy the benefits of all that went before. We must all make mistakes. That way, you know what it is like to fail and so you are able to at least be prepared for the future when the same set of circumstances could come to you again.

Every day, I thank God for all the so-called wrong decisions that I made, because now I have a loving, caring and beautiful wife, a bright and healthy daughter, a son whom I fought for from the beginning, who one day will win a Tony or an Oscar for his many Broadway and film performances (at least, that is what he told me, and I would never doubt him), an eldest daughter who has given me a grandson, and she has all the hallmarks of her determined and argumentative dad, and a middle daughter, who made mistakes but who made it through showing tremendous spunk and tenacity.

Living alone above a shop in London was not how I imagined it all, and to have travelled so many miles to be in what seemed like a dead end was not the most uplifting of situations. Although knocked down, I was not about to be beaten. I had to get ahead, no matter what.

At least I was talking to Jewel and she was agreeable to my seeing the kids often, but these were just an initial agreement.

We had already had an order issued against both of us that restricted us from molesting or interfering with each other. A joint order meant that at any time, either one of us could accuse the other of looking strangely at them and be hauled up before the courts.

I made arrangements for access through Ebony, because it was not possible for Jewel and I to communicate with each other. Ebony was always excited by our meetings, and so was James, but he could not be taken home unless he was tired and had fallen asleep. He was withdrawn and his mother tried to suggest that I stay away from him, but I could not entertain that thought, so we tried to make other arrangements, like seeing the children on weekends. This was agreed, but many times when I called to see them, they were suddenly not available.

However, 15th April 1986 was different. When I arrived, Ebony was at school, James was in, and I stayed for a while with the childminder looking on. When it was time for me to go, James would not let me leave; he clung to me, he cried, and he was so distressed, which made me feel awful. What was I to do? I stupidly suggested to the childminder that I would take him to stay a few days with me. What was I thinking! I used my heart, not my head, but this played into Jewel's hand, and it hit me like an express train.

After taking him home, I tried many times to get hold of Jewel but she played the part beautifully, and I could not locate her, so on the Thursday, six days later, I took James home. No one was home. Not on Friday, Saturday or Sunday, either.

Nine days later, there was a knock on my door, and when I answered it, Jewel stood there with her solicitors. James screamed and refused to go with them; no matter what Jewel said, James was not budging. I took him to her car, but he just screamed and screamed, so I took him home in my car and after a lot of persuasion and reassurance that I would return, he decided to stay.

Later that week, Jewel and I discussed James. She said that she had not realised how much he loved me and maybe we could share his needs 50/50. A few days later, she called to say that James was consistently calling for me and that he kept putting on his coat and heading for the door. That evening, I went and took him and Ebony out.

In court in May 1986, her side of things was very different. The courts heard both sides, and ruled that I submit my passport, and the kids were made wards of courts. Interim care and control went to Jewel, and I got every other weekend, 7.00 p.m. Friday to 6.30 p.m. on Sunday. Access arrangements did not work, and for the remainder of that year, I saw the kids less and less.

I continued with my exercise classes, which had grown in popularity. I was now being asked to teach in different locations, but living on my own saw me at a new lowest point in my life. I went home to an empty flat and an empty bed, and all I did was mentally return to the old house, with all its problems; but there was also laughter and fun and togetherness, at least with the kids, a place where my heart was, and where my children would run in and give me cuddles.

Why do we, as adults, find it so hard to be like children? You may get upset with the young ones, but a few moments later, no matter how mad you are with them, you are cuddling, reassuring and reminding them of your love. So different when adults are involved; the anger, disappointment and fear of losing territory keeps us from ever saying words that would put the situation right, such as, "I am sorry".

Many a night sleep failed to come. When awake, I tried various other distractions. I longed for female company and I sought this but it did not give complete satisfaction; there was always one ingredient missing, the complete warmth that you feel afterwards when you remain in each other's arms and wish that you could stay there forever.

But that is how things are in life and what one has to do is make the best of any given situation, otherwise you fall under a bus, and what a waste that would be.

After a year of turmoil and missed visits with the kids, I wondered whether there would ever be a normal relationship with them. Carolyne was a little bit sheltered from all that was going on, and whilst she was at private school, she was out of harm's way.

Chapter 6 - Finding My Roots

Once again, at a low point, out of the blue an opportunity came up and propelled me forward.

In 1986, I went to Jamaica for my usual visit to see the folks and to continue my search for my real parents.

Popa was still trying to make it as a farmer, and although the pension that he received monthly from England went a long way, his generosity required additional income to assist those in need. Popa found it hard to say no, to the detriment of his family. Many times, they went without so that others could benefit.

Popa and Auntie had never attempted to hide the fact that they were not my real parents. From a very young age, I knew, and when I tried to find out about my dad, nobody could give me any concrete evidence of who and where he was, but I continued to ask.

I was told my mother had been a chambermaid in a hotel, and in the early fifties, she had gone to the United Kingdom to attend to my grandfather, who had been very ill. But no one could tell me where she was. Her aunt who lived in the area told me all she knew was that my mother was in the UK.

On this trip, I also insisted on the identity of my father. But no one knew very much about the whereabouts of either parent, and whilst they thought relatives of my mother lived across the road from us, I still drew a blank. At home, I spoke to Lynn, our helper.

"Do you know who my father is?"

"Me 'ear 'dat he is a butcher."

"Where does he work?"

"Everybody a say dat he in a de market in Christiana."

"What is his name?"

"Me no sure, but dem a call him Mass Fred, and a 'im dey say use to visit yu madder in de 'otel dat she work, de 'otel call Villa Bella."

Armed with this information, I went in search of this elusive father. I arrived in Christiana, a noisy and congested market town with a main street that ran straight through it.

This road carried all the through traffic, and with the close proximity of makeshift stalls, the road was narrow, making it a very dangerous place to walk down. Often, a lorry and a car trying to pass each other had great difficulty: both sides of the street had varying arrays of shops, and the smells were pungently obvious, some leaving much to be desired.

As I wandered through the street stalls, seeing all the wonderful fruits and vegetables, I was struck by the fact that everyone sold basically the same things: lettuce, oranges, plantains, bananas, yam. Most of these people, with sundried faces, came up from the country the day before, and slept right where their goods were being sold.

Life was tough, but what choice did some of these people have? About 99% had never ventured further than where they were sitting; they had heard the sound of an aeroplane overhead but never had the opportunity to get on one. Many would have travelled to the next parish on a special visit – marriage or death – but would not dream of going any further.

The name Alfred Evans was on one of the meat stalls. I stood back and looked at the man. He was a man in his fifties, with a red-skinned complexion; that was what someone who was of mixed black and white blood was called. He had on a well-worn, wide-brimmed hat, and was dressed in blood-stained work clothing.

I waited. I thought, why do I need courage at this moment? If he is my dad, then all I have to say is, "Good to know you." If he isn't my father, then, "I am sorry, I seem to have made a mistake."

All the evidence that I had pointed to him; he even looked a little like me.

It seemed like ages, but he did not notice me. I felt braver, so I took a few steps forward, and then he saw me. He promptly placed some discs against the various cuts of meat, because, as I realised later, he thought that I was a food inspector, checking whether the meat had been passed for human consumption.

I caught his eye and asked him whether I could talk to him. He left from behind the counter and a young man, who turned out to be another one of his sons (although much darker), was left to mind the stall.

We went outside. The sun still shone and I felt the warmth on my face. He lagged behind a little bit so I walked slower. I stopped and he couldn't wait to ask.

"Wha' u want?"

"My name is Derrick." I didn't say my surname, because that would have made him realise where I was heading, so I beat about the bush a bit; I had to get more admissions, before I could hit him with my suspicions.

"Can you recall 25 years ago?"

"Yeah, man."

"Do you remember a young lady called Enid Richards?"

"Now let me t'ink. A' t'ink she use to wok inna Christiana."

"Yes she did,' I continued. "Did you visit her at the Villa Bella hotel where she worked?"

"Yes man, she and me had a ting."

I hesitated again, but I was almost sure -

"You are my Daddy."

Everything seemed to stop. Everyone was frozen in time. There was a silence, and then, his arms flying up in the air, he uttered a few expletives. He looked like he was about to have a seizure, and the bits I chose to hear were definitely a denial.

"No man, a no me, go weh!" which basically meant he was not my father and I should make tracks. I wanted to calm him down so I lowered my voice and I said calmly, "I don't want anything from you. All I would like to know is, are you my dad?"

He became calm. The world started to move, and he looked like living again.

He took me to meet my three other half-brothers, and three sisters and his wife. I was his first child and they all treated me well. In a short period of time, I became the big long-lost brother. I also got to know that there were many other siblings in existence all over Manchester. Every good-looking girl that I admired turned out to be a sister! I also now had thirteen uncles and, as you can imagine, many, many cousins.

In playing big brother, I found that there were numerous problems that needed my attention. Ignorance and lack of education was rife amongst my brothers, and so many had left school or had failed to attend any. Their literacy was very low. The fist and the knife all played a part in their lives and their very existence. I had to get in between many a confrontation. I left Jamaica with that feeling that some more of Derrick's jigsaw puzzle had been put together, and also one of completeness.

I mean, I met a man who drank and smoked too much. He womanised, and had few qualities that I admired; but at least I was able to identify some of the DNA that made me. Was he a good example? I think not, but at least I could now say I had met my father, although I was not sure how much time I would want to spend with him. Going on first impressions, he epitomised a character that I had always strived not to be.

I have very fond memories of my new family and I intended to get to know my brothers and sisters, especially Michael, who until I arrived was considered the eldest. I developed a real soft spot for him and, with his large frame and soft-spoken voice, I was sure that we would be great friends.

I arrived back in the UK with a mixture of happiness and sadness, because I was faced with further crisis. Mid-January, Jewel arrived at the office and we discussed my moving back to Southdene (the family home). I was very tempted and for a while I forgot all the bad points that existed when I left. I was convinced that I needed to try again, as I was not one for giving up. So we agreed that I would move back in - when, was another matter.

My keep-fit classes were expanding and growing demand for me was high. By March 1987, I was teaching Monday, Wednesday and Thursday, and at the end of each evening, I would still play squash as well.

Chapter 7: Building New Horizons

Evans Builders

For my financial protection, I looked at a number of options, and it was about this time that I came up with the idea of Evans Builders. Here was an opportunity to try something different and make some money in the process. I knew others with successful companies. Easton Howse was one such person, whom I had stayed with when I first came to London. He was extremely successful in buying, renovating, and selling diverse properties. He kept a large portfolio of properties, and I hung out close to him to try and learn the ropes.

Eventually, due to the need to make some money, I put in place my plan. There were contracts to be won in the East End of London, so I went after those. I did not have a team of guys – no plumbers or carpenters – but so what?

I wanted to try and do it. I saw others come from nowhere and establish themselves in a field which was awash with cowboys - and I felt that I could do better, give people a well-executed job, and value for money. I was inspired, and I was going to do it.

I got in touch with the local council, which had a list of conversions that needed doing. Armed with my list, I made my plans. I knew an architect and he was very willing to work out the costing for the very first job that I tendered, to an Indian gentleman in Bethnal Green who needed a side extension. We won it!

I quickly put a team together of carpenters, plumbers and labourers, and we arrived on site. That was the beginning of Evans Builders.

Most of the time, I was freezing; standing around overseeing, while learning a trade that was alien to me. With my long johns, leg warmers and many layers of clothing topped off by the head gear and gloves, I looked the part.

Just before the job was finished, I got to the point most builders get to – some earlier than others – the usual problem; my client started to find invisible faults, and attempted to get us off the job. We seemed to be moving too fast, and therefore we must have overcharged him.

We argued, he held up payments, so we made one last-ditch attempt to get at least our final payment in, albeit with the profit element missing. He agreed to make payment to us if we returned to the job. We did, he paid me in full, we completed the job, and then moved on. That was the last day that we would be seen in the Green. We did not make a profit, but I certainly learned a lot.

This first job started a roller coaster ride of different jobs, and to this day, I cannot figure how we were able to convince so many people that we were proficient builders, but that is just what we did.

Before I knew it, we were working on a block of flats in Maida Vale owned by an Arab. He wanted five flats converted and this was my first exposure to heights. We completed the job to a high standard, but once again it came to the snag, a list of things that should have been completed before the final payment. An argument ensued about 'he said, I said.' Payment became a problem, I was called a liar, and I saw red. I don't know how it happened, but he was on the ground and my knuckles hurt badly.

By now, I had Reg Johnson, my mate from Leicester, and my nephew David, working for me. We did quite a number of other jobs, one of which was a shop in Cricklewood.

That was an odd job, the one in Cricklewood. It was a video shop refit and after we had finished, the customer, who also owned the two floors above the shop, asked us to create some mirrored cubicles, a lounge and a bathroom on both floors. I couldn't understand what this was for and when I asked, he explained about an area of human behaviour that I did not know anything about.

He was a transvestite, and so were many of his friends, from doctors to bank managers, and they all wanted a discreet place to carry out their fantasies without the knowledge of wives or co-workers.

We completed this job and moved on to many more, which served to embellish my reputation for high-quality work.

But this was not me; I did not enjoy it. Even though I was making money and able to meet my expenses at home, all that I had proved to myself was that, as long as I committed myself to anything, I would always succeed.

I made the building business work, but the only way for me to have had real, sustainable, income, required that I go into buying, conversions and selling. I did not have the funds to do that, so until I was able to, I just continued doing different jobs.

At the end of one pretty ordinary trip to Jamaica, I returned to London via New York. I recalled this flight in particular, because I was amazed how a chance meeting could open up doors that otherwise were locked shut.

I was sitting in economy class when a well-dressed man came on board, followed closely behind by a woman with a broken leg who was briskly wheeled off to first class.

He sat beside me. He introduced himself in a rather posh American drawl, as Jack Brinsley Motto. For the next while, he told me how he ran offices in Italy, dealing in the financial market. He was apparently responsible for making money for his many clients, and also a lot for himself. He had done so well, in fact, that he owned a number of houses around the world, one near Buckingham Palace, which he said had a view of the grounds of the palace.

Oh yeah, I thought.

I told him about Evans Builders, and he liked the idea of buying and converting, then selling at a profit. We spoke about many things, but I felt something did not fit. Here was a man, supposedly with so much money, and yet he was sitting with me in economy class, and then he explained.

"Never waste money and pay full price for anything, when, with a bit of manipulation, you can get it for a cheaper price." He continued, "I always buy an economy ticket, then on board I offer the stewards some money for an upgrade. But, as I am enjoying talking to you, I will stay where I am!" I partially believed the explanation, but, as I was to learn later on, this was just one of his eccentricities.

At the end of the flight, he invited me and the wife to come and see him at his home in town, the one that he said had a lift and a butler. We said our goodbyes, and as I looked on I thought, "Well, at least he made the flight time go quickly."

I did not expect to see him again, but as the weeks went by, there was the occasional message at home saying 'Call Jack'. I had thrown away his card and forgotten who Jack was, until one day I answered the phone and heard, "Jack Brinsley Motto here". As soon as I heard that voice, it jogged my memory. "Derrick," he continued, "I have been calling you, 'cause I enjoyed your company so much, I would like to catch up. I'm having a dinner party, so come on over." I thanked him for the invitation and told him that I would be there.

I had difficulty finding his home. It was in a small mews that I could hardly find on the map, just round the corner from Buckingham Palace. I knocked loudly on a large teak door with very shiny brass knobs, which was opened by a butler. I enquired if I had the right house, and he said they were expecting me. As I stepped in, I marvelled at the opulence, which I had never been exposed to. Everything was lushly rich and way over the top. We climbed into a lift and got out at the first floor, which opened into a drawing room, with leather chairs and antique furniture.

I was asked to wait there, and, as I casually looked around, I saw from a window into the grounds of Buckingham Palace. I knew then that I had misjudged him.

I turned as I heard his voice. He greeted me warmly. His garish clothes contrasted sharply to my understated attire. His wife smiled broadly, and said she had heard good things about me, and wanted to hear more. She had invited a friend of hers who had just flown in to make up the numbers. This stunning lady was a well-known black model who was one of her dearest friends, and she wanted me to look after her.

We all had a drink, and over the rim of my glass of orange juice, I tried to take in all that was in front of me; what forces are at work here? Just maybe, opportunity was knocking at my door.

The chatter flowed freely around the room, and then we all moved into the dining room where we sat at a large oval table, me facing this gorgeous model.

This model, I learned, shared much with both of them.

I learned that Jack loved to ski, so he was always off following the snow. His wife, on the other hand, preferred the sunny climes and sought warmth across the world.

Dinner was great, but as it was nearing time for me to take my leave, Jack said something interesting.

"Derrick, if you find any good investment property, let me know and I will invest." He said he would be willing to buy the property, stump up the conversion cost and share the proceeds 50/50. I was grateful for his confidence in me, and so I thanked them all and left.

Everything was all a haze on the way home.

I did buy a number of properties, which he never saw. We converted them and sold them, I made a profit and I gained the experience.

One property that we bought in Wood Green proved to be a real problem, and it was the one that caused Jack and me to differ. He was not happy with the problems we encountered with a particular sitting tenant. He wanted them out of the premises, but it did not sit easy with me working up ways to get the tenant out; with patience, they would eventually leave. Jack wanted them out by any means necessary and so we went our own ways, never seeing each other again.

What did I learn from this experience? Well, opportunity does knock at the door, but you have got to be prepared to open it. Also, never judge a book by its cover. I had totally misjudged Jack; he was egalitarian, but because of my station in life, I had assumed that he could not possibly want to speak to me.

The year 1987 was a great year. No matter what I did in the building game, I made money. I bought and sold houses in many parts of the East End. I met various individuals who all wanted a part of my business, many came and went; to some, it cost money, but in general, I made money for a lot of them.

Bed and Breakfast

I also took on the lease of a building in Kingsland High Street, three stories above a furniture shop. I had seen how high the demand for bed and breakfast accommodation had become, and I seized the opportunity.

I converted each of the six very large rooms to hold homeless people. This property was to be managed by Moses, a man about 60 years old who I had sort of adopted a few years before. He was helping a carpenter who was working for me, but Moses had become a little disenchanted and was looking for a change, so I took him under my wing as a kind of general helper and odd job man.

He had his work cut out keeping the residents in order, but someone with his approach to things was able to manage the mix and variety of characters that we had staying with us. We provided them with the basic needs – after all, it was a bed and breakfast – with most tenants spending the days away from their rooms. The local council paid us well for the accommodation as there was not much governmental provision for young, single, homeless men, and as long as some form of accommodation was found for them, the council was only too willing to pay for them. After all, that was one less person on the book of the homeless statistics.

We tried to provide the best in terms of clean rooms, running hot and cold water, carpets, heating and a good breakfast, but from very early on, we found that these people seemed happier to be in squalor than live in a well-maintained place. Moses also had numerous problems to do with their behaviour; he was ill-equipped to do any better but he managed. He was brash, rough and tough, and that manner often won the day, getting tenants to do exactly what he wanted done.

We made quite a good income from the B&B. I stayed away most of the time, due to the fact that I could not stand the way in which the place was treated, and I was just not comfortable with the dinginess that became the norm.

Misery at Home

When I returned home, there were no bells ringing, no fireworks display, and no fanfare. Jewel and I tried to pick up the pieces of our damaged relationship, and, although I so wanted to be near the kids, it wasn't long before I regretted being back in the family home. Yes, I was near James and Ebony, but I was far, far away from Jewel. We tried to discuss and agree on many things, the first of which was that Jewel did not want Carolyne to live with us. Can you imagine? Carolyne was my 15-year-old daughter, the first love of my life! Well, I couldn't agree, and so we fought, physically and mentally.

We had so many disagreements; it seemed nothing was right. I could not sleep in the same bedroom with Jewel anymore, and although I was still living there, I was concerned for my safety. David, my nephew, had to stay in the home with me and we slept in the lounge, but I was so afraid of Jewel's wrath that the only way I felt safe was to prop a chair up against the lounge door at nights. I lived in this one room for the best part of a year but, as before, something had to change.

In the meantime, a rigid exercise programme helped me endure, but by 1988, I was asking my solicitor to prepare divorce papers.

I had a dream of setting up my own health club. I found a location and I did the budget. On paper, it looked good, but to get things going, I needed help. I got this needed assistance from a man who I knew who ran a travel agency with his son; Jeff and Max Petars were friends of mine, and when I mentioned the project, both were keen on becoming part of it.

At Brent Cross, there was a trading estate called the Atlas Business Centre, run by the Sulkin brothers. They had made their money by buying or leasing run-down warehouses, breaking up the premises into different sized units, refurbishing, and then subletting to different companies and individuals. I had located the best of the available units.

Jeff and Max knew the Sulkin brothers and, against my better judgement, I agreed to a licence on the premises. This arrangement gave us no long-term protection, but Max assured me that due to the friendship, it would not be necessary. This proved to be a mistake.

It did not take many months for me to put into place all the elements for what I knew would be a very successful business. The Studio, with our motto 'Fitness is a way of Life,' was a different kind of gym, wall-to-wall mirrors and lino flooring, large Olympic gym and sauna rooms, and a bar and meeting area. It changed the way people exercised.

Max knew Frank Bruno, and through this friendship, the big man performed the opening ceremony. It was a great day and there was a tremendous turnout. I taught a class, and most of my other teachers did the same. Afterwards, all I had to do was seek great teachers, and I was always on the lookout for new fitness regimes. We were on our way.

Overnight, news of The Studio began to spread. We attracted everyone, from every nationality, age and gender; they came from near and far. We were open every day and all classes were well attended, so naturally it wasn't long before we were looking to expand.

I spent more and more time away from all the hassles at home. Jewel did not approve, but at least I was able to meet all my financial commitments; she could not grumble at that. I didn't see the kids as much as before, but when I got home, seeing them just made my day.

As I came in, they would all congregate around me in the dining room, while their mother stayed in the TV room. It wasn't long before she would wander in and send them to bed. Many nights, I came home and there wasn't any dinner available for me, or there were her friends - one in particular, John Carr - at the dinner table enjoying the fruits of my labour.

Carolyne was about to leave Oakdene school with a number of O' and A' level. She had grown up into a lovely young lady. She developed my argumentative attitude, and was known for her entrepreneurial spirit at school. I remember her borrowing money from me to finance a tuck shop business. On my regular school visits to her, I had to take supplies to replenish her shop. This went on for a number of months, then she decided to give it up, because she had allowed too many schoolmates to take goods on credit that eroded her profit, and I was buying more and more goods with no repayment. She had, from this early enterprise experience, gained valuable lessons about business.

So now she was wondering what to do next. The most natural step was to help me at The Studio, which she did well and which suited me as there was no one else that I could trust to hold the fort when I was away.

One such time was when I had to leave very urgently for Jamaica. Auntie made several calls to me at the beginning of that week, but each evening, due to the time difference, the calls came whilst I was asleep downstairs. Jewel hung up each time and didn't tell me. It wasn't until much later in the week that I took a call to find out that Auntie had been calling and asking for me.

David, his mother Cherry, and I all left to see her with a heavy heart. Auntie had suffered much over the years; she was a brave old soul, who never complained. But she was near the end now.

Auntie Dies

We arrived in Kingston on Thursday, the first flight that I could get, and got to Pike quite late in the evening. All the lights were on as I climbed the steps to the house. I was met outside the bedroom, only to be told that I was too late. She could not wait any longer for me; she had been asking desperately for me to come and see her, but alas, she slipped away earlier in the evening.

I went in to see the only mother that I had known and loved so much. She was the person who had cared and looked after me as her very own, while being the quiet, strong backbone behind Popa. Auntie was always there; washing, caring, crying and laughing with us. She had done her best. Now I was getting ready to lay her to rest and I know she had found peace.

I left her room and told all the family members that I wanted to see them the next day, to make all the arrangements for the funeral. When we met, however, I received no contribution from the rest of the family: that was the norm; if you come in from the UK, there is an expectation that you are awash with cash.

Back to the UK

I buried Auntie and left Jamaica to return to my problems. When I got back to the UK, it was back to The Studio, and a marriage that was now on its last legs.

The Studio was just one great buzz. Membership had grown considerably; all the classes were busy and members could be seen sitting in groups in different parts of the building. The pink and grey walls had created a wonderful setting for exercising and socialising.

The home front was truly very bad now. Jewel's anger was directed against the kids, especially Carolyne. She wanted Carolyne out of the house and out of her life. The poison that came out of Jewel was incredible and I fought back saying no, the only person who was going to leave, if anyone, would be her.

One day on leaving The Studio, I saw some black bags by the front door. I opened them to find they contained Carolyne's clothes. I took them back home and was greeted by a confrontation. Another time, the door at home was locked and Carolyne's clothes had been thrown out of the window.

Jewel was also a regular visitor to The Studio, not for exercise but to enforce her position of part ownership by marriage. Her jealous presence caused major upsets, both with staff and clients. I cannot forget her spitting in the face of a business colleague of mine because she did not agree with what he had to say. He just took it and said she was lucky she was my wife.

The time came when things finally exploded. We had a blazing row on 25th October 1988, culminating in the police and lawyers being called. It was at this point I realised that there was no point in trying to continue any longer. I had walked into the house, very annoyed about her trying to move Carolyne out yet again. Jewel immediately started raving, and although she was only dressed in her bra and pants, I picked her up, put her out the front door and locked it. It was cold outside, and I needed a minute to calm myself down, but she was shrieking with rage, so in fear of the consequences, I let her come back inside.

She went crazy. Before I knew it, we were arguing and being violent to each other on the stairs. She hit me in the back of my head with the heel of her shoe. I retaliated and slapped her across the face. And as we struggled with each other, her profanities and violence increased, leading me to try and restrain her, but somehow my hands ended up around her throat. As I hoisted her up in the air, I felt her getting limp; it was then that I got a hold of myself and said, "There is no way I'm going to jail because of you."

I released her and thought that was the last of it, but she came back, throwing perfume into my face. I couldn't see and the kids couldn't hear me from their rooms. I grappled in the dark until I managed to get to the phone and called my lawyer to get on to the police.

I shouldn't have done that. When the police came, they refused to believe that a tiny woman like her could inflict on me the kind of damage that she had.

As a result of this argument, we went to court and I was ousted from the matrimonial home. I found myself with nowhere to live; I still had the offices in Cricklewood Broadway but I couldn't go there because most of the rooms were being used for running all the things that I was involved in

I contacted a guy who owned a bathroom fittings business in Harlesden. He did quite a lot of property conversions and also managed homes owned by wealthy Nigerians who periodically lived in the UK. He had a large unfurnished house in Brondesbury Park, which was way out of my reach. It was a five-bedroom double-fronted house on a large corner plot, with carpets and chandeliers in every room. Every bedroom had an en-suite bathroom. I left Mill Hill with Carolyne and our dog, JD, a large Rottweiler. We moved in and slept on the floor, but we were warm and comfortable, and at least we were at peace.

I needed to go forward. I had so much baggage that was holding me back, and, no matter what, it needed sorting out. But I wondered how many things I could do at once; I was not sure I could keep all the balls up in the air at the same time.

Divorce was in the air.

In the meantime, demand for my on-stage workouts increased. They were great opportunities for increasing membership of The Studio, which was now flying. We employed five part-time workers and a number of full-timers.

Terry Clarke, one of my instructors, and I took part in many different exercise classes and the experience was life-changing; all of a sudden, I realised where my future was, and I now wanted to be the very best exercise teacher there was, and all because of what I observed at some of the gyms that were in the area. So I investigated fitness conventions and found information about the International Dance Exercise Association (IDEA), and we flew out to Anaheim. I found that while there was excitement at the convention classes, after a while they were all the same. Most teachers did not instruct, but were more intent on showing off how complicated their workouts could get.

There was one lady, Karen Voight, at the convention, who was different from all the rest. She owned a studio called the Voight Centre; here was the goddess of fitness. She was single-handedly responsible for many new exercise regimes. Out of her studio came some exceptional exercise disciplines. As we wandered around the club, every class was full, but only one class took our breath away. It was bursting with people sweating, grunting, screaming, and laughing all at the same time.

The conductor of this class was a plump black guy with great rhythm, Billy Goodson. I was transfixed by his movements, and I knew there and then what my visit to the USA was about. I knew immediately what I was going back into the UK to teach.

I was so glad of the experience that I had gained, as it helped me to formulate a model for my classes, which touched on attitude, content, class awareness, and enjoyment. I am convinced that I coined the phrase, 'If it's not fun, don't do it.' On the return journey, we set about writing down all the moves, and Cardio Funk UK was born.

On the first day back, my usual class was different and it bore all the marks of my newly acquired skills. I floated on the response from my class members, the clapping and the smile at the end of my class. It was when I truly knew that I had arrived.

Tessa

In May 1988, I wandered outside to retrieve something from the car, and saw someone who looked familiar to me. I recognised Tessa Sanderson, a former Olympic javelin athlete. I started a conversation with her and her friend Wendy Hoyte. They were visiting a nearby recording studio and I persuaded them to come into The Studio. They did for a short time, but they were in a hurry and soon left.

Two weeks later, Tessa arrived at The Studio unannounced, and stayed until classes were finished. She joined a group of us, including my children, at a Chinese restaurant that we went to regularly.

Sometime after, I called Tessa to see how she was getting on, and she invited me to her going away party to the Seoul Olympics, which was at her home in Essex. Carolyne and I got there quite late, and so had missed most of the festivities and people were beginning to leave, so we didn't stay long. I had only met this woman a short while ago, but felt comfortable visiting her home, then visiting her in hospital for an injury that prevented her from going to the Olympics. Everything moved at quite a pace.

We discussed her changing her current manager. Tessa felt that in order to progress, she needed to be in charge of her own affairs, and that ultimately, having her own public relations company would be a good move. Not only would she look after herself, but she would also be able to offer a similar service to other athletes.

Before we got very far in dialogue, I found myself rising to the challenge of running a PR business. I knew nothing about it, but that had never stopped me. It would only be a new challenge, and associating with Tessa could only bring good things to my business, and more clients to my studio.

Together, Tessa and I poached a lady who worked for her former manager to run the office. Tessa then took on a lease for an office in the same estate, and before I knew it, she was next door to me. The pace at which things moved was incredible, but during all this time, nothing romantic had happened between us. I was still smarting from a failed marriage, and business was business. I was not about to miss a golden opportunity to move forward.

Terry Clarke and I set up teachers' training classes at The Studio, which was attended by many teachers who took to Cardio Funk like fish to water. We did a number of masterclasses around the UK and, although they were successful, there was a marked difference in our sense of rhythm and style, she being Caucasian. To be an exponent of

Cardio Funk, you needed some Black Soul. It wasn't long before we went our separate ways and I continued the classes by myself.

For reasons that were not clear to me at the time, just gut instinct I suppose, I started to speak to a number of TV stations, and before long, I met a man called Julian Aston, who ran New Era Television. Through him, I met his wife Penny, who I convinced should do an item on Cardio Funk. She came to The Studio, interviewed me, and filmed the class, which was shown on the cable station. Julian was impressed by it all and offered me a job with Penny to present a fitness and health show. Before the deal could be ratified, New Era was taken over by British Sky Broadcasting (BSB) and the deal was off. But I had gained a lot from this; I now had something for a showreel and I had developed a taste for TV.

It seemed a lot of people did see that very first exposure on TV. With all the press activity, membership of The Studio increased and I could see that it was on its way to great success. The B&B was also doing good business.

The Beginning of the End - DIVORCE

I was lonely living on my own; I had neither time nor energy to develop any long-term relationship, and I needed to resolve the situation about seeing James and Ebony. Since leaving Mill Hill, everything between Jewel and I had become very sour, and now I could only make arrangements to see the kids through Ebony.

My divorce papers were filed. I knew it would be contested but there was no point in putting things off.

I have to say that nearly ten years of litigation almost made me lose faith in human nature. All I ever wanted after the break up was regular times when I could see the children – not in a room with other people, and not just for an hour. I wanted meaningful time with them, and I wanted to be an integral part of their future.

The courts, as I realised, were less concerned with the rights of the father, so they failed to enforce their own orders and the mother was at liberty to break all the rules without getting her knuckles rapped.

I felt the courts should have given me the necessary support when they saw how dedicated I was to taking care and being with my children. But even when Jewel flouted a ruling, she should have had to answer to the courts, as would any father who was not willing to take full responsibility.

I went through a level of pressure unimaginable. No one could have been prepared for what I was about to go through. After a number of years, I found myself questioning my reasons for fighting so hard. Was it because I was given away? Was it because I never got the love of my biological parents? Was it just something that my adopted parents instilled in me? I don't know, but what I do know is that I fought for the right to be part of my childrens' lives.

By December 1988, I needed a break. I had to get away from it all so I made arrangements for The Studio to be looked after and for the B&B to be attended to. Tessa wanted to go on holiday as well, so we went to Jamaica.

The trip to Jamaica was good, and the weather was warm and revitalising. Carolyne was getting to know and like Tessa more and more, and so they shared a room.

When we got back, we began to come to terms with how circumstances were forcing us together. Tessa was pushing for something more and she was one of those people who did not take rejection lightly. We had some kind of bond but the essential ingredients of fire and passion was missing on my side. She was relentless, and I knew what she was looking for, but while I was not prepared to give it, there was nothing to stop me benefiting from an association. It is amazing how circumstances can dictate our actions, so I began to feel that maybe there was something worth pursuing.

In our discussions, we looked at the many advantages of being together; she needed to make a new name for herself and to establish a new career, as the Olympics had been a disaster for her. And so it was that I convinced her to let me look after her interests.

I wondered though, would I be able to cope with her possessive nature?

I rented a beautiful little cottage, and occasionally Tessa would stay. We seemed to immediately fall into a stage of being together, a man and wife position I had just moved away from. I was a bit raw from the nuclear fallout of my divorce proceedings, and the last thing I should have entertained was living with another woman. It was all too soon.

However, Tessa was a lady in a hurry, and she was running up the altar before I was able to take a breath. It is sad; we were two people heading in different directions and working to timescales. I met her parents – nice folks – and was also exposed to her so-called celebrity friends, most of them from the sporting field. Anyhow, I absorbed it all; I was now representing Tessa, and at the same time, I was developing a new circle of contacts.

The New Tessa

All said and done, home life was good at that time. The cottage was owned by a retired widowed lady, and was annexed to the larger house, situated in a substantial, well-maintained back garden. It was close to The Studio and was at the same time a midpoint for Tessa to get to work. I had been spending time re-sculpting and re-modelling Tessa. With a new hairstyle, streamlined body, and the right clothes, she looked so much better than before. Most javelin throwers are usually on the large side; Tessa was not, but her femininity and gentleness were not readily apparent.

Tessa wanted to be a marketable commodity and offers after her retirement were not coming in. I knew that she needed a new image, and so I made it my mission to help change some of her physical assets.

She responded well to my method of training, which focused on cardiovascular and strength development. I was amazed to see the radical change to her body.

The very first job that I negotiated for Tessa was as a sports reader at the new satellite provider Sky Television. She did fine, but was just lacking in something, the ability to stand out from the rest.

Tessa also liked the idea of appearing in an exercise video, and she was doing more and more interviews, which gave credit to my exercise regime as the reason behind her new-found figure, which, of course, it was.

I appeared with her regularly in newspaper articles, getting column inches, and all of a sudden, being noticed. The Studio continued to flourish, but as membership blossomed, there were rumblings that the guys who owned the estate were considering selling. Max, my partner, assured me that we had nothing to worry about if they were to ever sell. He was their good friend and because this friendship went way back, we would be protected. I worried, but I left the lease and licence situation to Max, and I continued to work at membership retention.

You see, I believe that the more a company focuses on the retention part of a business, the more it will succeed, and it is more able to afford incentives that keep it so. Too many organisations concentrate on attracting the new, as opposed to finding ways to keep what they have. At The Studio, I believe that we had it just right. The atmosphere was relaxing as there were areas where you could chill. The pink and grey colours were pleasant to both sexes, and the staff was second to none. We cared about what we were doing, and this care and concern went into our teaching.

I made a point of knowing all the clients, whether members or drop-ins. New people got a 'buddy', an established member who introduced them to other members to make them feel comfortable.

I knew that a decision to get fit was a big step, but the biggest was walking through that gym door. In those days, everyone wore leg and ankle warmers, stretch pants, headband and sweatbands, all matching. Wasn't that intimidating?

I also started taking coachloads of people to Margate for the day. We would leave on a coach early in the morning, with big picnic hampers, music machine, and smiles on our faces. When we arrived on the beach, armed with the council's approval, we would set up the sound system on the beach, and everyone would work out with us.

After an hour's workout, it was into the sea, then on to the local fun fair, Bemboms, for an afternoon of rides and ice cream.

At twilight, it was back on the coach for a sleepy ride back to Staples Corner. Definitively, these times were what gave me the experience that later proved invaluable when exercising with large groups, getting everyone moving and just getting the very best out of all taking part. I began to develop a knack for motivating people, and the bigger the group involved, the more animated I became.

Tessa came to all my classes at the gym, and this I found stifling. She gave me no space, no freedom, and I felt trapped. However, there were many new opportunities coming our way. I was asked to perform my Cardio Funk routine all over the place, from Butlin's holiday camp to warming up a fun run in Hyde Park.

Cardio Funk

I had written the concept for two potential videos: *Cardio Funk* was a dance exercise routine, and the other, *Body Blitz*, was a tougher routine based on a pyramid system of working out. This is where you start with one exercise, and then add another to each repeated routine until you get to at least eight exercises being done in sequence. Tessa liked the concepts and introduced the first one, *Cardio Funk*, to Video Gems, a video company that had on its books none other than the diet guru, Rosemary Conley.

A deal for a video was agreed and Tessa came to the table as Tee & Dee, splitting our share 50/50. I was to go away and do the scripting, and find a location, plus willing participants.

Not very long after, Scarborough beach was nominated as the best location. We would have to pray for sunshine, but I was able to get a group together for the shoot, which we had estimated to last two days. I was able through contacts to get about 30 people together and then we set about working out the final scripts and the clothes we would wear.

My pink and lilac full lycra suit, with Tessa wearing complementary colours, was the look we decided upon, and with the full package in place, we were on our way.

I was on cloud nine. More than ever, I was starting to get the recognition that I had secretly craved, and all I had to do was keep my head down and go quietly for it; the opportunity was there for the taking.

Before all that, I still had some more locations to go to with the Cardio Funk roadshow. When I say roadshow, this was paid PAs at different locations. I did some 20 cities, and it was so well received that keeping up with the demand was difficult. Tessa's presence created increasing tension between her and Terry Clarke, and the situation became unbearable. Terry had to go.

She read between the lines. It was never my intention to include Terry in the videos, as I did not see a fit; there was not a place for another instructor. When Terry learned of the impending video and that she would not be included, she bowed out gracefully. Filming was difficult, and with such a large team of extras, it proved to be a nightmare. We had to rehearse a section and then film, then we would do it time and time again so that the camera could be moved and take shots from different positions.

I was to learn later on about the importance of continuity, and that delivering lines to camera was not easy. Tessa had a large number of retakes on her introduction to the video, but I too had my challenges. I was a little bit nervous and unenthusiastic. I did not say very much in the beginning but as the filming progressed, more of the real Derrick emerged, although Mr Motivator was not yet ready to come forth.

We did the job and I went to the edit. Thankfully, the day had been sunny and the arena, which was an old amphitheatre, came out well. Everything looked great, but if you were to look closely, you would see people in one shot and when the camera had moved, they were missing, but all in all, it was fun. It was a great learning curve and I had come away with a product that would lead, later on, to another being commissioned.

Video Gems released the video and it sold fairly well. It was bought by many teachers and the public alike, and though we were not going to make the money we had first thought, we had arrived.

Sneaky Meetings with James

I had a whole load on my plate. The divorce from Jewel was long and drawn out. We contested everything. I had to hold my ground because most of all I wanted access to James, and I was having a difficult time getting to see him regularly.

On the many times when she failed to allow me access, I enlisted the help of Ebony in sneaking James out, and we would meet around the corner at the local Happy Eater. I remember dropping them back at the corner one day and asking him, "James, surely after all this food, you won't be hungry when you get in?" He said, "Sure, I won't eat."

"So what will you do when your mum puts the food on the table? I mean, you can't let our secret out, otherwise she will know that we have been meeting!"

"Oh Dad, that's easy!" He laughed. "When she's not looking, I'll just chuck the food over the fence and let the dogs next door eat it!" I smiled, because children can be so devious.

This did not continue for too long, as by the end of the year, the courts had awarded me every other weekend.

Chapter 8: True Love

Cardio Funk had given me numerous experiences to hold on to. I was invited to teach at leisure centres across the UK. They were not regular, but when they happened I would find myself in a hall with 300 people eager to work out. I was in my element, and as time went by, demand for the Derrick Evans type of teaching increased.

Every one of us has that one chance when things can change for the better. The saying is, 'Opportunity knocks at the door but once, disappointment leans on the doorbell.' When the knock happens, it is important to listen.

Palmer, the love of my life.

Palmer

Palmer is great. She has been the strength behind all that I do, and together we have shared so much. We share a great love, and the passion still burns.

I remember when she first walked into my life, in 1989, when she came into The Studio seeking membership. She was being shown around by one of the teachers, but I took over and continued the tour. I was taken by her wonderful clear eyes, and beautiful complexion, although she was carrying quite a bit of weight, which was what she wanted to change. Sandra Palmer was her name, and I knew from that very moment that I wanted to know more about her.

I was sometimes staying at Tessa's house in Essex; other times, we both stayed at the rented flat in Brondesbury Park. She continued to do well; I was involved in getting her a sponsored car, as long as she attended a number of events each year for the company. I also accompanied Tessa to a number of social events, including one of the garden parties given by the Queen.

The atmosphere was not very healthy. We were living together, and with her office next door to my Studio, we were working together. I found myself escaping more into my work and spending much time at the office.

I was also running my fitness weekends in Norwich. These weekends were a neat way of offering club members more reasons to belong to The Studio. Everyone enjoyed the relaxed family approach, and at the end of each day, it was difficult to get members to leave.

I inherited many people from other classes. This was at a time when health clubs were few in number, and most teachers made their living from running classes in schools and church halls. Sandra was now a regular club member; I had obviously said something right to her when I saw her that first day. She brought a smile to my face each time I looked at her. As she opted for weight training, I gave her extra attention. She stood out from the crowd; there was something very different about her and I so wanted to know more. She did not reveal much about herself, which made me even more inquisitive; she seemed to come in, train, and go.

I persuaded her to come to my classes. She hesitated, but it wasn't long before she was in there, working out.

After a while, she started to linger more. She formed friendships with other members, and occasionally she was in the last group to leave. Our eyes met in a different way now, and our conversations became more than a brief, "Hello, let's get training." The weight that she was carrying began to disappear, and right in front of me, I could see her stamina, strength, and shape improving.

With the changes in her body shape, Sandra's confidence soared. She was initially at the back of the room, but started to move further forward, until she was at the front row of the class, and being more vocal when I asked for a count against each exercise.

Each day, I longed to see her. I wondered if she noticed that I was giving her more attention than most. Had she noticed how I lingered when I looked at her? She had spoken of a boyfriend who had never entered the gym. She knew more about me now than I knew about her, but I found comfort in her attendance and I longed for more.

There were more and more occasions when she was one of the few members lingering after class; was this just coincidence?

I will always recall one evening, knowing that she was the only one left in the ladies' shower. I was next door, alone in the men's, and we started to chat. Before I knew it, as if my legs were propelled by remote control, I wandered into the ladies. I thought, if she catches me peeping at her, I would just say I did not know that she was in there.

She was in the open shower, and was a sight to behold. A warm feeling came over me and I was transfixed. Why was I so drawn to her?

She continued to talk to me, not realising that I was standing right behind her with my arms folded. I took all of her in and I was engulfed. She turned round and the emotion of the moment took us into the sauna; temperatures rose and the heat made us sweat for hours.

The year 1989 had started well. But emotionally, my life was more complicated than ever. I was now having a clandestine relationship, and I was already in one that seemed to need more of me than I was prepared to give. The Bible says that no man can serve two masters. But now, more than ever, I realise how true that is.

I had never truly thought that anything I was doing with Tessa would be of interest to any newspaper. All of a sudden, that changed dramatically, and it would influence her life and change mine forever. Our whole situation became very public, and very traumatic. It would also give me a real insight into how the British press works, how you can be exposed across the media, how one can influence and manipulate it, and how the press can provide an invaluable service if used correctly. At this time in my life, however, that meant very little to me.

In March 1989, I received a call at The Studio from a *News of the World* reporter and then *The Sun*, to say that a woman was going around

Fleet Street trying to sell a story about Tessa Sanderson. Initially, we were unconcerned because we weren't doing anything wrong, but the phone calls kept coming in. Tessa was about to start working for Sky TV, and as the newspaper was part of the same group, we were told that full details were being held back. But News Corporation was worried, and as they wanted to minimise the likelihood of a rival newspaper printing anything, they would be willing to do something in anticipation of what might be said.

I advised Tessa that there seemed little point in reacting to something that had not and might not happen, so we just remained silent. I, of course, knew who the lady was. I told reporters that no matter what she was saying, little truth was to be found in it. A few days later, the *News of the World* called to say the rumours were now much stronger and there would be something in the papers on the coming weekend, unless we acted soon.

On the way over to Tessa's, I sensed I was being followed, and as I turned into her road, I was sure that the two cars behind me slowed down. I did not alarm her with my suspicions, but I had noticed a red Metro and a Rover.

The next morning, I peered out of her bedroom window and saw the usual cars parked on their driveways, but there was also a camper van parked about 50 yards away on the opposite side of the road. I thought it strange that someone would have a van with curtains drawn and parked in this road, so for a while, I stood and watched. Then I realised that we were being watched; the curtain moved, and I was sure I saw a long lens.

I ran out of the house and managed to look in a corner of the van window. I saw a man lying on the floor, apparently asleep, but surrounded by an abundance of camera equipment. I got so angry, I ripped off the van's mirrors and rocked the van. He shot up and got into the driver's seat, trying desperately to get the van started, which he did, and sped off, but not before I ripped off its aerial.

The whole street woke up at the commotion; windows, curtains and doors were being opened. I had made a public display and they now knew even more.

A few days later, I was outside the cottage I rented with Tessa, who had just returned from the Sky TV launch party, when Jewel arrived with James and her sister. Inevitably, an argument ensued, and, for a while I thought it was going to become a slanging match and a fight. Jewel had travelled to argue with someone she did not know, and James was right in the middle of it. I tried to maintain a level of calm, which worked for a while until Jewel proceeded to describe Tessa as butch and that I was only around her for fame and fortune.

Eventually, it all broke up and Jewel threatened that the newspapers would be involved.

Tessa drove off and I went inside, knowing that all hell was about to break loose.

To try and squash things, we instructed Tessa's solicitors to send a letter to Jewel's solicitors and the *Mirror's* solicitors, denying anything other than a business relationship with me. Of course, this was not the truth; we just wanted to get them off our backs and out of the way.

I had organised a party at The Studio on the Saturday evening, but we were not enjoying ourselves very much, so we left for King's Cross Station. We wanted to get the early Sunday papers, and as I picked up a copy of each, I did not know what to expect. I secretly hoped that it would not be there; I prayed that my solicitor's letter had done the trick.

It was there. I did not want to see the article, but I also needed to read its contents.

We sat silently as the headlines hit home: *'Tessa Stole My Husband'* glared at us, *'so says beautician wife Jewel Evans.' 'How could she?'* it asked. Neither of us could break the silence that enveloped us; we didn't know where to look or turn. Tessa sobbed, and although I comforted her, strangely, I did not care about the story. The accusations were stupid; how can you steal someone? In any case, I was separated and in the process of divorce before I even met Tessa.

I was philosophical about it all, and I thought that there was no such thing as bad publicity. I saw that all of a sudden, Tessa was to be noticed, and where many people had forgotten what year she won her Olympic medal, they would now be reminded about who she was.

I remained calm as Tessa became more upset. She felt ashamed; all of a sudden, her world was at an end, and worse, her name was about to be dragged throughout newspaper land.

Her private life had become public and she felt emotionally exposed. She started asking herself questions that she should have asked before: why had she not gone for someone who was fully single? Why had she gone into that gym on that fateful day? Why, why, why? She didn't just want to bury her head in the sand, she wanted to disappear, she wanted out.

Conversely, though, she felt that she had hit the jackpot. She wanted to sue the newspapers; there were a lot of untruths in the articles, spread across the *Mirror* and repeated in small columns in the *Sunday People*. I advised her to leave it alone, but she was intrigued by the possibility of a big payout that she felt could amount to six figures. I disagreed with her; some of the payouts to other celebrities had been huge, but they were household names, and importantly, they were white.

I had also noticed a change in the climate and the courts were under the microscope. There was still a desire to punish the newspaper proprietors, but not to give a jackpot payout in cases of libel.

We did not go home but stayed in a hotel in Watford for five days. When we did venture outside; I was conscious of everyone looking at us, whispering, talking, smiling, nodding heads. Truthfully, I did not mind; after all, I was not doing anything abnormal – guy meets girl, relationship develops and they are together. But that was just me.

Jewel was trying to do harm, but, although we did not know it then, she was also about to do Tessa and me a favour. I was still having difficulty seeing the kids, and after the article, it became even worse. I missed them but my efforts to get access would have to be put on hold for a short while.

I could still walk down the streets unnoticed; after all, who was Derrick Evans? Of course, only when Tessa was with me did the alarm bells go off in people's heads. I could get peace; she, however, was always out there, and although everyone says it will be tomorrow's fish and chips paper, tomorrow seemed to her a long way away.

Tessa was now dressing to show off her new figure. She had been a challenge. I not only worked on her physical size, but also on her hair, clothing, and make up.

She was a good pupil. She was willing to adapt and change, and she achieved great results.

We both had calls from abroad about the article. For maximum effect, Jewel had bought loads of copies and then sent them to anyone who knew me abroad.

Tessa made up her mind to sue the *Sunday Mirror* and the *People*. I thought this was brave of her, but I did wonder what was spurring her on. Was it to protect her reputation, or was it the allure of big money? After all, things were getting quieter, and she had not seen a downturn in work. In fact, I got more requests for her appearance at events. She had suffered, but only she truly knew how much.

Advice to avoid litigation was coming in thick and fast, but she was determined to try and reinstate her damaged reputation. She was advised that any attempt to do so would bring lots of things out of the woodwork, things that had not been mentioned before, and the tabloids would turn over every rock and prod every cranny. Who knew what would come out? It would be a driverless express train; would she be prepared for the crash?

She sought advice from a firm of solicitors in Euston, who told her that there was a case – but then they would, wouldn't they? Litigation costs would be high, far more money than Tessa could afford, but they were sure she would win – how much would be another matter.

Bindmans and Partners took on a barrister who was reputed to be brilliant, but he would eventually be up against one of the most formidable lawyers, George Carmen, a man renowned for getting people off even when it looked like all the chips were down.

The phones kept on ringing and the opportunities kept coming in. All of a sudden, attention was on me. I was doing far more radio, TV and press than ever, and Cardio Funk was all over the place. I was also teaching or getting requests for appearances at various health clubs and exhibitions.

I became involved in a new exercise competition called Reebok Championship Aerobics, and appeared as the compère at many events around the country. It was an American idea, and I began to get products from Reebok through a lady who was to become a great friend of mine, Chantal Gosselin. Over many years, she was to provide any amount of trainers, socks and the like, that I required.

Sandra had become Palmer to me, and she was secretly sharing my every waking and sleeping moment. There was a passion in all our encounters. Across the room and at The Studio, her appearance made my heart skip a beat. Her figure had changed and her dress sense had evolved; skirts were short to show off her lovely legs and she had lost so much weight that everyone marvelled at her appearance.

I could not get enough of her, and at every moment we were to be found together. Everyone suspected and Tessa knew too, even though when we were confronted, we denied it. I was spending so much time with her, more than I had ever spent with anyone before. She was at all my classes and events, and any little thing that I needed help with, Palmer was there. I depended on her and I wanted to be with her more than ever.

We discussed our situation, and I fretted: how could I leave when so much had happened to Tessa? I felt that the least I could do was to be around to support her. She had a career which would be in tatters if I did not help her get through this fight.

Palmer was philosophical about it: no matter what we wanted, we should enjoy what we have, one day at a time, because it won't make any difference – if something is right, it will work itself out.

I loved her for that, but it still highlighted another, more physical issue. I could no longer serve two masters, or should I say two mistresses. I therefore developed a medical problem to avoid confrontation, and for a while, this served to keep Tessa away from me. I knew who I wanted to be with, not just for now, but forever. I wanted out, but I couldn't tell her. I pretended and I waited for the right occasion.

Palmer became my all. I thought of her constantly, and I longed for her at every moment. There had been many relationships in my life but none such as this. I was struck by lightning and the electricity that flowed through my body left me charged. I was helpless without her.

She offered me love and attention, not for what I had, but for who I was, and still am. She represented so many things to me, and whenever she could leave work during the day and we could be free of prying eyes, she would be there with me. I was hooked and I wanted more of this explosive loving that was physical, emotional and mental.

I did not realise how long it took to bring a libel trial to court, but it seemed like forever. A year went by. In that time, I went again to Norwich Sports Village with another group of willing participants, and whilst there, I decided that to further my career, I should go and get qualified. I went out of town and enrolled on a short intensive Royal Society Arts certificated course.

I passed the RSA Exercise to Music exam with flying colours, although I did bend a few rules, because I could not agree with the way in which they expected everyone to teach.

I could only teach my classes based on the atmosphere that I felt in the room when I arrived. I could not lesson plan, and I basically made it up as I went along; that is the way it has always been. You will never see me arrive at a class with a structured lesson in place. I don't even know what music I will use until I pick up the vibes from the people in the room.

I explained this to the examiner who understood and accepted it. Because of that, I was able to throw away my previously planned lesson and I freestyled, much to the applause of those attending.

Inevitably, Palmer was there to see it happen.

Legal Wranglings

Mr George Carmen was the infamous lawyer who had been responsible for getting off Ken Dodd, MP Jeremy Thorpe, and Jeffrey Archer. He was representing the *Sunday Mirror*, and his reputation brought fear to every competing lawyer.

He flung out a list of prying questions, demanding diaries and supporting paperwork. This was just the beginning.

Tessa's lawyers wanted to be assured of my attendance and support, so I was subpoenaed by her lawyer, Mr Hartley.

The *Sunday Mirror* made an offer of an out-of-court settlement of some £20,000. This was a strategic move designed to weaken Tessa's resolve and also a procedure widely used to minimise the defendant's exposure to large expenses. If Tessa did not accept the offer and the final award was £20,000 or less, then Tessa was liable for all court costs. If it went the other way, the papers would pay all costs. Tessa's lawyers advised her to say no.

The build up to the case was frantic and press attention was more than ever. The papers revelled in Tessa as this case was to be heard at a quiet time in the media. I just stayed in the background. We had to make plans for arrival at court and for the pressure of the days that lay ahead. It was going to be a very open and visible trial, and there is nothing better than gossip. With me by her side, we arrived at court dressed to kill. The photographers were out in force and we hurried from the front entrance into the high court, and quickly passed security to the sanctity of the hallowed halls.

This was my first time in the high court, and was the start of many further visits to that place. The main hall had tremendous, high ceilings – beautifully decorated, and imposing. We followed our solicitors to the main court in which the case would be heard.

Tessa had many solicitors, all with clerks, and then her lawyer with his entourage. He was very elegantly dressed in a wig and robe, carrying nothing – all papers and files were on a luggage trolley.

Jewel was there, of course. She was the star witness, and also dressed very elegantly. She stared at me so fiery I should have been burnt to a cinder.

The opening remarks were made by George Carmen, indicating that he would prove how Tessa, by her own action, had destroyed her reputation by hooking up with a married man, and when this was drawn to the public attention, she was seeking to get paid for something that was in the public interest.

Mr Hartley, on the other hand, stated that the *Sunday Mirror* had sought to suggest that a person can be stolen from another, and that the article was an incorrect portrayal of Tessa's relationship.

Each day, as we came out of court, the press was there. The most difficult part of the day was lunchtime when we had nowhere private, so we were invited into the renowned Wig & Pen, the lawyers' den directly across the road from the high court, to find momentary peace.

Jewel's behaviour on the stand played right into the hands of Tessa's lawyers. She was her usual venomous self and she showed that she was out to cause maximum hurt. Basically, she confirmed that we had a failed marriage that went back years before. When the pressure got to her from the questioning, she was difficult and rude, her head would start to turn from side to side and then she would offer help at a time when she should have continued to object.

She single-handedly won the case for Tessa, and now the papers had a difficult time proving their case: she was their star witness, but the aggressive, argumentative, rude, vile and vindictive way she behaved was most damaging to their case.

Tessa had a grilling, and so did I. After two days on the stand, I was tired; I had been painted as an opportunist and a liar.

But although I had a rough time, the issue was not about me. Before the jury went out, the judge gave guidelines on what could be considered a reasonable sum to award Tessa, a sum that was not to be a pool's win and not as low as a good Chinese meal, more than a holiday, but not a financial punishment to the newspapers.

Tessa's lawyers were stunned at the direction given by the judge, and for once they felt that her award may be short of the magical £20,000.

The jury walked in. We stood and heard the verdict for an award of £30,000. Tessa was disappointed; she had won, but the sum was a lot less than she had thought and what she had been advised it was worth. Also, an appeal would be made by the papers, which would serve to delay final payment.

The *Sunday Mirror* had paid Jewel for her story; was it all worth it in the end?

Tessa was gutted. On the way out, she smiled for the cameras, but we sat in silence on the way back to my flat. What was it worth, all the microscopic attention, all the baring of one's most intimate details? What would be the eventual fallout?

Palmer had been in the gallery most days. I glanced at her whenever I could. Work for Tessa did not slow. She was busier than ever. I received quite a lot of calls to do radio and some small TV appearances.

The Studio was having problems. What came back to haunt me was the fear that I had from the very beginning. We did not have a proper lease, and Max Petar's assurances about his friends, the owners, were to prove that in business, you shouldn't mix business with pleasure.

The owners were in negotiations to sell and the new owners only wanted tenants with a proper lease. We had to make plans to relocate, so we stopped taking memberships until such time. Funds dried up so we couldn't pay all our creditors, and very quickly I was closing the doors for the final time. All equipment now belonged to the suppliers.

The Studio became a ghost town; we still had Tessa's office and her business continued to run. I had the dull, dark rooms that once used to house Cardio Funk, and the hundreds of members to reminisce over. The only comfort I had was from Palmer, but I still felt lonely. I had spent the past two years developing a business that I thought would survive all the traumas.

When the final equipment we had leased was taken back and all the mirrors came down off the walls, my heart sank. Had I gone backwards? Was I going to sit here and mope over what may have been, or was I going to fight back. "Never wait for your ship to come in, swim out to it."

Max had lost money based on guarantees that he had given. I was left picking up rates and rent that were owed, and after the closure of The Studio, this was the last I saw of Max, but not the last that I heard from him.

Mr Motivator says: *When you set up any business, slow is the pace that wins the race. It is never gonna be easy, but the starting point is to first write up the concept, then you must do a budget. This provides you with the framework and also a snapshot of your business idea and potential. It gives everyone a focus and also it helps you to plan. If I had done that, most of the financial worries would have been avoided.*

In business, things don't always go well first time out, so be prepared for setbacks; these backward steps are part of the learning process. It will work out in the end; hard work never killed anybody. Just remember that the more you practise, the better you will get, and also this has a way of increasing your luck.

Life has a way of working out: keep on trying, striving and focusing on being the very best that you can be. Many will look on and give negative criticism. Some will tell you that you're on the wrong track, and others will tell you it will never work. Believe in yourself; the more you spread your wings, the more you will soar. I know, as I had so many who told me it could not be done.

You cannot do it alone; having a team behind you is great: think of the tennis pro or the Olympic athlete; they have support staff to guide, advise and help.

Your team may consist of just you and your better half, but doing it all together will reap rewards and lots of successes. A problem shared is a problem halved and a success doubled.

I told Tessa that I was no longer able to look after her career for free; I would have to charge her a percentage of her income. This got a negative reaction, which I admit I was surprised about. After all, her money was her own, and looking after her affairs took a lot of my time. I felt it was a reasonable request. When she had an agent, she was required to pay a commission. But this time, she refused, saying that as we were in a relationship, she should not have to pay.

My heart had nothing to do with it. If I was required to represent her interests, then she should pay. Nothing came of the repeated discussions and arguments. The rift had begun, and I was glad; it would make things easier for me.

I went looking for a place to do classes, and found a church hall in a location that I felt would be temporary. I contacted as many members as I could and started to do classes again. It felt a little bit like going backwards. I had started my career in a church hall and here I was, back there again.

I felt that better things would come along, as most of the die-hard, members, the real exercisers, remained loyal, and to this day, most of them are still with me.

Due to my association with Reebok, I got a number of opportunities. There was to be a TV show in the Midlands called 'Look Good, Feel Great', and I was asked to be on it with a group of girls who had competed in the Aerobic Championships. I met the Green Goddess, Diana Moran, and we were on air for two to three minutes performing a rehearsed routine. Each show took place in a different shopping centre.

I also did a monthly class at the Heathrow Penta Hotel on a Sunday. The hall was packed out with a hundred or so people, all eager to do Cardio Funk. It was at these times that I ran into lots of exercise teachers who were there to pick up new moves and ideas. I remember seeing Carolyn Brown, a very good exponent of fitness who went on to do her own Cardio Funk video and also became Princess Diana's personal trainer, and Lydia Campbell who ran, and still does, weekend breaks to Butlins.

I got into personal training and picked up a number of wealthy clients, but I was determined not to get burnt out, so I limited the number of classes and clients I was prepared to teach. Demand for my Cardio Funk workshop across the country had not waned, and I travelled many miles to continue its demand.

With The Studio out of the way, technically I had more time on my hands, and it meant that I had more time with Palmer. We steadily grew to love each other very much. The passion was and is always there. I had found my soul mate and it would only be a question of time before we were together fully.

Body Blitz

The video company was pleased with the *Cardio Funk* sales. I didn't see very much of the money but I did have a concept for *Cardio Funk 2*. This was to be a much tougher non-dance routine that would use a system of circuit training without weights. This class format was well tried and tested; I used it in a class that I taught to rugby players on Tuesday nights. It was a class that generated loads of interest and was popular to the point of having equal numbers of men and women.

I drove them hard in this class, a bit like the sergeant in *An Officer and a Gentleman*; they were never allowed to eyeball me! The harder I pushed them, the more they wanted one and a half hours of hell. What with the intense pace of the music, and my constant cajoling and pushing, this was not a class for the faint-hearted.

The new video looked good on paper and I was ready to be occupied in something different. Filming was to take place in Docklands, an area of East London which was under development, on the decks of an old ship in dry dock.

Filming was a problem on two fronts. We had to wear these small ear pieces which picked up the music we were working out to. This was to try and avoid our mikes picking up the music. It gave a very clean audio track. The principle was great, but it failed to work because the music level could not be increased sufficiently and we all seemed to hear the music at different times.

The second problem was that the week in question was freezing, it being November. If an exercise required clapping hands, we couldn't do it without inflicting severe pain. We were all dressed in thin, skimpy lycra that showed up the cold in various places! I was unable to get motivated and this affected all of us taking part. We could not see the funny side of any jokes and when Alan and David, two friends of mine who also appeared on the video, tried to cheer us up, we were not amused.

In the end, the video looked better than I had expected. Watching it, no one would have known of the problems we experienced.

It went on sale with no proper promotion, but we did achieve some sales, and it is still selling today.

Chapter 9: Kidnapped

On 24th July 1992, I spent a good day with James, Ebony, and Carolyne at Thorpe Park, and I was sad as usual to be taking them home. It became increasingly hard each time to return to the old matrimonial house, and we would stop around the corner and play our usual game.

I was never quite sure who would ask the question but during the quiet moments, waiting around the corner of the cul-de-sac, someone would say, "I wonder if she's in?" Then there would be a course of rapid betting on the outcome. I would edge the car forward inch by inch, all eyes on the lookout to see if her car was outside the house. If it was, there was a sad response, "Oh no!" and if the car was not there, a sense of relief came over all of us.

There was something very different about this particular day. At that moment, I just couldn't figure out why.

Her car was there, and yet we remained in the car. We knew something was not right, and so our goodbyes took longer than usual.

Ebony and James headed towards the front door. Carolyne and I waited and looked on as the door was opened, and they would both then go in with just the very slightest look back while we waited for a while, letting the memories of the past years flood over us.

We were sorry to see them go but we knew that this was for the better. In the meantime, we continued to see them every other weekend. I knew my day would come, but my fight for defined access was proving very difficult and expensive.

We drove back to Tessa's in silence. So many things had led the family to this position. The years had been varied and bitter, and the family was now apart. It seemed it would take a miracle to put us back together again.

All Jewel and I did was meet across the courtroom arena. The fights were bitter, and although I firmly believe that the price of success is perseverance, the continual legal wrangling took its toll on all of us.

When it suited her, I would get the children for a day here, a day there, and occasionally for a weekend. If the court order said from 5.00 p.m. Friday, I would wait outside forever before she would allow them out, but woe betide if I was ever late taking them home! To avoid that, we would purposely arrive early and play in the Happy Eater around the corner until the appointed return time, all to ensure that she could not return to court and get me for breaking the order.

Why do men who want so much to share in the lives of their children have to jump through hoops to see them?. Why do the courts treat the mothers so leniently, even when a court order is in place? The women break these time and time again and the courts do nothing. This was how it was for men; we were at the mercy of the mother and who did the courts always believe? Not us.

The next day, Ebony was on the phone. She spoke very quietly, in an attempt at ensuring that her mother would not hear.

"Dad", she said, "I know it's late, but there's a lot of noise coming from downstairs and there's been loud banging from the attic. I don't know what she's up to, but it seems serious. What shall I do?" All I could suggest was that she stayed calm and just keep me informed. Somehow, we would get to the bottom of it.

Ebony was now 14 years old, as she was born in 1978. The next day, there was another panicked call. "Dad, Mum has got lots of cases packed downstairs. The lounge and bedrooms are all empty. In fact, it looks like everything has been taken away. It looks like we are going away!"

I reminded her that there was a court order, which forbade her mother from removing her and James from the family home.

She whispered that she would call me again as soon as she was able.

Later that morning, she was on the phone again. I could hear airport announcements in the background. "Dad, we are at Heathrow and Mum is taking us away. But I don't know where to and Mum won't tell us. All she said is she's fed up with all the pressure you have been putting her under, so she's got to get away fast."

All of a sudden, the gate number came up on the board and Ebony realised that they were on the way to Guyana. She pleaded with me to do something. "Dad, you must get here fast!"

The phone went dead. I frantically dialled 999 and when I got the police, I yelled, "Officer, I need some help. My children are being abducted, and if you don't hurry, they will be on the way to Guyana!"

They took all my details and said they would get back to me. I felt like my world was collapsing. What now? All hope almost went away.

The children were wards of the court, which meant they were not to be removed from the country without permission, but here was my estranged wife taking them away. I felt powerless.

I was very tired; I had not slept the night before. Ebony's phone call had set my mind racing, and I thanked God for her; she was always the one who came forward. James, as the youngest, was a bit more sheltered.

The officer was back on the phone. "We can't locate anyone on the flight answering to those names."

"There has got to be." I replied. "I just spoke to my daughter and they were about to board the flight."

"Well, Mr Evans, we checked and the last flight to Ghana left this morning."

"I am sorry, did you say Ghana? I made a point of telling you Guyana!" The phone went dead. A few moments later, he was back.

"Yes, sir, we are at the desk now and the flight has just taken off for Guyana, and the log says that they were on it. I am so sorry for the mix up."

I was livid; how could he make such a mistake? This was no time for me to be understanding. I wanted my children, and him saying how sorry he was did not satisfy me. The phone fell from my hand and I entered a temporary state of depression. I did not know where to turn.

Once again, the authorities had failed to protect the interest of James and Ebony, and also they had failed to protect my rights. What was I to do?

I immediately started fantasising about an action plan, where SuperDad goes into the jungle after the captured children, fights off all opposition, and takes them back to safety. But that was just a dream and a wish. In the real world, there are laws and regulations. I couldn't just go to Guyana and take them back. I had no choice, so I waited.

It wasn't long before I heard again from Ebony, who was on the phone crying, pleading, and begging. "Dad, we are in Guyana. I don't want to be here! Help us, please!" What else could I say, but be patient? I told her to bear with me, and we would win in the end.

"I'll call as soon as I can," she whispered. The phone went dead. It took a while before I was able to put the handset down, her last few words lingered and echoed in my ears. I had to do something, but what?

I reported it to the welfare officers and my solicitors, but they said they could only take action when she returned; these were words I did not want to hear. I was dejected, surely the authorities could work through the Guyanese government and do something. That was too much to hope for. They just said that maybe she had gone for a week or so, to give her a chance. I knew differently. The house had been emptied, and not just of clothes but all the furniture. Those were not the actions of someone who was going away for a week or so. I was banned from going into the house as per a previous court order, so I only had Ebony's word to go by.

The next time Ebony called, I got her to paint a picture of what life was like and where she was living. A plan was brewing in my head and making it work meant I needed to know as much as I could about her movements and those of the rest of the family.

In secret, over the next few weeks, I learned she lived in a house where she shared a room with her mother and James. Her auntie lived across the hallway, and all the rooms led into the lounge of a part-wooden house in the country.

Most days began with her and James going off to school, either walking or by taxi. After school, she sometimes visited an uncle. Then her mother would pick her up. She enjoyed going to see her uncle, because it took her away from her mother.

She hated school and the whole atmosphere around the home. James missed me badly, but he fell into the swing of things and did not seem to mind very much, so long as he was outdoors. He was now eight years old.

I knew by now what I wanted to do, and in spite of Ebony's pleading, we were not going to hurry my escape plan. It could only be done at the right time.

Weeks went by, then months. During this time, I felt empty, and I only thank God for Palmer; my world would have been even emptier if she had not been there. As a childcare officer with nearly 20 years' experience, she knew a fair amount about what parents would do for the sake of their kids, but also what they would do to deprive the other parent of seeing the children.

Palmer was also going through a tough crisis; both her parents had been diagnosed with terminal forms of cancer. She was chief caregiver, especially to her mother who was bedridden, and although she had the physical and emotional pressures that caring for the terminally ill brought, she kept my spirits up and reassured me that all would be well. Children are more astute than they are given credit for, and as long as they were assured of my love, they would be able to 'put two and two together,' and come up with the right answer.

The summer of 1992 was not pleasant; it was a lonely time for me. I had given up the cottage and put most of my stuff into storage. I rented a small office behind the old studio, and this is where I retreated to when I wanted peace and quiet, and some privacy. I was there without anyone suspecting that I was sleeping in there. Palmer shared this store room/office with me many times and when it was cold, we put the Calor gas heater on, and warmed each other under a duvet. Occasionally, we woke up feeling extremely groggy, and wondered why we had slept for so long. Eventually, we worked out the reason: in the enclosed area called our store room, the oxygen was been used up by the gas fire. After that, we started leaving the doors open.

I didn't see Tessa very much; I started to make myself very scarce. She failed to pick up the message that I was not man enough to give her straight. She hung in there like a trooper, and no matter what I did, no matter how I tried to hint at where we were, she still could not see which way the wind was blowing. She wanted to stay with me.

I was at a crossroads in my life. I knew who I wanted to be with, but I delayed the inevitable. This was Olympic year and Tessa was busy preparing for it; there was no way I could drop the bombshell on her. It would have destroyed all her preparations, and the fallout could have been devastating.

This was a comeback. She had won an Olympic gold, and for three Olympics, she had tried to regain that world stage. There was no other medal that meant the same as an Olympic medal, so her training took on a new meaning. She needed to be focused, but she had numerous problems with her Achilles heel and had operations on it.

She was pain-free but I started to question whether she was just going through the motions, the determination with which she performed in her previous competitions was not there.

One reason was that she had not been able to get any proper sponsorship, so funds to take her to the Olympics were tight. She had not had a very successful four years in the build up to Barcelona, and therefore she had been unable to get the appearance money she was usually able to command, but Tessa was someone with good contacts and I was always amazed at who she knew and also those who knew her. She was held in great respect and was well liked by all.

Tessa's charity work took her to many areas of the UK, and she went about her appearances with great attention. Everyone always marvelled at the way she was so accessible. I learnt from these qualities and I admired her for her generosity, and when I was out at these functions and watched her doing her celebrity bits, I stood back and applauded her for what she was doing.

This was to be her last Olympic challenge, and although she had made the effort, the demands that throwing the javelin made on her body were very high. While flexibility, strength and a strong back come into play, after years of throwing the back and knees eventually let all javelin throwers down. This is where Tessa's body was; winning was impossible, but she wanted this to be her final stage.

Accommodation in Barcelona was a problem. Anyone staying in the village as an athlete or trainer was fine, but hotel space was short and, when available, was expensive.

Tessa received an invitation from the public relations people at Coca Cola to stay on a cruise liner they had rented for the duration of the games.

They offered her a double room on board over the long weekend that she was competing, and travel to the games for her partner. Of course, she accepted. I had never been to an Olympic event, but I felt very honoured when she gave me the invitation.

I was in turmoil over not seeing the kids and I did not want to be away from them any longer. I had to get them back.

I really loved these kids. Carolyne was growing up so fast. Ebony had such an independent air about her. She was popular and charmed her way through any situation, no matter how difficult. James, on the other hand, lacked the years and so he always seemed vulnerable. From the moment he was born, so small and so fragile, I was very protective of him. His little voice echoed in my heart, and I had to do more than was in my power to get him back. Money at this time was tight; in fact, I had not felt it so bad. With The Studio, a stream of income had disappeared, and now my main income was from the few classes I did each week, plus some personal training. Each time I went to court fighting for custody or access, I got hit with a bill that ate voraciously into my income.

To go away to the Olympics was fortuitous; it gave me a break and opportunities to network, and who knew where that could lead. We arrived at Barcelona Airport and were taxied to the waiting ship. What a size; I had to stand back and marvel at how it was possible for something so large to float, a city on the sea; there were so many people on board.

I climbed the gangplank, and it seemed that all the athletes knew each other, or at least they pretended to. This was my first real exposure to the 'Meerkat' principle; as they said hellos and greetings, their heads swivelled around all the while looking for more important people than you.

I was introduced over and over again, but I had not won any Olympic medals. I was not a hopeful, and so I was largely ignored. I longed to be in the safety of the cabin, lost in the secret knowledge that in 1965 whilst in Leicester, I had won 1st place in the high jump – I laughed; a feat that would never be repeated.

I was truly glad of the experience of being on that floating city. It was a wonderful feeling to be in the stadium watching Tessa compete; she bowed out gracefully and had done her country proud. She had brought honour to an event that had attracted many drug cheats. She for one could hold her head up high.

I came away with many wonderful memories: the passion in each event; the winner standing on the podium; the cheers and the sadness when fourth place was not quite good enough. I had been to an Olympic event, something I had never imagined that I would ever be able to achieve or afford. I also met some interesting people: George Foreman, Spike Lee, and Gail Devers.

My heart was not there, though. It was split between London and Guyana. I longed to be back to the task that needed my attention. I wanted to be back as soon as possible, so I could go and get my kids back.

I was in the audience while Tessa appeared on the *Richard and Judy Show*, and I got talking to a producer called Gail Torr. I told her about an idea that I had for a three to five minute slot where Derrick Evans gets released on the streets and he gets everyone around exercising and working out. She liked it and told me I would hear from her.

Early the following week, the phone rang, and it was Gail. She wanted me to come up and do exactly what I was proposing. Tessa was not happy; she wanted us to do a TV thing together.

We had already filmed our own pilot for a health show with Yorkshire Television. Tessa was the main presenter and I did fitness snippets throughout the show. Paul Dunston, Tessa and I had conceived the whole format; YTV wanted first option, and we filmed it at the local electricity board. It looked good, but was not what the great British public was looking for; so said the governing network centre body.

This new opportunity at *This Morning* depended on my abilities alone. I flew up to Liverpool on a Monday, stayed overnight and filmed it as a live broadcast early the next day. It was great fun being on the streets and in the shopping centres of Liverpool. I picked on anyone I could find, willing or otherwise. I created quite a stir, wearing my stretch lycra and a bumbag, and with my music blaring, people crowded around.

Richard and Judy had asked what I wanted to be called, and out of the blue, I just said, "The Motivator." The name stuck, and throughout the series, they'd say, "And earlier today, we sent Mr Motivator out on the streets. Let's see how he got on." They'd cut to me, and I would talk to camera and you would see me being in the one place that I came alive, when I am performing.

I have lots to thank Gail Torr for. She gave me that first national exposure.

More was on the way. I got a call from the producer of the *Gloria Hunniford Show*. They wanted a fitness expert to take on ten guys for a fitness spot. I agreed immediately. I had the freedom to select who I wanted to appear with me and so I brought along members of my Tuesday night class. They were so excited about being on television. We had a run through, did the item, and it felt good. I behaved as a 'friendly' sergeant, who drilled them to precision; as usual, I had asked them to be vocal and to smile through all of the items, no matter how much pain they were in. Gloria came over and was charming, gracious, and was satisfied with the show.

As a result, I became Gloria's personal trainer and travelled three times a week to her home in Kent. We stepped, did some floor work and we talked about opportunities for me and television. She just advised me to keep on going and eventually it would all come good.

I am not sure that she truly wanted to get fitter or whether the sessions where she was on the bike talking about a variety of different topics just gave her some time when she was free of being public, perfectly coiffed and made-up Gloria. I liked and admired her; I also enjoyed the two-hour journey there and back. It was far to travel, but distance did not matter; I needed the money.

My new showreel was beginning to look more and more interesting; there was quite a lot of variety on it. I made a number of copies and sent these out to various TV companies. Each came back with the same message; we are only looking for a blonde woman of 35 with two kids to do fitness. Oh, and she must be white.

Some years before, I visited the *TV-am* studios in Camden Town. The then-programme controller could be found with me on the floor doing the exercises that I felt should be shown on TV. The studio, however, had a well-established fitness portion with a lady called Mad Lizzie. She was contracted to *TV-am* for ten years and he was unable to break an established agreement. Mad Lizzie did a good job in helping to create greater awareness of fitness, in competition with the Green Goddess on the BBC.

He could not see a black man with spectacles doing fitness on television. I kept at him to no avail; he was not about to make a corporate decision to introduce such an image.

Reunion

September started well. I knew what I had to do. Ebony and James' routine was set. Each day, they went to school without their mother, and after school they would go over to a relative and stay until late. Jewel did not check when they were late; she just assumed that they must be at some relative's home.

We now needed the passports. They were held in the safe; Ebony knew where the keys were kept and felt that, at the right time, she could get to them.

Everything else was in place. She needed to get ready to leave on the Friday. A lot depended on Ebony; she would be taking chances, and I did not know what problems she would encounter, but we had to try and make it work as I had made the reservation for leaving on the Friday. I wished her the best. I told her that I would see her on Saturday.

This was a last-ditch attempt; I hoped she could do it. I was sure that anything that could go wrong would, and I would be helpless to do anything in the future. I should have had more faith in a 14-year-old who had seen her education messed up due to a vindictive mother who had taken them away to punish me.

I had started teaching classes in various school halls, and on a Saturday, my class was held in John Kelly Girls' School, Neasden. To everyone attending, this was just a normal Saturday morning class. It was packed, which was usual and, to everyone, except Palmer, I was being my usual myself.

The atmosphere was charged. I was trying to get the best out of each of them, but I was full of apprehension. I could just about hear the sound of the mobile phone ringing above the noise of the workout music.

I could not stand the uncertainty; would they be at Heathrow airport?

Carolyne had gone to the airport instead of me. I was sure it was Carolyne on the phone, so I broke off from the class, walked over very slowly to the table and picked up the phone. All I heard was the words, "Dad, I've got them!"

The tears streamed down my face; I dropped to my knees, saying "Thank you, God." The excitement of the moment totally overwhelmed me and a great weight fell from my shoulders; the relief was immense. Over the years, there had been many joyful events, but nothing as rewarding as this moment. After months of planning, tomorrow, tomorrow, tomorrow... I was beside myself with joy. I was sure that the fight with my ex would continue, but I did not care.

I forgot where I was, but my class understood as the tears flowed down my face. I could not finish the class so I went and relaxed as best I could at the home of two friends of mine, Glen and Laura.

An hour later, they arrived, Ebony with a smile that said, "That was easy," on her face, and James, who in short trousers exposed some seriously skinny legs, seemed smaller than usual and somewhat confused.

I hugged them both and I knew that this moment would be etched in our memories forever and that no matter what, I would fight tooth and nail to ensure they did not get away from me again.

Ebony's Tale

Ebony started to tell me of her exploits. I was dying to know how she had pulled it off.

She had needed to get to the documents, so on the Thursday night she did not go to sleep. Early on Friday morning, while the house was quiet, she crept into the lounge, and with the creaking floorboards and the stillness of the house, where the least little noise seemed to echo much louder than normal, she managed to open the safe and took all the passports, including her mother's tickets and whatever money she could find. All these would be necessary at the airport. There was no going back now.

She had packed only enough things for the trip and this bag was hidden in the garden of the house next door. She did not want to oversleep so she sat up and waited for dawn. Her aunt woke early and asked why she was in the living room so early. Ebony gave a polite story of illness.

She got ready for school. James moved at his usual pace putting on his clothes, and she had a nervous breakfast and they said their goodbyes. She picked up the bag from the garden and got into the first cab she could find.

The first part of the journey had begun. On the way to the airport, James asked about the direction that they were going in. Ebony managed to keep him calm but told him nothing in particular.

They arrived in plenty of time for the check-in, but the first problem arose; James could not travel because he did not have his own passport, he was on his mother's.

Ebony was told that the only way he could leave the country was to be put on her passport. She showed her mother's passport, which we had decided she should take and which would give her mother problems if she wanted to follow.

The check-in clerk said that the travel document was no good without the owner travelling at the same time. The only way was for her to go to the High Commission and plead her case. Ebony left in a hurry by taxi to the British High Commission.

She was in a hurry, so tears were needed and out they flowed as she was hurried into the commissioner's office. He tried to calm her but she sputtered, "Sir, I am in a hurry! I must get this flight back to England! An urgent health problem has developed with my dad and we can't locate our mother. She is in the jungle, travelling."

He was consoling and comforting, with a sympathetic tone in his voice. Extraordinarily, he granted permission to the changes and had James' name put in her passport. Ebony made it back to the airport in time and before long, she was on the plane taxiing off to England.

I am, and will forever be, grateful to Ebony. Believing that you are blessed is the very first step to being blessed. So many things could have gone wrong, but nothing did; instead, everything went right.

Amongst all the commotion and uncertainty, I had not made any plans about where they would be staying. I felt that if we had to camp on someone's floor, that was what we would do.

While I sat there holding these two prodigal children, returned sound and well, Tessa was on the line. She said she was happy for me and that we could always stay at her home. I felt there were a few logistical problems about that, but until I could resolve those properly, I took her up on her offer.

It was two months of being in Tessa's home before I was able to move. I had to go back into the old matrimonial house to get the kids' school uniform and books; it meant breaking a court order. When

Jewel eventually got back to the UK, she had me arrested and brought to court: I was fined £250.

Imagine that! I did no one any harm. I merely wanted to get the kids back into school as quickly as possible. Jewel, on the other hand, had absconded with the kids, so breaking an equally important court order, but was she fined or threatened with imprisonment? No, but she was allowed to get me arrested. She was allowed to contest the residence order that I was awarded after she broke the original order. Life is so unfair, isn't it?

Soon we were in front of the judge, for her to plead her case for the return of the children. I was clutching at straws; the only lifeline I was given was that the judge wanted a welfare report before he was willing to look properly at the future of these kids.

This meant that I needed to get away from Tessa's home as soon as possible. Those early mornings – leaving Essex, dropping the kids to school, picking them up, and them coming to class with me, only to arrive home tired and irritable – would have to change. I knew it, but I needed somewhere to live. Funds were tight; I could not buy and I could only afford a certain amount for rent.

Palmer offered to help me look, and it wasn't long before we saw a three-bedroom house in Meadow Bank Road, Kingsbury. The landlords were Greek and lived next door, but although it needed things such as bedding, utensils, curtains, it was reasonable, so I took it.

Glen, Laura and Palmer took on the task of cleaning up and ensuring that it was habitable. We moved into the house in November 1992, and at last we felt that this could be home. James had his own room, and so did Ebony. Life settled down, despite the continuing battles.

As I said, money was tight. Each court date used up funds that I did not have. Most of my income came from the one-to-one training sessions that I was doing all over London.

As well as Gloria, I now trained Paul Young and Stacey, his wife, who I had met at a Jackie Stewart event held at Gleneagles in Scotland. This was a charity event that raised thousands of pounds for the needy – anyone who was anybody was there, from Royalty to me! Paul has such a talent and he became a close friend of mine – but the voice! Oh, what a voice! When he sang *Wherever I Lay My Hat*, he moved so many people. As a person, Paul is a real example to the rest of those rockers out there, staying true and faithful to family and home. He was not the rocker type, but a man with lots of worthy values. With Paul and Stacey, we worked on stamina and strength, lots of weights and we used anything around the house as exercise equipment.

After exercise, we used to sit down and over breakfast or lunch, we would discuss TV opportunities. As always, he reassured me that things would come good in the end.

I also had a number of business people and housewives on my books. Together with the odd TV or radio appearances and with my classes, this was how I made part of my living. Of course, I had my Center Parcs weekends as well.

That Christmas was the first for four years that I spent with the children.

Palmer came around and we all enjoyed the special moments. Life, for a while, felt good. There was some sadness, but my cup was three-quarters full.

Custody of the Children

All year, life with the ex-wife had played out like a soap opera. Ebony and James had left her behind in Guyana, without a passport or money, but it was not long before she was back, snorting smoke and spitting venom.

When the kids came back, I had gone to court and was awarded temporary care and control. This was a luxury, considering for nearly ten years I had not had any court recognise my control over their future.

In breaking the court order, Jewel had played into my hands, and from then on she was required to prove she was worthy of being awarded custody. While the kids were with her, the onus of proof was never on her being a good mother; it was on me to prove that I was a better father and mother all rolled into one.

The courts were very one-sided and they always seemed to assume that the kids should at all times remain with the mother.

The chronology of what happened over the year is too much to go into here, but suffice to say that over that period, we went to court at least ten times. Every court order in my favour was challenged; every welfare officer's report; every official court solicitor's report was contested on grounds of being biased and groundless. It was implied that I had mesmerised them into giving me a favourable bill of health.

James Visits Mother

James had seen Jewel about eight times over the year. These had to be supervised, as James wanted re-assurance that he would not be taken away again. Jewel suggested David Thompson, my nephew, for the supervision, as I am sure she felt able to manipulate him.

The visits went well for a short while. David took James twice a week to his mother. But after several visits, he did not want to go and became very distressed. When I asked David why, it became evident that Jewel was the cause. There were times that David felt uneasy about the way she was behaving and the questions she would ask James. He felt that she should be making each visit, which was fairly short, a fun time, a time to make James feel at home and at ease. Instead, she continually badgered James with the same questions: "Why are you staying with your dad? Why don't you want to live with me?"

Jewel could not accept that James was living with me, and so she pressured him. As a youngster of ten, he tried to cope with it. Eventually, when this came out in court, via a report, Jewel attempted to discredit David, by making baseless accusations against him.

A court welfare officer was appointed to report on the relationship between James, Ebony, Jewel and myself. She submitted her report with a final recommendation that some visiting contact every other weekend should be made, even though James wanted reassurance by having David with him. Jewel refused to see her son with supervision, so the supervised visits stopped and she did not see James for quite a while. Eventually, James started going to her home one afternoon fortnightly.

I desperately tried to keep this distraction outside the home. We needed, as a family, to be at peace, and I also needed some peace business-wise. I had a mode of escape; I had classes in a school hall, and also classes at a number of companies, but better than that, things were due to change for the better. The impending change was to prove the turning point in my life, as in August 1993, I got my slot on *GMTV*.

So, I was then able to continue the court battle, and paying my way was no longer an issue, no more scraping the barrel. Previously I was not able to get legal aid as she did, so almost all that I earned went into fighting for the kids. I had come too far to give up. If they went back to living with Jewel, then all would be lost. I would have failed them and for that I would not be forgiven.

They had shown that they wanted to live with me. In turn, I needed to put together a loving, caring, supporting, and most importantly, a stable environment for them.

The visits got so bad that one day – I do not know how the mistake happened – we arrived at the matrimonial home on the wrong day. James got out and ran to knock on the door. His mother opened up, and, rather than being happy to see him, asked him what he was doing there. She did not welcome him. Instead she started to argue that we did it on purpose and she was not ready for his visit. Consequently, she did not let him in, so we left, James being very upset, of course.

Had the shoe been on the other foot, I would have grabbed him up with open arms and been happy that he was there to see me. Not his mother.

I realised that kind of rebuff was all part of her not being prepared to move on with her life. The poison inside of her was just eating away and eventually, she would lose all that she was fighting for.

Jewel stopped at nothing. Whatever she could do to try and distract me or to put people off me, she did. The final straw that led me to take out an injunction was when the *GMTV* duty room started receiving calls from a woman who said the person on TV calling himself Mr Motivator was a fraud, not properly qualified to teach exercise, that she was a qualified teacher and the exercises that he was giving people to do were not good for them, but downright dangerous. These were ignored, but we all knew who was calling in repeatedly.

Jewel Again…

With all the delays, after the decree absolute in 1991, two years later the financial settlement for the divorce was not yet agreed or finalised. She would have some entitlement, but work was needed to arrive at an agreement. She had done her homework and I received a list of all my companies and details of all bank accounts, past and present.

Everything was geared to causing me maximum inconvenience and cost. Most of the time, she insisted on representing herself.

I had to disclose very personal information, but I complied, in the belief that I might finally get rid of her. Therefore, I did a supporting affidavit, which detailed my income as at the end of 1993.

After this disclosure, I decided to fight back. I hired a private detective who revealed that Jewel had one flat in Kilburn in her maiden name. She was receiving rent rebate, even though she was not resident there and had rented out the property. In two affidavits, she had not mentioned that she had purchased this property under the right to buy scheme.

She had also procured a property from a housing association which was also rented out; again, there was no mention of this property in all previous affidavits for disclosure. In fact, when I drew attention to the existence of this property, she denied it and stated, "I have not applied for, nor have I ever had a tenancy at this property."

I also found out about the purchase of a property in Guyana, which she denied under oath, even though we had copies of correspondence from her solicitor confirming the intended completion date. We also found evidence of her claiming state benefits in different names from different addresses. But by the end of November 1993, she admitted that she had misled the courts.

Finally, my lawyers suggested that she give up the former matrimonial home as a clean break between me and her, that I would not make any claim against her for maintenance, and I would not be making any claim through the Child Support Agency.

She would not agree to any of this, and so it seemed that our court appearances would continue for a while yet.

Initially, all the money I was making at *GMTV* and elsewhere went towards court costs. Jewel had legal aid, and because she often represented herself, she was able to take me back to court time and time again.

But my financial status was to change drastically. I could not have imagined how much money I was about to make over a very short period.

Chapter 10: Finding My Way

The New Year of 1993 opened with the usual flurry of guilt that most people have after Christmas overindulgences. You know how it is; we all have a little bit too much to eat and drink, and then the New Year's resolutions start, but with the best will in the world, by the end of March, most resolutions are broken.

I was busy, but I felt incomplete. My life was at a crossroads; I just did not know where to go, what to do, what to say and though God had always played a part in my life, right then I felt I could do with any kind of guidance.

The Spiritualist

I drifted aimlessly for a while, and then I had a chance meeting with Sylvia, a woman whom I knew very well. She said to me one day – not that she knew about anything that was going on in my life – if I ever felt a little bit lost and needed some independent advice, to call this spiritualist, and she gave me a number.

Little did she know that this introduction was to become one of the best things that she would ever do for me.

Although I did not believe in spiritualism, I thought I would keep an open mind; it wouldn't make matters worse.

I called a Nottingham number on a Tuesday, and a lady called Joyce Lane answered, and gave me an appointment to call her the following Friday.

I called Joyce at the agreed time. She answered, in a very calm and charming voice, and I asked her if she minded if I made notes. She said she would make a recording for me.

And then she started. You have to realise, I had never met this lady, but yet she was able to dissect my life.

"You had a dog, a black dog, which is no longer with you."

"Yes," I said.

"Well, it is on the other side."

I did lose my Rottweiler. When I first moved out of the matrimonial house, I had taken the dog with me. One day, she went missing and was never found again.

"You are also in a relationship where your other half is at the front of the stage and you are behind. For some time, you have wanted and longed to be at the front, but this lady takes all the limelight. If you are to ever get on and get to where you truly belong, then realise this affair is holding you back. You have another lady friend who supports you, and so you must make a choice and a decision." I listened intently.

"I see people looking up to you, following what you do. It is something to do with physical health and well-being. They love what you do, but the front of the stage is where you need to be, to be successful. I see America and it is calling.

"Oh, I see new keys. You are moving, or have moved. I see water."

I had just moved into a road called Meadowbank and it was near a body of water called the Welsh Harp.

"You will be signing new contracts by August of this year. You have done an advertisement. I don't mean for baked beans or anything like that, but it shows what you do, and people are looking at it."

I had done a showreel of the work I had done on TV, made numerous copies, and sent it out to many stations for them to look at.

I had always been sceptical about spiritualism, but she was credible; she had mentioned many more things than I can mention here, and I was convinced – to a point. I thanked her and I sent her a cheque for £25 the next day, but I needed more convincing. So I told Palmer about her, and Palmer gave the number to her sister. The result was we were convinced she was gifted.

I received a call from the producers of a new Chris Tarrant show called *The Main Event*. They wanted me to be part of a team of fitness experts who would compete in various rounds against other contestants. On the plane going up to Yorkshire with my team members, The Green Goddess and Mad Lizzie, I found myself sitting next to Eammon Holmes, who had just been employed by *GMTV*, the new franchisee of the morning show. Eammon was with Lorraine Kelly, previously a presenter on *TV-am*.

Eammon and I spoke for most of the journey. He knew of me through Gloria Hunniford; she had done a good job of advertising me, and Eammon wanted some personal training sessions. I told him I would call him.

The show itself was not a great success, and went only as far as a pilot.

On the way back to London, Mad Lizzie started to talk about how she was about to be offered the fitness slot on *GMTV*. My heart sank. Why, I thought, would they inflict on the general public more of that type of fitness. She had been around for about ten years, and I felt it was time for some new blood. I wanted that job. I knew that I could do it, but I was not sure how to go about getting that break.

I felt as if I was still drifting and needing some direction, so I said to myself something that was probably the one statement that spurred me on. They say there is power in words: "If, by the end of the year 1993, I have not achieved a good measure of success across all areas of my life, I will leave Britain and try elsewhere."

I said it, but what did it mean? How was I going to measure it? I just felt that I would know when I had arrived.

If you think about it, I had been slogging away for many years, but I had nothing to show for it. I had a house that was worth quite a bit of money, but I couldn't even look at it. I was living in rented accommodation. I had no money left in the bank; all of it was being used to fight for my children.

I did not have a career; I did bits and pieces. This is where I was – NOWHERE! I was barely looking after my children, and to add to all of this, I had failed all around in sorting out my emotional life. So this was the state of my life in 1993.

I had to let go of Tessa. We had lost each other years before, but we were afraid to admit it, so finally I hinted enough that I wanted out. In my mind, we broke up fairly amicably.

With her out of the picture, I felt more settled, and all of a sudden, things started to change. The first was that I felt less pressured. By the summer, I started training Eammon Holmes. I would arrive at the studio in South Bank for 9.30 a.m. and he would come out, changed and ready for action.

Some mornings, we just walked; other times, we ran along the River Thames and then back to Jubilee Gardens, where the London Eye is now. We would train for an hour in the park, and no matter the weather, he worked hard, so very quickly, we began to see results.

But word of this outdoor class began to spread, and soon Lorraine Kelly joined us. She enjoyed the camaraderie; she is such a natural person. This party eventually increased to include Sally Meen, the weather girl, and Martin Frizell, the news reporter.

I enjoyed these sessions, but I always hoped for the chance to get indoors. At this time, *GMTV* was the lowest-rated morning TV show; Chris Evans and Gaby Roslin at Channel 4 were knocking them for six. Even the BBC was ahead of them, and with low ratings came low income, because advertisers didn't want to be seen on a station that was not bringing in the viewers. They were desperate for something to give them the edge. In the old *TV-am* days, they had Roland Rat, who grabbed the younger audience, and once the youngsters were hooked, no one else in the household could make a choice.

Channel 4 had Zig and Zag, another puppet comedy pair, capable of commanding most of the younger viewers – and so *GMTV* lagged behind.

I sat in reception at LWT waiting for the gang to come out for their session, and occasionally I saw presenters of other shows, who would come out and head straight for their waiting car. I felt poor, aware of our differences in lifestyle, but never envious. Their perceived status just spurred me on to try harder.

I wished that I had the same opportunities they had been given, but ringing in my ears was the former head of *TV-am* telling me, "Derrick, you are wasting your time. The only person who could do fitness on TV is a white woman, mid-thirties, with two children. You have got no chance; you are not white."

That was not the first time that someone had told me that my colour mattered. The editorial head of *This Morning* also confirmed this opinion. Tessa's agent, Jacque Evans, once told me I could make it in TV, but it would take at least five years. I was not prepared to wait that long. It seemed everyone else could see my ambitions doomed to fail, but I couldn't see it. I could hear the knocking on the door; I just needed to find the key to open it.

Unknown to me, it was all going to start and I would not know how to control it.

For ten years, I had religiously watched *TV-am* and Mad Lizzie; I had watched the Green Goddess. I had seen every attempt to get fitness on TV. I had watched all the North American programmes on fitness; I had bought just about every fitness video, most of them done very badly.

I had gone to every fitness convention that existed. I purchased every magazine with items on fitness. I had immersed myself in the arena, and I knew what the new trends were. I lived and breathed fitness.

If Jane Fonda had new leotards, I knew about it, so focused was I on my craft. My Center Parcs weekends had grown to three per year and the numbers were beyond my wildest dreams. We now had between 200 and 400 people attending. But real public recognition kept eluding me.

GMTV had started the year with Linda Lusardi, who was the darling of Page 3 girls. She did a kind of sports fitness in the early morning. This slot did not survive for long. Then in came Tonya, who the press dubbed 'thunder thighs'. The knives were out, and it was not long before she too was let go.

One morning in July 1993 as I sat waiting, I saw a man walking towards the reception. He was small in stature but carrying a lot on his belly. His hair was a little untidy. I felt I had to get up, my legs propelling me towards him, and we met just as he arrived at the reception desk. He was about to pass me and – I do not know what was driving me – my finger shot out and pointed towards his belly. I said, "You need to look after yourself and do something about that."

"Who the hell are you?" he said, making a move towards the lift, but I was blocking his way.

"I am the person who trains most of your GMTV presenters."

"Oh, you are the one who is responsible for working them out." And with that comment, he made his way towards the lift. When he was out of sight, I asked the receptionist who he was. She looked at me and said, "I think you just blew it!"

I said, "What do you mean?"

"Well that was the programme controller of *GMTV*, Mr Peter McHugh."

I looked at her and smiled. I later met Eammon and Lorraine for our training session.

The next day after training, I took my exercise bike from the back of the car up to the third floor, and as Mr McHugh's office was empty, I left it in there. A few days later, I returned and knocked on his door and I went in. He said something like, "Oh, it's you again."

"Well," I said, "you've got my bike and it's time you used it."

"I am not interested," he replied. "And more important than that, I don't have the time. My priority at the moment is to get this station to make money."

I called to his secretary Gill Stacey, and I enquired whether there was space in the diary for him to do some training. She had a look, "Yes, I am sure we could find space. How much time do you need?"

"About 15 to 20 minutes every other day."

"Well, he can do Tuesday, Thursday and Friday at 11.45 a.m.?"

"Ok, book me in."

All this conversation took place as if Mr McHugh was not in the room. I left before he could say anything, poked my head back round the door and said, "See you next Tuesday."

At precisely 11.45 a.m. on Tuesday, I arrived at Peter's office and knocked. He opened the door, and to my surprise, he had changed into a tracksuit and was ready for action. He started very gingerly, but as he climbed on the bike, I had a feeling of satisfaction. I had persuaded someone, who, I was about to learn, had a serious aversion to exercise.

He'd had a difficult time with his health; he smoked and had suffered a heart attack. You could argue that he should have started exercising a long time ago. Exercising now was not too late, but he was not the very best person to try and get fitter.

After about five minutes, he was panting, sweating, and out of breath, so I slowed him down. I reminded him that 'slow is the pace to win the race'.

We continued every other day, and as the weeks went by, I noticed a change: Peter was not panting as much as when we started, he was looking less strained in his face and, the acid test, he was able to continue a conversation with me while he worked out.

About four weeks later, out of the blue, he said, "Motivator, any person who could convince me to start exercising I am sure could get the great British public to do the same."

I listened and nodded in agreement, but I was waiting for him to say more. I just love compliments, but I also love people to tell me what I know already, and I have been ready for years to get the UK moving.

"I am going to give you a chance to be on screen."

My heart skipped a beat. Those were the words I had wanted to hear! All I could say was, "Thank You!"

I waited for the next session, but he did not mention it again, and I couldn't work out whether I should remind him.

And then I was walking through the production offices when I overheard a lady talking on the phone saying, "I want the Keep Fit Association of Great Britain to do some fitness on screen for us."

I felt rooted to the spot and then I approached her. I introduced myself as the trainer for all the presenters. She introduced herself as Loll Ingham.

I knelt down; I was grovelling and I have never done that before. Anyhow, I was pleading and I said to her, "Give me a chance, I can make a difference!" She looked at me and said that she would talk to Peter about it.

That weekend was the longest I have ever been through. I debated if I had done the right thing in being impatient, but I consoled myself with the fact that I had been patient for too long and I needed the opportunity to pursue my destiny.

I needed that break. It meant not waiting around for people to decide when they felt was the right time to give me bread for my table: that was the reason I had been working on my own for so long. After God, I am in charge of my destiny.

Loll called me the next week and the news was positive. Mr McHugh suggested that I be put on screen for one week, but she was pushing for two. When I saw Mr McHugh, he said that it would be for one week, but they needed to talk to the sponsor of that slot.

He said not to worry and that nothing would happen for a few weeks because the 'Fun in the Sun' roadshow was still going on around Britain, although due to all the rain they had been having in each location, it should have been called 'Noah in the Rain.' They were looking at the period after the roadshow ended, but there were some obstacles and resistance that they needed to get over.

I wasn't sleeping much. Each morning, I would be up for the start of *GMTV*, sitting there, transfixed and apprehensive. I would watch Tonya as she tried to get the crowds to do a routine she had worked out but which, unfortunately for her, did not create the impact that was needed. I knew that she was just not right for *GMTV*, and so I waited in the wings.

In early August, while we were training, Mr McHugh said he had some bad news. The sponsors of the fitness slot did not want a man doing fitness on TV, and they would pull their sponsorship if I came in. I was devastated and convinced it wasn't that they didn't want a man; it was that they didn't want a black man. The chip that I had been avoiding landed on my shoulder like a plank, and it was very heavy to bear.

Mr McHugh offered some hope, saying things have a way of working out; I just had to be patient. There was that word again – I was beginning to hate it.

By the end of the second week in August, Loll came to me. She said that there was going to be a two-week break when advertisers would not be sponsoring that spot. Tonya would be on holiday for those two weeks, returning when *GMTV* started its autumn season.

This meant that the sponsor had little say in what went in that slot over those two weeks. It was on for me again. I prayed for no more disappointments.

Loll called me to go in for a run through at the studios, as they used four cameras and the director wanted to see how I moved and what I would be doing. When I arrived, I stood in front of the cameras, but I could not do things the way they wanted. I had always taught spontaneously; I never rehearsed what I was going to do. I explained to Loll that being in front of the cameras was no different to being in front of my class. I preferred if they told me which was my main shot, and which camera I should look into for a close-up; all the rest could be on standby. They would know to do a close-up of my legs as I would say which muscles were being worked and that would be the cue to zoom in or switch to a better shot.

She said that it was unusual, but if that was the only way, then they would try it. A car was to pick me up at 4.45 a.m. to be at the studios by 5.30 a.m. With that, I left for a very nerve-wracking weekend.

Normally, I could get up in a class and not feel in the least bit apprehensive, but this time, I was not confident. I was downright nervous.

That Sunday was a beautiful day. Palmer came round and we had a family barbecue. I enjoyed some good laughs despite the tension I was feeling. I told everyone that I was about to be on morning television and they should watch and make sure they phoned in.

GMTV

It was not yet 4.00 a.m. on Monday 23rd August 1993 when I realised that I had not slept; I was too apprehensive and excited. I got up, my legs wobbling ominously, but after a shower and a few stretches, I put on some casual clothes and prepared for this day.

I heard the car coming down the road, and peeped out the window to signal to the driver I would be out in five. Palmer wished me luck and we kissed, and I left. The driver opened the door for me and I got in the black Ford Granada. We headed down the Edgware Road along a route that would become as familiar as brushing one's teeth every morning.

It was strange; I now felt sleepy, but I also wanted to stay awake to savour this new journey I was on. There were very few people awake that time of the morning.

It was an easy drive to the studios. I got out and went to reception; they all wished me good luck. Into the lift and out at the third floor, I walked through the production office. Loll Ingham met me and took me down to the squeeze of the dressing room area. On the way down, I said hello to Eammon and Lorraine who were doing their programme preparation.

I put my bag on the floor, and before long I was called into make-up. She recommended an anti-shine product, but I declined and said I would just wipe my face before I was due to go on.

Back in the dressing room, the wardrobe department asked if I had anything to be ironed and could I show them what I was wearing because this would need approval from the director, just in case it would cause any 'strobing'.

The sound engineer came in to mike me up and asked me what music track I would be using. I put on my unitard; it was black with Reebok Trainers and white socks that matched, a rare occurrence.

I was called to the studio. My heart skipped a beat as I walked the winding corridor. I felt that my destiny was unfolding. I knew that the success of this opportunity was in my hands.

The warning on the door said, 'Do not enter when red light is on,' so I waited outside with Loll. Then we were allowed midway between two doors, and then I was in. There were the four cameras, and there was the sofa I had seen so many times before. We were on the advert break which meant I had two to three minutes to be seated on the sofa.

This early part of the show was called *News Hour* and was presented by Mike Wilson. It was a heavy news programme which needed a little light relief at the 6.50 a.m. slot before the magazine-style programme of *GMTV*. This was where I came in. As I was seated, Mike smiled pleasantly through his beard and welcomed me.

I was definitely nervous now; I hadn't done any preparation. I was relying on my knowledge of exercise to take me through.

I heard Mike say, "So, Tonya is away for a few weeks and you are standing in for her?"

"Yes," I said.

"And what will you be doing?'

"Motivating everyone to exercise, and getting people to look at their bodies differently."

"OK, take it away, Derrick."

I had the confidence that with all my experience, all the knowledge I had accrued, I was now prepared to be put to the test.

Nothing distracted me. I was focused and ready. I heard the music and as I started to move, the rhythm just allowed me to fly. I felt like water running over glass; in control, in step, in time, and the words just started to flow.

It wasn't something I had practised, but I found that I was able to move arms, legs and body in different positions, keeping up a stream of dialogue, cajoling, inspiring, and motivating, all at the same time.

I knew that if there was a gap in my delivery, people at home would get distracted. I was not going to have viewers wandering off and so I heard myself saying, "Everyone go 'Huh!' And again! 'Huh!' Everybody say 'yeah!' Everybody go 'OW!'"

And then – I don't know if it was what I said next that mobilised people, or whether they were just moved by the freshness of this new face on television – I said, "If you would like more of me, if you would like to get and feel better about yourself, give *GMTV* a call, let them know that you need my body, 'cause I need your body!"

Behind the cameras, I could see people moving. Mike was rocking, and when I repeated my, "Everybody say 'yeah!'" the entire studio responded, "Yeah!"

Mike thanked me, and I floated into the green room. Loll hugged me, and everybody had huge smiles. I took a drink and went to get changed, but before I could, Loll called me back, telling me the phone lines were jammed, everyone asking for more.

I said my goodbyes and went to my waiting car. I was still in a world of my own; no one could invade that moment. The journey home seemed shorter than usual. Palmer was there, and she was ecstatic!

Wherever I went that day, it seemed as if I was already being noticed, but I put that down to my euphoria; it is catching!

GMTV was miles behind Channel 4 in the ratings and most mornings they were lucky to beat BBC1. They were desperate for a change in fortune. The rule was, in morning TV, get the kids watching and you are onto a winner. Kids dictated what the household watched every morning.

I had calls that day from my friends, who had all made a point of calling in. Lena, a good friend whom I had turned onto fitness, was the instigator of this minor civil disturbance. She and her partner Brian had mobilised the troops and raised that morning's income for British Telecom.

The next day was easier; the format was about the same, and as soon as I had finished, again the phone lines lit up. Things were going so well, *GMTV* was unable to contain the flood of calls they received; they had to keep the duty room open until early afternoon to cope with all the enquires.

Wednesday was the day I was totally convinced I was onto something. When I came off air, Mr McHugh wanted to see me. He said he felt that I had got all my friends to call in. I assured him that I did not have that many friends. He was very happy. He had done many things in his time and he knew that the public was reacting very favourably to me, and he now had a plan of action. Peter informed me that on Thursday I would not only come on at 6.50 a.m. but I would have another slot in the main show. I was in; I knew it, and I left that morning silently thanking God and all those people who tuned in to my show.

What started as an impromptu filler was going forward at breakneck speed. Ratings were up and the reaction to Mr Motivator was astronomical. Now we just had to work out how to move forward.

It was a special day on 23rd August, as it was also Carolyne's birthday, and while that was a good way of remembering when I started on GMTV, it was 26th August, the Thursday, that became exceptionally special.

That morning, I was thinking that there was only one more day to go and the week would be over. If I was going to seal my place in TV history, I needed to pull something extra out of the bag. Yes, I was making an impression, but I was not making a statement. I needed to change something, but what?

I went on and did my 6.50 a.m. slot. A lot of people saw that early item and the phone lines were still busy. The duty log had, "Mr Motivator, give us more," time and time again. But what was to happen when I went on at 7.35 a.m. in the main show?

I was interviewed by Eammon and Lorraine, but it was mainly Eammon and I who played verbal ping-pong with each other. We had a laugh before I settled into my music, Bob Marley, and in the middle of my routine, I spoke to Eammon and he moved his body to the music; in fact, everyone moved that morning. It felt like every foot in the nation was tapping.

I was on a roll. I felt the energy; this was different to the 6.50 a.m. slot. I knew that thousands were watching and following my every move and word. When I looked behind the camera, everyone was rocking. I was on cloud nine. Mr Motivator had arrived at last. That moment was mine, and no one could take it away from me.

I left the studio on an extreme high. Loll ran over and hugged me. She had stuck her neck out over this, and would eventually give *GMTV* viewers many presenters such as Dr Hilary Jones followed by Beechy Colclough, Simon Biagi, Reverend Steve Chalke, but I was her prize catch, and she knew it.

I walked up the stairs to leave, and the production office, of about 80members of staff, all stood up and applauded me.

Mr McHugh wanted to see me.

He shook my hand and asked me if I would I like a permanent job. I enquired about Tonya, who was still on holiday. He said, "Don't worry about her; we will sort her out."

I said "No!" jokingly. He laughed.

I told him I would get my agent to call him. I did not have one.

As I stood in reception on the ground floor, I turned and looked at the pictures on the walls of all the other presenters, and I knew that mine would be up there soon.

Fame and the Media

Tessa's agent, Jacque Evans, the same person who had told me it would take at least five years for me to break into television, was glad to receive my call.

I was supposed to have been offered a contract for two years as per Peter McHugh's directive. But Simon Davey, the company accountant, was cautious, and so he gave me one for six months; a mistake, but he was not as convinced as Peter was about my longevity. I had been on *GMTV* only a few weeks when the power of the media became evident. I was now the hottest thing in town, and overnight! I went from school hall exercise teacher to fitness guru.

My life was on a roller coaster, but I was ill-equipped to be on this ride. I did not know how to cope with all the attention that was coming my way, so I leaned on the only people who understood the media, and who could teach me what to say, how to say it, what to do, and when to do it.

The press office was run by Janie Ironsides-Wood, ably supported by Nicci Johnceline; both were fabulous people. They had great knowledge of the working press. Janie's professionalism was exceptional. I admired her and was very grateful to her. I looked up to her, and gained valuable knowledge about this business. For the rest of my time at *GMTV*, I was able to lean on her for guidance.

Before I knew it, I was posing for photographs to be sent to the Press Association, followed by cards to sign for my expanding fan base. Just imagine, at age 40, receiving 100 fan letters a day. I worked hard at answering them, and in the end, someone in the press office took over this job. My head swelled, but I felt so honoured. Everywhere I went, people were coming up to me. I left the studio one morning and went into a sandwich bar where I ordered a cheese roll, only to be told by the owner that there was no charge. I asked why, and he just said that I brought pleasure to his early mornings and gave him a new reason to get out of bed. This was humbling, and I thanked him.

GMTV put all they had behind me. I was on screen about every 20 minutes doing something. If it was not some kind of workout, it was saying "hello" to people at home or just larking about. Eammon and I had a comedy duo going; just before my spot, he and I would enter into some quick fire dialogue. There were calls on the duty log suggesting that Eammon did not like me, based on some of the comments that he made, but I saw this as just good fun.

Before the end of October, advertisers were clamouring to be featured around my spot. There was also the opportunity to sponsor my workout items, and, after some negotiations, St. Ivel's Shape provided sponsorship with a series of small, seven-second adverts showing a very flexible lady doing different stretches. This became the way everyone knew that I was about to come on. Households across the UK tuned in just to see what I was doing, and also what I was wearing next. *GMTV*'s viewing figures went up and up, and before long, we were neck and neck with Channel 4.

I will always remember listening to Steve Wright on Radio 2 one morning; he described how he was in a hotel room, and I came on. He shot up and started doing his thing to the beat of the music, when out of the corner of his eye, he caught a glimpse of himself in the mirror, and realised that he was naked. He said it was a sight to see!

I found there was no hiding place; there just seemed to be an abundance of articles and TV interviews to do. At my Center Parcs weekends, people attending acted differently. Before all they wanted were photographs with me, but now it was autographs, photos, hugging. Oh, the attention! And I lapped it up.

I had to employ a West End accountant to handle all my affairs. His first job was to get me up to date by sorting out all my bank accounts and back taxes for the past nine years.

I soon negotiated a deal for my story with the *News of The World*, but the crowning glory was a two video deal with Weight Watchers. I was to choreograph the video, and select most of the participants; they wanted their Slimmer of the Year included in the video. I wanted all exercises endorsed and covered by an exercise physiologist, so Kathy Fulcher, my friend of many years, came in to do that.

We spent days rehearsing and going over all the exercises for their safety and execution. The team was put in place and we set about working with them. It felt strange working to a set routine when I have always freestyled. I have always felt that to make exercise fresh, you need to do it spontaneously.

We filmed indoors in a studio setting, each item done over and over again until it was right. For the next five days, I went to *GMTV* and did at least five items on the show, then I made my way to Bushey and filmed until 5.00 p.m.

That month, I also appeared on *Kelly Live* in Belfast – believe me, you had arrived when you were invited to this show.

I designed exercises for the *Daily Mirror*, *Chat magazine*, *Me magazine*, *Woman's Own*; any number of local magazines up and down the UK, plus I compèred the Aerobic Championships in Birmingham.

One particular morning, Eammon asked me if I did not have any clothes to wear, because all he ever saw me in was exercise gear. I pretended to cry saying, no, that was all I had. A week later, a call came from Ciro Citterio, offering me a whole wardrobe of clothes. I accepted, and for the best part of five years, whatever I wanted they provided. All I had to do was go into any of their branches and make my selection. To this day, I wear clothes from Ciro, and I will be eternally grateful to Mr Peter Fitzpatrick.

September was an exceedingly busy month, and before the end I was in Jersey filming for a whole weekend. *GMTV*'s focus was on getting me out of the studio as much as possible: meeting the people was important in the ratings war that had developed between them and Channel 4.

They scheduled my slot to coincide with Channel 4's Zig and Zag – after all, Mr Motivator was almost like a cartoon character; he was energetic and animated, and had his own catchy brand of 'speak'.

I was popular with the kids. I read out the birthday requests, which gave us the edge in the children's market.

I was now the hit of the station, and it became the norm for whoever came into the studio, especially celebrities, to work out with me, especially if they had something that they wanted to plug. Advertisers were queuing up to sponsor my items, and over the years everyone from Burton's Biscuits to St. Ivel's Shape were willing to pay large sums of money to be the seven-second sting that appeared before my workouts.

With Paul and Stacey Young.

With Kid Creole.

With Luther Vandross.

With Gary Barlow.

With Rachel Hunter.

With Steps.

In October 1993, Cindy Crawford came in for an interview about modelling, and of course, her videos received a high level of success. We got talking and I suggested that we did an exercise slot together which would go out every morning for a week. Production loved the idea, and so it was that I had Cindy all to myself.

The chemistry was right and I teased her throughout all the items we did. Each time I look back at it, I have to smile. The station was only too pleased, and it played out time and time again.

That same month, I also worked out with the full cast of *Starlight Express* on rollerblades; sadly, this Andrew Lloyd Webber musical is no longer in the West End.

I wanted to do a fitness video, and so I suggested it to *GMTV*. They wanted a treatment and I set to work on it, and after a very short period of time, I had come up with a concept that had not been done before. Most exercise videos featured someone like Jane Fonda, or a soap opera celebrity, flanked by a trainer. Credibility was missing from most of these, which seldom showed a fitness instructor who knew what he or she was talking about.

GMTV wanted a word by word treatment and description of each exercise, but I needed to make this video as spontaneous as possible, which meant a bare-bones script and no rehearsal. They took a lot of convincing that I could do this, and we set about discussing the title that I had come up with.

To most people, BLT meant bacon, lettuce and tomato, but to me it was Bums, Legs & Tums; after all, these were the key areas, the main body parts that most people, women especially, were worried about. *GMTV* agreed, and so the title was set: *Mr Motivator's BLT*.

Management could not see why I wanted to travel abroad. Videos needed a glossy cover and then the exercises could be shot in a studio. I had hated doing the Weight Watchers video indoors, but I needed the money and I was not yet big enough to make demands; but *GMTV* needed me. I needed them too, but I didn't let on.

Studios have the advantage of control of the elements, cheaper costs, and time restrictions – quicker in the long run. I believed that exercise videos should be inspirational: there must be sunshine, water, good music and preferably a tropical island setting.

Costs kept coming up time and time again, so I asked if I could find a way to cover most of the overheads, would they all agree to my proposal. There was a unanimous, "Yes!"

First Video – Bums Legs and Tums – BLT in Jamaica

With my image now complete, *GMTV* was ready and I was willing to be exploited, so off we went for two weeks to Jamaica to shoot my first video. We arrived at Montego Bay and were met by Sue McManus and our driver Mr Clue.

We arrived at our hotel, Jamaica Jamaica in Runaway Bay, which would be our base for the next two weeks (this hotel is now called Breezes). We were all allocated very good rooms and this was a first rate hotel.

We had three cameramen and a director who had never filmed an exercise video of this type before.

We used most of the well-known locations around Jamaica. The infamous Dunn's River Falls was used as the backdrop that opened the video, where I said my first words and set the scene for the rest of the video.

Doing my first video in Jamaica was very poignant; I had returned to my place of birth. I was a star in so short a time, travelling with a full entourage.

I was chaperoned by Janie Ironside-Wood and Nicky Johnceline from the press office, as we had a *Sun* reporter with us, and he was looking for a story.

Each evening, he sat with me for a story on Derrick. When there was a break in filming, we went and visited my adoptive father, and so his story developed.

We filmed sections on *The Zein*, a yacht belonging to Zein Issa, one of the daughters of the Issa family, who owned a large chunk of

Jamaica, the successful SuperClubs chain of hotels, and an upscale car dealership brokering Mercedes Benzs, Audis and Volkswagens.

The Zein was a beautiful seafarer. I was very pleased to be given permission to film on it, and to enjoy the sensational, ever-changing backdrop of the coastline as we filmed.

We also filmed at Ricks Café in Negril at sunset. This is a famous Jamaican landmark where thousands gather to witness the spectacular setting of the warm Jamaican sun into the ocean.

Although I was very green for my first video shoot, I knew what format to follow, but I did not have the production experience to guide Simon, the director. We ended up with a product which was mine – the idea, the exercises, the music, and the outfits, yes it all looked good. But when we were finished, I knew that this was the final time I would allow full authority to anyone in the production of my videos. I knew how I wanted it to look, the angles for shots of the exercises, but I lacked directorial expertise. I would learn quickly how it should all be filmed.

The first real newspaper story feature was a two-page spread in the *Sun* newspaper, with pictures by Alan Olley, who became the photographer that I was most comfortable with. He shot the majority of my magazine and publicity work, together with pictures of Popa and my humble home; I was happy with the outcome.

I remember sitting in my room at the end of a very hard day of filming. The shoot had gone well, and as I sat on my bed, quietly listening to the gentle crash of the waves, I looked back and reflected on what had gone on that year.

I had been training about 25 of the staff at JVC for a while, and classes were going well. I was also training the staff at Chrysalis TV, and the immaculate Gloria Hunniford was still part of my early morning regime on Tuesdays and Thursdays.

Personal trainers, like hairdressers, become the confidant of their clients, and I often found my clients would develop a relationship of trust with me and use me as their sounding board.

GMTV was starting to win the ratings war. I was compared to *TV-am's* Roland Rat, everyone from the young to the baby boomers were tuning in, and they all continued to keep the duty room busy.

The *BLT* video went straight into the charts and held its position for nearly 18 months. *GMTV* was ecstatic, and so was I. *GMTV* was raking in the money, and, as I was to learn, every artist loses on their first video or album. You live and learn. Later on, I signed a deal that blew my mind and disappointed *GMTV*.

I looked at improving how I presented myself. Yes, the baseball caps were an eye-catcher, but I did not go for the rest of my gear that much. I had my unitards made by a gentleman from the south of England named Len White. I told him I needed to make more of a statement, so he combed the country to find fabric suppliers. I will be eternally grateful to Len. All I had to do was tell him the theme that I wanted, and he found the perfect choice of fabric. He had his work cut out for the next seven years.

The colours didn't matter to me, as long as they were bright. Other elements of my attire, including the positioning of my mike, were adapted for my specific needs.

Reebok had been providing me with trainers, and I received a large selection: after all, my feet were in sight for valuable minutes each morning. That was indeed money well spent for the company.

The Mr Motivator image was just about complete. With a few tweaks, I was ready for anything. How you market yourself is critical for long-term success; the look and the feel is all part of how you are remembered. The more I refined what would become the Motivator image, the more my confidence grew. There is a power when you stand in front of an audience and you realise that they will move however you want them to. You must never abuse that power, but treasure it as it can be removed as fast as it came. I had the handle on what works and I knew that to be remembered, you needed to make maximum impact each time. How many other fitness exponents do you recall, such as the Green Goddess and Mad Lizzie, but you would walk by them in the street now. Positive impact is critical.

Mr Motivator Says: *I am convinced that we recall these fitness exponents because they had a visual image and name that resonated with the public. Mr Motivator had to have a memorable image, otherwise he would go the same way of other failed fitness presenters.*

How you market yourself in life is very important. It is critical for success, and anyone who wants to achieve must concentrate on the visual part of their business.

You must also have standards that others will adhere to and want to follow. Look at Disney: their credibility is beyond question and they work hard at ensuring that the public trust of their product is never brought into question.

Get Up and Give

I cannot emphasise enough the need to give thanks for one's blessings. I had reason to link with the Reverend Steve Chalke, a dashing young Indian clergyman who had a passion for charity work. He gave advice from a Christian and moral point of view. He also ran a charity called 'The Oasis' and he and I shared many public moments together. His on-screen presence made many a woman viewer dust off her Bible.

Rev. Steve extended his ministry to relieving suffering. In 1993, there was a devastating earthquake in India. People were destitute, 10,000 had died, and another 14,000 were homeless. Steve wanted to make a difference, so he came up with the idea of an appeal.

And, as part of GMTV's corporate responsibility, the company moved on the idea for a fundraising event called 'Motivation Weekend'.

I was to do a series of appeals to exercise teachers and health clubs for them to put on events and donate the proceeds to this cause. This resulted in a spectacular mobilisation of the entire country.

The public got behind the project. Many of differing ages and occupations took part and raised funds for the cause. After registering, volunteers would be sent a Body and Soul Pack. I was the body and Steve was the soul. Cliff Richard lent his support, and he and I also did a series of workout spots.

On the weekend in question, I would drop into different locations and work out with the gathering throng.

A helicopter was put at my disposal, and we commenced the marathon of dropping in on workouts, starting on the steps of St. Paul's in London. From there, we went to Birmingham, Scotland, Wales, and finally by ferry to Ireland.

It was a fantastically brilliant weekend. The end result was the raising of nearly £600,000.

What a weekend! Thousands had responded; exercise teachers across the UK held classes, and there were tea parties galore. With the money raised, more than one hospital was built in India, with enough money left over to maintain them for years to come.

Popa

I was thankful that I'd spent a good Christmas in Jamaica visiting with Popa. His pains were getting worse, and I knew it would not be long before he followed Auntie.

Since her death, he'd drifted along, and although the house was not empty, the loneliness in his heart was beginning to tell. I took him to Kingston for some treatment; his kidneys were giving problems and he needed a catheter fitted.

To illustrate the innocence that existed in the lives of rural Jamaicans, two things stood out on this particular Kingston visit. We stayed at the Pegasus Hotel. After we had checked in, we proceeded to the elevators. When the door opened Popa asked why our room was so empty, so I explained the function of this 'room'. But he did not understand because when the door opened again for us to get out, he could not fathom that we were on the 11th floor and could not figure how we had got there so quickly.

Once inside the room, I called Carolyne in the UK and gave Popa the phone to say hello. He didn't know which way around to hold the handset, and spoke into the earpiece.

It was to be the last time we were together. We went to the hospital and later spent a good few days just enjoying each other's company and sightseeing. I will always remember the expressions on his face. It was like watching a child being given a new toy, his eyes opened wide, thrilled at all that he saw and did.

Although this year was just the beginning of many wonderful things, at least Popa was able to see some of my success. He saw that Derrick had at last come into his own, and was able to carve his own destiny. In his understated way, he was proud of me, and my Auntie would have hugged me, and whispered some words of encouragement.

I learnt a lot from them both and I would not let anyone spoil or defame the wonderful memory I had of them.

As 1993 came to a close, I was happy, excited, apprehensive, worried and saddened for the future. These emotions were whirling around in my head, and I knew I would have to learn how to cope with them quickly.

Celebrities

I had interactions with several celebrities, who all wanted to be on my exercise slot. Cindy Crawford worked out with me, as did Elle the Body. Whether they had a video to sell or not, in they came to *GMTV*, from John Denver to Luther Vandross and Danny Glover - every star or group wanted to appear and work out with me.

I was invited to be on a LWT show called *An Audience with Shirley Bassey*. This was a show filled with hundreds of well-known personalities. Shirley was given prearranged questions by the audience, and the one on fitness should have been asked by me, but wasn't.

At the after-show party, Shirley came up to me and indicated that she was disappointed that I had not asked the fitness question. She also said she was a great fan of mine and she hoped we would meet again.

I felt the energy from her and I knew that she was genuine. That initial meeting was not the end of it. Because of our synergy, I suggested to *GMTV* that they should start negotiations for Shirley to appear with me. It was not long before the deal was done, and the stage was set for us to meet and do an item together. The plan was as follows; we would meet at my favourite restaurant, and when I came in for lunch, this person would be sitting in my usual place. The restaurant would be busy, and therefore we had to share the same table. I introduce myself to her; she knows who I am, and I pretend that I have no knowledge of her. She reminds me of some of her well-known hits, and I continue to mistake her for Whitney Houston. She tells me of a James Bond hit, but I still continue my pretence of not knowing her.

I suggest that maybe we should have a workout together; she agrees. We get up and dance the tango, then I snap my fingers and immediately we're changed into exercise gear, and we begin our workout.

The whole item went wonderfully and it was very funny. The station networked the footage, and it was promoted after *News At Ten*, a prime advertising spot, and the build up to it created an amazing air of anticipation.

Her publicity machinery was pleased and her record company very thankful. I got so much mileage out of anything that I did, and my column inches in magazines and newspapers increased; no matter how small, it was written about.

This was not the end of my association with Shirley Bassey. The next week, an invitation came through her press agent for me to come and visit her in France, but I declined. I was surprised to be told by her press agent that she wanted me, and what she wanted, she got.

Some months later, an invitation came for me to come to a restaurant where Shirley was having a dinner for a few of her close friends, and this one I accepted. Palmer and I went to the location, just off Charlotte Street, and we were shown upstairs to a private dining area. I was surprised to see a very long table of strangers. I was introduced to everyone and I remember several Lords and Ladies, and other eminent persons.

But what I found disturbing was the fact that although a place had been set for me, next to Shirley, there was no place for Palmer. There was a reshuffle at the other end of the table to fit her in. So picture this. I am at one end sitting next to the host and Palmer is at the other end, sitting pretty uncomfortably, between elderly, non-English-speaking guests.

Small talk went round the table, and Shirley spoke to me constantly, but I was not really listening. I was just feeling embarrassed. I had the main course, then felt that it would be a good time to take my leave. I made my excuses to Shirley, and she insisted that I stayed longer. I was adamant to go, and she at last got the message. I air-kissed her and went to leave with Palmer. Shirley then stood up and said, "I have something for you," and right there, in front of all her friends, she sang me a love song. I cringed and I am sure her friends thought it was most inappropriate, but they were very polite, as they applauded loudly.

I thanked her and we took flight down to the comfort of the pavement outside. We looked at each other as we went to our car and burst out laughing.

I never did get another invitation from Shirley.

Chapter 11: Projects 1994

'Fun In The Sun' in Spain

GMTV wanted to do a roadshow in Spain called 'Fun in the Sun'. In previous years, they had done a roadshow, but this was not successful. It failed to excite the viewers because the UK weather was always guaranteed rain, and when viewers were already experiencing rain in their backyards, they were not prepared to see rain on TV as well.

The station guardians decided that by going to Spain, they would achieve something better. For a start, the weather would be great and what was better than sunshine beaming into your home on a rainy and dismal day.

The plan was that we would have the studio as a back-up. Eammon would be holding the fort back in London; he just did not fancy Spain. Fun in the sun, he was not, and anyway, he was a serious presenter, and to be taken seriously he could not be seen in shorts on a beach abroad. That was his argument. He seemed unable to understand that *GMTV* was not a serious news programme – for that, you tuned into the BBC. Our team of presenters would be Simon Biagi, part-time weather presenter, employed by Loll Ingham for his rugged good looks. He was a model in Scotland and together he shared this position with a blonde named Sally Meen.

Word had it that a high percentage of people working at *GMTV* were gay, earning the nickname Gay Men Television. I am Jamaican by birth, and most Jamaicans are homophobic and intolerant. For me, what you do in the privacy of your own home and is harmless to others is your business. I had a high gay following, as many of my letters indicated, but when they found out that I was straight there was many,

"What a shame". I have no problem with people's lifestyle; it is up to them who they wish to court; who am I to dictate who you choose to love or share your life with? I say live and let live.

The stubbly kisses I get on the cheek every year I see as a form of endearment and it just shows me that people love me, so why should I not show the same love in return? The problem with Jamaicans is that they focus on the sexual act, rather than the person.

There still exists in Jamaica this church-led and cultural negative attitude towards gay people, which I do not understand. We have very high incidences of crime against children and women; why don't those same people speak out about that practice?

So that was the low down on the Spain team. Obviously, there was the full production and make-up support team. But there is someone I omitted from the equation. Anthea Turner.

I remember Eammon talking about how good this person would be for the station. He had given her his blessing and he felt that her fun personality was exactly what the station needed. She had been around for a long time in children's television and she had experience that would prove valuable. She would be a good sidekick for Eammon. Mr 'Serious Presenter' would do all the serious interviewing and she would fill in and just sit by his side and do as she was told.

Eammon made a serious mistake. She was no pushover, and she wanted to be the face.

A press conference was called before we went to Spain. I thought that most of the questions would be directed to her, but apart from, "What was it like leaving children's TV for the grown-ups?" there was little else the press wanted to know about Anthea Turner.

When it came to me, the questions came in thick and fast. Where did I come from? How did I get the job at *GMTV*? Did I feel guilty at ousting my predecessor Tonya? Every question they asked, I answered promptly, but there was one that would indicate the turn of my future: "Where are your skeletons? Are they in a cupboard somewhere?" I realised they would be checking me out, and they would be in my past faster than me saying, "Back to the future."

I bonded with Anthea, but then you had to. My friendship was based on air-kisses, hellos and "Is everything all right?" I realised that being a certain colour or gender provided certain advantages; there was a lot of pandering to her every need; being blonde and white helped. I was also friendly with Eammon; he came round to my home a number of times for dinner. Those were the times when he bared his soul about home life and also working at *GMTV*.

We flew off to Spain very soon afterwards. I was featured in a number of newspapers and magazines, and I was one of the main reasons for people congregating on the beach at that time in the morning. There were several different bands and acts performing on stage, but what was expected to give us the viewing figures were my antics throughout the show, and also getting a glimpse into the other side of the presenters.

GMTV paid for my family to be there, so when Palmer, James and I arrived at our hotel, I was dumbfounded. There were no phones in the rooms, which was small. We had three single beds, obviously made for pygmies. When we sat on any bed, it skated across the room. But worse of all, it was at least 40 minutes away from the location. I was so annoyed, I could not contain myself.

I looked for the other presenters and I found Anthea in the same state of annoyance. We went looking for the production office – and this is where the story gets even more bizarre – and we found them in a four star hotel just down the road from the transmitting location. As we walked to the reception, we realised that they had nominated themselves for the best that there was. We made our way to the production floor, and then waited in the outer room to be seen by Helen McMurray, head of programme presentation. Everyone else was too busy to even notice us; after all, they were making preparations for our time on air.

Helen greeted us, asking if we were ready. We told her of our disgust with the accommodations and she dismissed us with, "There wasn't any other accommodation available so we had to make do." She was now even more annoyed than we were. How dare we ask for a change of location. We would have to lump it as that was all the budget would allow. I told her we would not be staying in the current location, bid her buenos días and left with an amazed Anthea.

Later on that day, we found a hotel called the Don Poncho and we booked three rooms at a cost that I did not care about.

We were now within a ten-minute walk from the stage, and I had definitely put Helen McMurray's nose out of joint.

The first morning went very well. There were a few breaks in transmission, but throughout the show, I did a variety of workout items.

After a while, the attention of the crowd became unbearable. I was also having problems with an animal rights group. A month before, I had gone to Spain to do some publicity shots. The photographs appeared on the front cover of the *Sunday Magazine* of the *News of the World*, with me beside and sitting on a donkey. Unknown to me, this donkey had marks on its face. No one had realised this, but the animal rights people saw this as Mr Motivator 'abusing' animals, and, as I was giving publicity to this 'fun' pastime, they decide to send some of their supporters to Spain to picket the station.

To be honest, they were quite ineffective, but the station was not taking any chances. Nicci from the press office arrived in Spain with bodyguards to look after each presenter.

Audrey and Brian

We stayed in Torremolinos for one week, and by the end of it, I felt besieged. I had no escape from the continual attention; there was nowhere to hide, and I got no peace. I think it was on the Wednesday, as the show came to an end that I felt a tap on my shoulder. I turned round and a woman introduced herself as Audrey. She had a flat nearby that she and her husband Brian had bought some years before. They were regular visitors to Spain, and she said some words that I was very grateful for: "If ever you need some peace and quiet, and want to get away from it all, you're welcome at our place."

I said, "Thank you," and I gladly took up her offer. She made lunch, and it really was a great break away from the entire tourist scene.

Audrey and Brian have become our dear friends. They'd go to my Center Parcs weekends, and they've visited us in Jamaica too.

I did items on winemaking, sun protection and exercise. Whenever the exercise element came up, it was guaranteed a warm reception; everyone, no matter their ages, wanted to be involved. A large crowd always gathered at the location that I was in, so that each workout just became one big party. Getting people to perform together and to have a laugh; this is what I was good at.

Many a morning, we would come down to the stage to get ready, and couples could be found using our stage as a bed, and they would not stop their amorous activities, even when people were beginning to arrive.

Anthea and I did not spend as much time together as I thought we would; for the most part, I was on my own. Most of the guys were gay, and very much into their own company. If they were not, they were into drinking, and I did not feel comfortable with any of it. I kept to myself and after the production meeting, I made myself busy shopping, or as Anthea called it, Retail Therapy.

The summer road show was a success. *GMTV* was now the number one morning station, and for them and for me, there would be no looking back. I rested for a few weeks, but the public demand for my time was at times unbearable. There was no escape from the character that I had created.

Disney

I came back to the UK and the studios brimming with ideas. James and I had done some exercise slots aimed at the younger market. They had been a success, and now I wanted to do something more for the young as this was a growing market that I should get into.

James.

I was already doing slots on Saturday mornings on *GMTV*, and these two-minute items had seen me go around the world filming in different countries. Everyone knows that the attention span of a young child is very short and that is why our Time Out segments were of a two-minute duration – and they worked. So I wanted to do a video with exercise segments of no more than two minutes, and then slot in cartoons that had some kind of health message.

I spoke to Mark Wilson and John Beaumont, director and producer respectively on my Time Out items, and they liked the idea. The next port of call was Peter McHugh. He too saw some merit in what we were proposing.

David Briggs, who went on to devise *Who Wants to be a Millionaire?*, had joined *GMTV* from Capital Radio. He too came on board and the idea started to get some meat on the bones.

Mark Wilson had a lot of experience of working with children's programmes from his time at the BBC, and now he was running the children's department at *GMTV*. He was a small and intelligent man;his skills were numerous and I found him extremely creative. He had a way, as any good director does, of bringing out the very best in me. His vision and foresight was an inspiration, and I learned a lot from him about presenting. He was also a good example to his staff.

He took the nucleus of this idea and went away with John Beaumont, who was his sidekick and friend of many years, and together they came back with a storyboard that had us smiling and excited.

The idea was that I would be a school teacher, and as Mr Evans I was teaching a group of children about the body. One child would ask, "Please sir, how does your heart work?" and Mr Evans draws a heart on a blackboard, which opens up to Disney World, where the whole class is met by Goofy who takes up the story of how the heart works. He then introduces the class – and now Mr Evans becomes Mr Motivator – to the first cartoon, which illustrates the workings of the heart and love and emotion. Mr Motivator also teaches them to exercise. Cut back to classroom and onto the next lesson.

This idea became the proposal that was taken by Peter and David to a meeting at Disney. At the end of August, they came back with an agreement to pursue the project as a joint venture, with all costs being mutually agreed in advance. *GMTV* would produce, and Disney would market and distribute the video.

This project would be huge. It would be the first time that anything like this would be undertaken. Prior to going ahead, market research had to be done to determine its viability and potential, and whether the launch of the video should be pre or post-Christmas.

The research was very favourable. The public saw that there was a synergy between the Disney characters and Mr Motivator. In fact, the under-fives felt that Mr Motivator was a cartoon character.

Disney was excited and wanted to go along with the project. They said they would consider promoting this new video on the back of the *Lion King* video launch. All that was left to be resolved was the costing. In the meantime, *GMTV* was to continue with the video plans and finalise the storyboard.

Mark set up auditions for boys and girls to appear with me on the video. Most of the kids came from stage school, with James as one of the many selected. We did our shortlist and I went off to Orlando to film my inserts.

James, some of his school friends and Palmer came to Orlando for the week. We stayed at the Yacht Club, and our shooting took us to many Disney locations, from Mystic Mountain to Wilderness Safari. We filmed with Goofy, Donald Duck, and many others. We also went to Universal Studios and filmed there.

When we got back to the UK, we found there was a snag. *GMTV* was short on funds and complained about some of Disney's demands. In the end, the problem was not resolved, much to my disappointment. I was to get a 30% share of this project; the sales potential was enormous and everyone would have benefited. I was amazed that *GMTV* allowed such an opportunity to slip through its fingers. I became convinced more than ever that only I and I alone could look after my interests. I felt that maybe my demand for 30% of the action had made *GMTV* back off, so I knew that in the very near future, I would have to put my plans in action for Mr Motivator looking after himself.

Sales of my *BLT* video had gone through the roof, exceeding everyone's expectations. There were numerous newspaper articles highlighting its phenomenal success: *Motivator outsells Clint Eastwood's 'Unforgiven,'* and *Motivator has three videos in the Top Ten.* So it was decided partly by the press office and partly by management that we should hold an award ceremony at The Sanctuary in the West End.

We took over the whole place and invited a lot of celebrities. On the evening in question, I paraded around the place in my cream suit waistcoat and no shirt, and enjoyed the attention I was drawing. The press was in full attendance, speeches were made and the party continued into the early morning.

Chapter 12: 1996 - The War Wages…

1996 was a significant year in my life and in James' life. He was now 12 years old, old enough to say when he wanted to see his mother, although the courts were trying to regularise his visits. James got very stressed about these visits, and he wanted to go less and less. His confidence in her was shattered and he did not trust her. But every time he refused to go, Jewel took me to court saying I was behind his refusal to see her.

Court welfare officers and solicitors had been appointed to provide a deeper insight into us, and also into what James really wanted to do. When these reports were submitted, Jewel insisted that the writers were biased or star-struck. She had forgotten that for many years, I was the one faced with the adverse judgements.

James was starting to put his foot down. He remembered what had gone on before, such as the fighting and being taken out of the country. He also saw that his mother regularly tried to get me arrested. He was starting to say, "No!" One incident that I believe brought him to write about his true feelings happened after an arranged visit to his mother.

On the way to his mother's house, James was quiet. I knew that he did not want to go. However, the arrangements were made and he went in. All day, I wondered how he was, but James was not allowed to call me. I arrived back at his mother's house for his evening pick up, but there was no answer.

I waited until 7.00 p.m., and then 8.00 p.m., all kinds of things running through my mind. Was he being taken away again? Would I be able to see him again? What should I do? In the end, I decided to call the police and report him as missing. He was a ward of the court and anything could have happened.

The police came, and soon after, Jewel arrived with James, who was in tears. Ignoring all of us, she went inside with him; she would not acknowledge the police or me, or James' tears. No matter how everyone pleaded and cajoled, she just closed the door.

We waited outside and about 20 minutes later, James came out, so upset he could hardly talk. He was affected badly by this incident, but although I reported it, no action was taken to change the court orders when Jewel broke them.

The only thing that happened was that contact broke down. She would not accept anyone that we put forward to oversee James' visit to her. There was a genuine concern that she might try to abduct him so all future visits were at a contact centre. These visits were stressful for James and he was reluctant to go.

I was so grateful for Palmer. She afforded me the space to be myself but also the support that I needed at times such as these. She was that constant pillar that was there for all of us. Everyone benefited from her presence and without her, things would have been vastly different. She was slowly bringing stability to the home.

She offered to take James for his visits to the contact centre, and she tried to make these times as stress-free as possible. Her experience as a childcare officer was a blessing; she was able to use her knowledge of dealing with kids from broken homes. He knew she was only in the next room, and no matter how the visits went, she made sure James was happy and smiling when he came home.

Tessa's Kiss and Tell

It amazes me how adults behave when things are over and long gone. I say this as one who has been through a disastrous marriage, and borne years of endless litigation, arguments and hurts. I thought that Tessa was long gone, but not so. It served me right to become successful. Tessa was jealous of what was happening to me in the public arena, and one particular Monday, I had a call from the press office to say that Tessa was about to do a 'kiss and tell' story of my time with her, and would I be prepared to tell my side of it, to counteract the effect of any revelations that she was about to make.

These things usually came out in the *News of The World*, but she had done a deal with the *Sun* newspaper for a serialisation of our time together. It was to be printed over three days and she was being paid approximately £50,000.

I found this hard to believe. The one thing Tessa always said was she would never want to be like my ex-wife, and secondly she would never want to see what happened to her happen to me. Many times, she expressed her disgust at women who paraded themselves in the tabloids, spilling all their intimate details, and how no money would ever make her stoop so low – so she had said.

Her attitude towards such things impressed me, but circumstances change and people change.

I have never commented before on what was stated in the article, and although I had been pressed by many people, I kept my mouth shut. I now feel that the time is right to say something here.

I was curious about the article. I gathered from a source that the friendship between the *Sun* and *GMTV* had soured and that was why this was appearing. I never did find out what *GMTV* did, but whatever it was must have been serious.

In the articles, she had nothing bad to say because there wasn't anything bad to say about me. She did try to paint a picture of me as an opportunist but, I say now, if in life you do not have the ability, then no matter how many doors are opened for you, as soon as you enter, you will be at a loss. After three days of articles in the *Sun*, I became more popular than ever. It is true there is no such thing as bad publicity.

I know that in life there is not one decision that I made in the past that I am sorry for. Meeting Tessa was not a mistake, but just part of the pieces that make up Derrick's jigsaw of life. Very soon after Tessa's article, the *News of The World* saw an opportunity to get in on some of the action. Their feature writer wrote to Jewel Evans on 28th June giving her the opportunity to tell her side of the story. There was one line in their letter that shows how devious they are: "I know that you are not another Tessa and I also know that you have retained your dignity over the years since the court case, but I wonder if you could spare the time to give me an insight into what he is really like. The other thing is my boss would be happy to give a substantial amount to either the charity of your choice, or yourself, for your help in my article." This deal did not materialise as there was a stipulation in the court's financial settlement barring any such publicity stunt.

Christopher

This one day in 1996 was a most inspiring event. It was the day I had the honour of presenting Christopher with an award for bravery at the highest level. He was just six years old, and indeed a remarkable young man. I travelled to his school and surprised him. I was apparently his idol, but the feeling is mutual.

His joy and smile touched my heart. At that time, I did not fully notice that he was in a wheelchair. I noticed his bald head, which was not by choice, as chemotherapy had removed his flowing locks.

The story is that cancer of the thighs had made him weak. But he was determined that the wheelchair was only for a time. This very determined young man wanted very little to do with the chair; he felt and knew that with support from his family, the Fosters – father, mother and brother, Richard – he could rise up out of what he regarded as a temporary situation.

The whole day was a day of awakening and I left them feeling wiser and happier than when I first arrived. I had been blessed, and the impact of a young man of six who exuded such courage had a humbling effect on me.

Christopher.

On the way home, I knew that adoption was to be my next move, and not just Christopher but the whole family. I invited them to most of my Center Parcs weekends and provided them with a villa for their stay. I proudly introduced Christopher to everyone.

I was happy to see the family support, and I was so proud to have also been adopted by the Fosters. Sue, his mother, would for years continue to update me on Christopher's progress. Miraculously, he had got out of the wheelchair and was now able to play football. His hair had also grown back. In 1999, I had a call. Sue told me that one leg had to be removed and he would be nearby in Stanmore in hospital. I went to see Chris, who was having physio; everyone was optimistic and the feeling was that the cancer had been arrested.

He recovered very quickly, and before long, without the offending leg, he was taking part in a circuit class. He became fitter than those with all their limbs. I would push him hard;it mattered not as he rose to the challenge, dancing on one leg, with more rhythm than those with two feet. He became for me a real inspiration.

Chris continued to come to at least one of my Center Parcs weekends each year, and I watched him grow as he rose to every challenge. The family came and stayed with us in Jamaica, and each day Chris would swim, and if the family was going away for the day, he would rather stay behind and eat and swim.

With his passion and determination, Chris soon represented Great Britain in the fields of cricket, football and swimming.

I have kept in touch and in early 2007, there was a scare. Chris was not well. He was diagnosed with stomach problems brought on by exams. He would be fine. I spoke to his mum to get an update and she said that everyone was doing great. She said Chris wanted to go on to university to become a sports physio.

Richard, his brother, was nearing completion in his quest to become an actor. He is an amazing person in all respects, supporting Chris in every way he could. There was never a time that he was envious of the obvious extra attention that went to Chris instead of him.

Their father, Martin, worked tirelessly for his family. Sue was the epitome of motherhood. She was also a great storyteller.

The Fosters are an inspiration to me and, quite possibly, all who come in contact with them. I consider them real friends and I have learnt many valuable lessons from their lives.

An Audience with Freddie Starr

An invitation came in for *An Audience with Freddie Starr*. Everyone in the industry knew how unpredictable he could be. Faith Brown, the comedienne, will always remember that night. Freddie came on stage with a large see-through bowl full of 'maggots'. He fooled the audience, scooping up a handful of rice, which we all thought was maggots, and threw that into the audience. It brought a huge laugh when everyone realised what it was, but as usual he always went just a little bit too far. Seeing Faith Brown with her revealing top, he scooped up a handful of what everyone thought was definitely rice and threw what we now know were maggots into her top. We all creased up laughing unknowingly at the expense of Faith Brown.

On this same evening, a bike was brought onto the stage. He asked for my help and I duly obliged. He told me to sit on the bike, which I did, then he asked me to start pedalling. I did, but very slowly, so he asked me to do it quicker. I did, and the lights went brighter. When I slowed down, the room got darker. He told me to go quicker, and the lights returned to normal. Then he started to sing. If I pedalled slowly, his voice got distorted, and if I went quicker, so did his voice. It brought the house down.

Polygram & Party!

As I stated earlier, I was not happy with my video arrangements. I was also still mad at *GMTV* for missing the chance of a Disney video. *GMTV* had made at least a million pounds off my first video. I had probably received about £20,000. Things were about to change. I wanted greater control on the videos I made, and so I started negotiations with PolyGram.

The intention here was not to cut *GMTV* out of the picture, but instead to leave them doing what they knew best, which was programming. I was in the strongest position and I knew the only way to recover and make some real money was to get my own contract with PolyGram.

So I set up a meeting with the head of their video division. He listened, and I was in such a driving position that all my demands were met, so on 3rd November, we had an agreement which was one of the largest deals they have ever done for a video.

This was to be a three-video deal. I would be paid £275,000 and my production company, Wicked Productions, would produce, capped at £97,000 per video.

I was happy! I felt able to move on in control of my life. That Christmas, I was in the mood to celebrate, so I asked Gill Stacey, Peter McHugh's PA, to help me locate a venue for a party. Everyone who had helped me was invited. I paid for everything, and so all the *GMTV* staff from top to bottom were there.

Music played, food and drinks flowed, and everyone was on a high. I was glad I did it. It was just my way of saying thank you to everyone who was there at the beginning: my friends who I grew up with, those at *GMTV*, even the cleaners were there. Halfway through the evening, Peter stood up to say something. He was very generous with his words of thanks, but whilst he was speaking, two people in particular were not listening or paying attention. In fact, they were being disruptive.

So while everyone else faced Peter, he asked for the way to be parted so he could see who was being so disrespectful. The path cleared just like the parting of the Red Sea, and who did we see at the back, laughing loudly without a care in the world, but Helen McMurray and Liam Hamilton, neither of them my biggest fans.

At the top of his voice, Peter shouted for them to shut up, and then he uttered some words that have remained with me from then.

"You may laugh and be disrespectful, but if it wasn't for Mote, you wouldn't be here!" I smiled and I felt humbled in a kind of big-headed way.

On saying something in return, I just used the words from McFadden and Whitehead, "Ain't no stopping us now, we're on our way."

I was to do this yearly party for the next three years.

Chapter 13: The Wedding

From the moment we met, I knew that she was for me. Bells went off in my head, my heart raced every time I saw her, or simply thought of her, and I couldn't keep my hands off her. With Palmer now pregnant, I felt an urgent and honest desire to make her my own, as we had become engaged a year before.

This was a passion that I had never known or experienced before and the ingredients were so right. It was time to seal a deeply heartfelt friendship.

She was my soulmate and she made me complete. I found someone who not only loves me, but likes me and was prepared to tolerate me, willing to accept me for the way I am. She was happy with what I had to offer. Now I believe the saying, 'Behind every great man is an even greater woman'.

Without Palmer, I would still have been successful, but on a scale of one to ten, I would have been a three. With her, I am a ten. I am not as financially wealthy as those of the *Times Rich List*, but I am so wealthy in other more significant ways with Palmer by my side.

I thank Palmer here and now, and I look forward to many more happy years with her.

Wedding Plans

I was in the middle of the Summer Roadshow in Spain when we made the decision to Jump The Broomstick. However, there was only one window of time and that was the weekend of 26th July. I spoke with Palmer at length, and we thought, why not? Let's do it!

I called Alan Ollie, a good mate of mine, who had travelled the world with me taking my pictures. He was sure that *Hello!* magazine would feature the wedding. Teresa, my personal assistant, put a call through to the Marquesa, the lady who made all the celebrity deals for *Hello!* She said sure, but it had to be exclusive. I asked what money we were talking about; she said five figures, and I agreed.

Palmer and I had decided to adopt a colourful African theme, and she set about designing her dress, the bridesmaids' dresses, and original African robes for James and me. The only problem we had was time; everything had to be arranged within a month.

The dressmaker knew of African designers in France, so James and I had our measurements flown out, while she proceeded with the bridal wear.

James was my best man, and Palmer would be given away by her nephew, Dean. Carolyne was chief bridesmaid, and my niece, Kerry-Ann, was the flower girl. Valerie, Palmer's sister, was matron of honour and her youngest nephew, Sherrick, was page boy. Charmaine, who had been our housekeeper for many years, was put in charge of organising the catering, and everyone else.

I came home most weekends to do personal appearances, but with only four weeks to go, I had a mission to find a church that would fit our requirements.

We wanted one that would marry a divorcé, big enough to hold about 250 people, something like a castle or stately home. We went to see Leeds Castle but we both felt that it was not what we were looking for, so feeling rather disappointed, we followed a sign for Chilham. Neither of us had heard of it, but a sign said Chilham Castle, and as we turned off the main road, our spirits shot up. We came upon a quaint 'chocolate box' village square, surrounded by old-fashioned shops and houses and, picture this, at one end was an imposing 'knights in shining armour' castle, turrets and all.

We drove up to the castle and were shown around by the manager. The lawns and grounds were spectacular, with distant rolling hills. We were pleased, and after watching the peacocks wandering around, we knew that this was the place.

We booked it and started planning an outdoor event. We were convinced it would not rain. We wanted clowns, jugglers, stilt walkers and jongleurs to keep everyone amused.

We would purchase lots of mats to put on the ground, and I would locate a steel band with African singers and dancers to entertain. A disco would also be in place.

Well, we knew where we would hold the reception, but where would we do the deed? The local tea house provided the answer as we sat enjoying a cup of tea. At the opposite end of the square to Chilham Castle was St. Mary's, a beautiful church, almost as old as the castle. When we walked in through the doors, we knew it was the place we wanted to take our vows.

Reverend Duncan led us through the church, explaining its history, and I found it refreshing to meet someone who didn't know of me. We explained the previous marriage situation and he said that would not be a problem.

We drove home realising there were a ton of things to get done in one month. What with work and the timing, Palmer and Charmaine would have to make most of the arrangements, although I wanted Palmer to know I was fully behind it all.

We were concerned about Palmer's age and being pregnant, so we arranged the very best medical attention. We were asked whether we would take the chance or go for an amniocentesis, but we felt that this would be too invasive, and even though Palmer was close to 40, we felt that we were blessed and that nothing would ever go wrong. In ordering her dress, Palmer had to take into account Abigail growing inside her. I then had to start giving some thought to invitations.

Adrian, a friend, ran a T-shirt printing business, and when I spoke to him about invitations, the possibility of doing an invite on a baby T-shirt was born. It was done in the form of a newspaper front page. It also mentioned that guests had to come dressed in bright colours, and as African as possible.

Myself and Palmer on our wedding day. Courtesy of Hello! magazine.

With the GMTV presenters. Courtesy of Hello! magazine.

I spent the weeks leading up to that eventful day in Spain during the week transmitting live into the UK. As soon as we came off air on Friday, I caught the earliest flight home. Responses were coming back from the invitations, and I had made a point of inviting anyone who had remotely shared in my life so far.

I flew to the UK from Spain on Thursday 25th July to get married the following day. It rained cats and dogs, but we still believed that the next day would be beautiful and sunny.

That evening, I checked into a hotel near the church with a load of my buddies, whilst Palmer was in a hotel just off the village square.

Our Day

Friday 26th July dawned and proved us right. It was the most beautiful day of the summer; our Lord was definitely smiling down on us. I did an early morning live workout on *GMTV* with all my mates, and after that I set about getting ready. My African robe looked and fitted great, and when James put his on, my heart swelled. He looked so manly and all grown up; I was so proud of him.

We drove to the church in our stretch limo. I thought that our exclusive deal with *Hello!* was well-protected. We had asked all guests to hand in their cameras, but when we arrived at Chilham Square, I was amazed at the crowds of people and photographers who were there; so much for secrets. We had a private security firm who were supposed to shelter us from prying eyes, but how much good that did was beyond me.

As I stood at the back of the church, I could see the result of all that planning. Palmer and Charmaine had come down previously to arrange the catering and flower arrangements. The local florist had had a field day. A riot of colourful floral swags adorned every pew, two huge arrangements sat at the altar, and everybody sported bright buttonholes and corsages. On my walk to my seat at the front, I also realised how much effort everyone had made: there was upwards of 250 guests gathered in the church; it was full to overflowing. Their clothes were amazing, with suits and hats of every colour and combination, and African wear featured heavily.

I sat down with James on my right but I was nervous, and anticipation made me get up and look around every minute. I just kept thinking the worst; what if she changed her mind?

The scene was set and all we needed was the bride, but why was I feeling so emotional? I was welling up inside and tears filled my eyes. I knew why I felt this way; I had married Carolyne's mother and also James' mother, but this time, I was marrying for love.

Then I heard the music. I looked and there she was, looking truly amazing and as radiant as I have ever seen her. Her dress was of African design, but made of ivory satin and beaded lace. She had fresh flowers of every colour in her hair, matching her cascading bouquet, and she floated up the aisle on the arm of her nephew.

Carolyne and Kerry-Ann looked beautiful in blue, but that's all that registered. I felt as if something was lifting me out of my shoes. I must have grown two feet in height as my bride came towards me. Suddenly, a figure in a bright red suit slipped behind the bridal party. It was my daughter Ebony, who we had not heard from or seen for a while, but I was glad she was there.

I was jigging from one foot to the other, and before I knew it, Palmer was by my side and I was kissing her on the cheek. We didn't hear the pastor's welcome. But we heard James' clear, ringing voice as he sang *Edelweiss*, reducing everyone to tears. He had the voice of an angel and did us proud.

It wasn't long before we had exchanged rings and our vows and, after signing the register, we did jump the broomstick! One of our friends, Kerry, who has now gone on to become a minister, placed an old birch broomstick in the aisle. This was an old slave ritual. In the old days when there were no vicars in the village, the local head man would place a broomstick on the ground and couples who wanted to get married would 'Jump into the promised land.' Palmer and I did the symbolic jumping of the broomstick. We hugged, kissed and thanked what felt like hundreds of people as we made our way to our car for the short ride across the square. The crowd outside had grown even larger so we had to be escorted as we drove up to the castle.

Red Hot Jam was on the lawn playing some jazz music, and drinks and canapés were served. Alan Ollie organised us for the photographs.

We took hundreds of photographs for *Hello!* magazine, including some that would never be featured. After all this came the reception, set inside one of the castle's banqueting halls. As we walked inside, the African dance troupe danced and sang loudly in the background.

We waited a moment as Rusty Lee serenaded us in beautiful song. Since leaving our TV screens as a cook, she had carved out a rather lucrative singing career on cruise ships.

Once again, I was amazed by the florist's handiwork. Huge, wildly-coloured floral arrangements festooned the hall, and the bridal table groaned under the weight of platters filled with tropical fruits, flowers and plants.

The medieval crier made the announcements and introductions, in fine Old English fashion. I was first; there were many others who had things to say, but I warned them about being brief. After all, everyone was hungry! I quickly thanked our families and friends, and then I made a special tribute to Palmer, using each letter of her name to indicate what she meant to me. She started crying before I'd finished the first letter!

Palmer and I danced to a song by Billy Paul that I particularity liked called *Thanks For Saving My Life*, sung by Ritchie, Carolyne's then-boyfriend and father of her first child, RJ.

The catering was set up in the grounds and it was wonderful to see our guests enjoying themselves. It was very informal so our guests reclined on silk bedspreads that Palmer bought. These were taken home as souvenirs, and likewise the flowers. They were so beautiful, people could not help but take them home.

The disco tripped in with beautiful music and with the open bar, we had the makings of a great festive evening. Palmer and I left soon after, waving our goodbyes as we headed to our hotel close by for our honeymoon.

Palmer and I had no parents left and most of our families were far away; all we truly had was each other and I was determined to make it work.

We were extremely happy and grateful for all that we had been blessed with; it was a special wedding day. The memories will be preserved on celluloid and in print for us to see in years to come.

The week after, *Hello!* made an amazing tribute to us with our photo gracing the front page and a further 17 pages inside, cataloguing the day.

Happy Birthday, Abigail!

As Christmas neared, we knew the baby was nearly due. I warned Palmer that the only date with a window of opportunity for the birth was Christmas Day; I would have to be on stage performing in a Pantomime in Reading on the afternoon of the 26th. Charmaine, our very good friend and housekeeper, promised faithfully that she would be there with Palmer.

Palmer still went about her business, although she was larger than ever. Water retention curtailed her exercising, but it did not stop her wanting to ensure the home ran properly. She insisted on driving and doing the shopping, to the point where supermarket managers would insist on her sitting down while they got her groceries, just in case she gave birth in their shops! Charmaine had a hard job keeping Palmer from trotting up and down stepladders and cleaning the attic, and we all had to run around after her getting things ready for the newcomer. She seemed to have researched every bit of equipment and accessory, and when she had made her decision, I just trailed after her to collect her choice.

Usually at Christmas, we have a lot of people in the house, and this one was no different. So, with a house full of friends and family, we set about enjoying ourselves.

Palmer kept calling herself 'The Blimp', but she reminded me of a majestic Spanish galleon in full sail, billowing around the house making sure everything and everyone was alright. She was in and out of the kitchen, helping Charmaine, a chef par excellence, both of them wearing Santa hats, laughing and dancing as they worked.

Everyone stuffed themselves silly, weaving in and out, dancing to the music as they drank and ate the day away. Although Palmer usually watched what she ate, she could not resist Champ's Christmas pud and brandy sauce; she was also seen nibbling on a huge turkey leg as she danced through the crowd. When the calypso music started, so did Palmer. She gyrated across the floor, belly one way, hips the other, amazing everybody and causing no little concern to Champs. She was on a high and she didn't slow down until the last person left. Moses took Charmaine home, and Palmer had just sat down with a cup of tea and put her feet up when she said, "Dee, I think I need to go to the hospital!"

James and I bustled about while Palmer sedately went and showered, taking her time, surprising us as she came out in a sleeveless summer dress. This was the dead of winter, but she was as hot as a boiler, and I was not arguing. I sent Moses off to get Champs to meet us at the hospital.

I wanted to throw caution to the wind and just speed along, but I couldn't; I knew that slowly and carefully would be the order of the day. I had called Mr Beedham, the gynaecologist, and we needed to know how quickly the contractions were coming, so I took off my watch, and gave it to James, but I was so excited, I couldn't hear anything. We think the contractions were about every six minutes.

Palmer was very quiet as I drove along the Western Avenue towards Edgware Road and Great Portland Street. I went over everything, but she had been well-organised, she had packed her case with everything she needed, even a note telling me what oils she wanted rubbing in to ease the labour, and a letter telling me to remember she loved me, no matter what she called me as she was bearing down. It seemed I was in for a bit of work.

I was totally reassured that Palmer would get the very best of attention. Great Portland Street had seen many royal births. Sarah

Ferguson went there with her two princesses, and if it was good enough for them, then it would be good enough for my Palmer.

All the hospital arrangements had been done months before, so there was no need for paperwork. Palmer was whisked straight up to her private room. They confirmed what we already knew; that she was in labour and had been for some time. The dancing earlier on had hidden the labour pains.

My one worry was, would I be there for the birth? I needed to get to Reading for the pantomime and this would mean leaving the West End by 12.00 p.m. I couldn't think where Champs was. We had arranged for her to be with Palmer just in case, and I'd been phoning her with no reply. Where was she?

I got ready for a long night. The contractions were coming hard and fast, so I held her hand. There are various methods available to ease the pain. Palmer, who wanted as natural a birth as possible, chose a TENS machine, which emitted electrical impulses to block the pain. After a few minutes of practise, my job was to sit there and get into the rhythm of turning the switch.

I don't know how effective the TENS was. All I know is that when a contraction came, Palmer's nails speared into my very delicate arms!

I did not visibly cry as she repeatedly gouged my arm. Through misted eyes, I asked, "Are you OK?" as each bout of pain passed. Not once did she care to ask me how I was bearing up under such pressure! I did have moments of respite. It seemed that between each painful period, it was as if I had been drugged by her nails, and I automatically fell asleep.

As regularly as I drifted off, Palmer woke me with her talons. I put on a brave face. I told her jokes when I could and had everyone laughing.

Eighteen hours later, the doctors and nurses were worried. Although all the signs indicated everything was ready, the baby seemed to be hitting against a barrier, and was getting tired. Palmer would need a caesarean section.

She was worried about the baby and very upset, but did not want to be anaesthetised, so she opted for an epidural injection. That way, she could be awake to greet and hold her baby.

James and I followed everyone down to the prep room and got scrubbed up and gowned. He made sure he had the camcorder ready to film this exciting, real live operation!

We watched them getting ready for the epidural, which incidentally was not a good thing. They were going to push what looked to me like a javelin into Palmer's spinal column. They explained the seriousness of the injection. She was to face me with her head resting on my chest and she had to keep very still. If the needle entered the wrong place, it could cause neurological problems.

Imagining all the things that could go wrong, a warm feeling came over me, then a cold sweat began and the floor spun all over the place.

Brave though I was, I needed to get out of the theatre before I kissed the floor, so I excused myself and rushed to the restroom. The cold water felt good as I splashed it over my face. Once revived, I knew I had to get back quickly.

Palmer waited for a period between contractions, and sat on the edge of the table while I held her close. The nurse had already inked the spot so the doctor pushed on home. Unfortunately, Palmer immediately had another contraction and she moved just as the needle was pushed home. The damage has remained with her to this day: she has nerve sensitivity and a little weakness along her right leg.

The injection took effect quite quickly. Palmer was laid on her back and the nurses erected a blue rubber sheet across her abdomen, ensuring she could not see what was about to happen. Good thing too. I will forever remember the sight of the incision, and the ensuing surgery. James did not have time to say 'action', but the camera was rolling and I can recall looking forward to the replay of the event. I was by Palmer's head.

Some psychological studies inform men to stay away from the delivery end to avoid post-pregnancy trauma, but not James. He was there and so engrossed, the surgeon had to kindly ask him to move over.

This beautiful, angelic, oh so perfect little girl emerged. I don't care what people say – newborn babies are usually ugly, especially if they have been squashed on the journey down that tunnel. But with a caesarean, everything is where it should be. We knew immediately she was a girl, and what a huge dumpling she was at 8lbs 13oz; and deserving of being named Abigail Jordana Theresa Julia Evans.

Thank God for all my blessings that year. I had lost quite a bit of weight, trying to tackle almost every job that came in. Consequently, my health started to suffer, reminding me of the saying that "So many people spend their health gaining wealth, and then have to spend their wealth to regain their health". I had to re-evaluate what was important. Changes were afoot.

James spearheaded one of the most influential changes. Aged 14, he had realised that his mother was trying to destabilise my relationship and my happiness. She was also trying to get me arrested. He also realised that if he missed a date to see her, or failed to go at a court-determined time, he would have broken the court order, for which I would be held in breach.

So after numerous appointments with court welfare officers, James wrote a letter to his mother and deposited this with Mrs K, one of those officers.

He told his mother that he loved her, but he wanted to be the one who dictated his visiting times. He would say what suited him and he wanted the freedom to change arrangements, including the regularity of each visit.

Most importantly, he did not want the courts involved anymore. He said he was fed up with the continual pressure, and would not attend court again. If the situation did not change, he pointed out clearly, he would not be going to see his mother anymore.

His mother received this letter, and needless to say, she missed the whole point. She wrote back to James calling him a 'whippersnapper' - how dare he tell her what to do? She would tell him exactly when she wanted to see him and he had no choice in the matter.

Once again, we went to court. The judge was unable to force the situation. He paid attention to the court officer's report, but most of all he noted James' letter and read his mother's reply.

The judge ordered a resting period, and that is how it has remained. James has not seen or heard from his mother from that date, and when I ask him if he would like to, he just says, "No, thanks." These days, I do not bother to ask. Jewel no longer features in our lives, and peace has reigned.

So, 1996 was a turning point in my life. As a family, we were moving on, and the future looked bright.

With James.

Chapter 14: More Projects 1996 -1998

St. Lucia

St. Lucia was the location for my next video. I chose the music of the legendary Bob Marley, renowned guitarist Ernest Ranglin, and Calypso music to accompany my exercises.

I had taken on many more responsibilities in 1996. After the summer roadshow to Spain, I had to get on with fulfilling my contractual arrangement with PolyGram. All the videos had been selling well, and now we needed to do one for the 1997 season. PolyGram felt that rather than going by my gut feeling of what would work, they should have market research done for the next video.

It is not that things were not working, but in television there is always a need to change things. The survey was done amongst small focus groups, and from the results, it was deemed that 'Mr M' standing with arms folded would not work, as this pose was not very inviting. The title needed to make the promise 'ten minutes for a new you' and the front cover needed to be a toned down, not as loud as before. And so attention was given to these findings.

Tobago

Apparently, the public did love my outdoor locations, and as Tobago was my choice, a deal was done with their tourist board. They were only too pleased to have me come to their island and Caledonian

Airways offered free flights for a mention on the cover and the credits. Accommodation was at Le Grand Courlan.

Tobago was one of the most beautiful places I have been to; the people and the atmosphere just blew my mind away. It was the inspiration for *The Treasure Island*, and if you visit there, you will easily see why. It's a very small island, totally unspoilt and unaffected by the problems of Trinidad. The video was a good product, but it was not as strong as my St. Lucia video which I will always believe was my strongest and best – although the first video outsold all of them.

It was not a fun time for me. Palmer, due to her pregnancy, was unable to travel that distance, and I missed her. This was the second project of its kind that she would not be involved in, and, although I knew that I had to get the job done, my heart was not fully in it. I missed home. Whilst there, I filmed a TV advert for the video, and one for 'My AbTech', the stomach exerciser, so we worked long days to achieve all that was needed.

These projects were the work of my production company, Wicked Productions. I was pleased with the outcome and came back to the UK to meet a rapidly expanding Palmer.

The Tobago video was well received and sales were doing well. I was being featured in many magazines, and the treadmill of personal appearances and shop openings continued.

Dubai

Dubai proved an excellent location for our filming. The *GMTV* crew and I were well provided for. Everything in Dubai was on a grand scale. The hotels were extremely well-equipped, and at the markets, everything could be found at a good price.

Our transmission into the UK was live every day for a week, and when I came off-air, I had to spend time filming my Saturday morning and holiday period 'Time Out' pieces. These were stored for use at holiday times, or as fillers for kids' programmes.

Barbados

After the Barbados MOT video, Ralph Taylor, at the Almond Beach Hotel, had invited me back for a holiday and that invitation was also extended to my family during the March half-term. I was tired and I longed to spend quality time with my family, who were now in Barbados.

I called *GMTV*. "I'm tired," I told them. "Do we have enough items in the can to allow me to be away for ten days?" The reply was yes. I called my agent to see if there were any pressing matters in my diary that could not wait. No.

British Airways said that they could get me on a flight the very next day, but only first class was available, so I booked it. I called Almond Beach, and they were to pick me up from the airport the next day, making sure they did not say anything to Palmer.

It had been a short trip from the airport to our room. I knocked, saying, "Room service!" The door opened and the shocked look on Palmer's face was a picture to behold! She leaped into my arms, and suffice it to say, we knew almost to the minute when Abigail was conceived.

We spent a great time at the Almond Beach. Most days, we ran into Frank Bruno and wife, and we had some quality time. I had great fun taking over some of the exercise sessions for the Almond.

This place became our March holiday location for several years to come.

I will always be grateful for the way in which Ralph Taylor looked after my family, and to show my gratitude, I was able to film a number of my TV and video concepts at the Almond Beach.

Pantomime

The pantomime was set to run from December 1996 to January 1997. The show was *Goldilocks and the Three Bears*, starring Mr Motivator as the Ringmaster. This was a specially written version of that very old fairy tale, set in a circus. Anyone and everyone of any worth gets the 'panto' offer. This was mine.

I would be the star with Wendy Turner as Goldilocks, supported by a large number of very talented theatre actors. I was blessed to be in such good company, and I learned a lot whilst being paid £60,000. I loved the rehearsals. This was new ground for me, and I found the whole experience a real challenge. I sang and I danced, and enjoyed myself so much. After it ended, I was offered the part of Chalky the boxer in the opera *Carmen*, singing that epic song, *Stand Up and Fight*. I did not do it. I felt that although they were willing to make concessions and allow me time flexibility, I could not make the commitment.

Mr M's BLT

In 1995, I did a magazine with *GMTV* called *Mr M's BLT*, which highlighted whatever I was up to, and gave the reader exercises for the problem areas. It sold exceptionally well and *GMTV* had prospered from it. I had been paid a one-off fee for my contribution, and although hundreds of thousands had been sold, I saw only £20,000.

However, I was determined to make my own way and soon the very first edition of the Mr Motivator magazine hit the newsstands. Produced by Highbury House Communications, it was a good read, full of fitness and health articles, and advertisers were keen to participate.

My production office controlled most of my business, and this was in the very capable hands of Teresa Poole.

The Derrick Evans Show

So much was going on at this time, and everything seemed to be going in the right direction. The offers came in and I just took it all in my stride. I was slimmer than I had ever been, but I had to keep going. I was never too sure how long it would last and while I had interests other than TV, this industry provided remuneration at a level that was difficult to achieve anywhere else. So I continued to say yes to all opportunities. I had a good offer from several bed companies to develop and sell a range of beds with my name attached. I went for airsprung. Their offer was in five digits and I would also be able to furnish both houses for free.

There was a regular weekday morning show called *The Time, The Place*, presented by the respected broadcaster John Stapleton. He was of the view I had a side that needed to be explored, so he offered me the chance to come on stage in front of 200 people and be quizzed by them about Derrick Evans and Mr Motivator. I agreed. I thought maybe this would illustrate my ability to hold the attention of an audience for 45 minutes.

I went on to the cheers of a crowd that enthusiastically asked my advice on fitness and individual problems. Palmer was asked how difficult it was to be married to me and if she felt pressured to be keeping fit all the time. Palmer told of my support and my lack of pressure on her to be any different to how she is. Abigail just smiled and cooed, which won everyone's hearts.

At the end of the show, I thanked John and, to show how small the world is and that you should always be as courteous as possible, a while later our paths were to cross again, as he worked for *GMTV* as a presenter of their early morning show.

It is said in TV that if you do too many appearances, you get stereotyped. I believed strongly that I had more to offer. There were few times that I had been given the opportunity to speak.

Not long after, I was in Yorkshire appearing on a quiz show, and in the corridor, I ran into the man in charge, Bruce Gyngell. I knew little of this man who was in charge of a major part of British TV, but he said to me that I was an asset to *GMTV* and if they failed at any time to recognise that, and I was unhappy or I found myself in need of a presenting job, he would readily offer me work. I thanked him for his kind words. He shook my hand and looked me in the eye and just said that he was serious. He was about to walk away when he turned and said he would prove how highly he thought of me.

I went away to film the show I was there to do. At lunchtime, we met again and he said, "What show would you like to present?" Immediately, I said a chat show on some serious issues. He smiled saying, "Let's make a pilot. I have a studio for a show called *The Calendar Show*. It is off-air for now so the large studio is available. I will put my team on it and we will be in touch."

Once again, I thanked him and went on my way, partially thinking I would not hear from him again. When I got back to London, I told my ace assistant Teresa Poole about this meeting; I also told her not to hold her breath.

Soon the phone rang with a call from a man called Nick Thorogood who worked for Arch Dyson, the producer. They had been told by Bruce Gyngell to make contact with a view to developing a show just for me. They were at my disposal and they would make it happen. I needed to think about what kind of chat show I wanted to do.

I wanted to cover one item; are we tough enough on young offenders? Because I had been in trouble when I was younger, I felt that this was a topic that I could carry off, and if they got creative, we could get the network centre's approval. After weeks of planning, we arrived at a format we were happy with.

In the audience would be representatives from the police, probation officers, politicians from both major parties, youth workers, and the population at large, including offenders.

We also would look at the issue of legalising prostitution. I would do a satellite link with a gentleman from the USA who ran a company called Sporting House Connection. He had set up the very first timeshare brothel. Uptake had been high and he felt that he had broken down many of the barriers around the oldest profession in the world.

I had been briefed well by Teresa, but sitting alone in my dressing room, for once I felt vulnerable. I was being exposed to a field that I had little experience of and now I would need to summon up all that I could to make myself convincing and credible. For years, I'd had a character to hide behind. Mr Motivator could do anything, say anything;. He broke down barriers and doors and had attitude, but most of all, he protected Derrick. Would he be there when I needed him?

I stood at the top of the stairs and peeked through a crack in the curtain that kept me out of the audience's view. I was shaking, but not noticeably... I hoped. I was not ready, but I had to be. In my earpiece, I could hear the organised confusion of the control room. Teresa was asking how I was feeling and I could not give an audible answer. I had forgotten one important matter: no one would see this if it was terrible, only 200 people would know this show had happened. It had not been difficult to get an audience together; there are always people who willingly attend shows. I felt this audience would be baying for my blood. They had come to see the fall of Motivator, but this was not the Motivator show, it was the Derrick Evans Show, and I had the ability to be whomsoever I wanted to be.

I was looking for divine help but everything felt incomplete and ill-prepared. I knew in my heart of hearts that although I should be able to carry this off, just maybe I wanted too much for it to be a success.

The new Italian suit felt awkward. It was the best that Ciro Citterio could provide. As the Best Dressed Man of the Year, I was given a vast amount of clothing to wear. I had been exploiting this privileged position for a long time. I was so fortunate to be able to do this. I would make a gift of clothing to friends whenever a new leather jacket got soiled. Even Palmer had a pinstripe suit altered to fit her. I was looking good, but with nowhere to hide. All of a sudden, my collar felt two sizes smaller and my shoes too tight. Palmer was in the audience, and I was sure I would see her embarrassment.

I was given that familiar count. I walked down to the sound of "Welcome to the Derrick Evans Show," and the audience started cheering and clapping. Then, I was at the lectern announcing what the show was about, simultaneously being briefed in my earpiece and reading from the autocue.

The debate began well. Young offenders were a contentious issue and stirred up many comments from the audience. I moved around like a conductor with a disorganised orchestra. As the programme went on, I began to feel more comfortable and the suit no longer felt restrictive.

I spoke to a female victim who had been set upon by some youths and heard her story. Then I highlighted the history of a young man who had spent time in and out of young offender's institutions. The local council in all its wisdom decided that he would benefit from an all-expenses-paid round-the-world trip. He was sent off and had the time of his life, one that he had never envisioned. Now much older, he was suing the local authority for creating in him a taste for a lifestyle he could not maintain, and for exposing him to something he probably would never have achieved on his own. In other words, their decision made him want to steal more. The audience agreed that the council had wasted money on a joyride.

Then we showed them a film of a group of young men breaking into a factory and getting away with very little loot. I then asked the panel what they would recommend for such a situation.

Some wanted to lock up the offenders, others wanted them to undergo counselling. I went over to the local Labour MP, and asked him what would be the Labour view. He refused to answer, stating that he was not there as a Labour Party MP, so I asked him what was his view then. He uttered these words, which I didn't like and will never understand: "I don't like the way people like you ask these questions." I asked him what he meant by people like me. He was not forthcoming with an answer so I moved away.

I directed everyone back to the video tape and we watched the young men up in front of a judge and the sentences being handed out. Only when my name was mentioned did the audience realise that the video was about me. I went round for a reaction, to see whether the panel had changed their views, knowing what they knew now. There were a few replies of, "Well, you are different."

That part of the show went well, my performance went better than I expected, so we came on to the second subject; whether prostitution should be legalised or decriminalised.

I felt more in control here, although this was something that I had no particular view on. But the whole basis of this pilot was to show that I could handle a number of different issues and the technical procedures involved in keeping a show alive.

With the show over, I was congratulated, but in truth I did not feel that I had given it the best. I was assured by the production people that after editing, I would not be able to fault it. But after viewing the video, I was not convinced, so I went back to London to await Bruce's verdict.

Bruce said that he would submit it to the Network Centre, the regulatory body that decided what was acceptable for public viewing. Up to the end of the nineties, the centre ruled ITV with an iron hand, and in many ways restricted the progress of several new talents. They had their favourites who came up time and time again, presenting a variety of different shows. Breaking into this upper circle, it seemed, would sometimes depend on something other than professional criteria.

They replied sooner than I thought. They did not critique the programme content, its direction or production, but instead their letter, which annoyed Bruce, just stated that it was good to see Derrick doing something different; however, they felt uncomfortable with the way in which he expressed his views so forcibly.

Bruce was livid; he said he would appeal. I told him not to bother, but he did not want them to get away with it. He thought it was a racial slur. He felt the confrontation between me and the Labour MP was not thought to be good television. I went away, initially convinced that Bruce was right, in that the panel had felt television was not ready for a black man questioning prominent white people. Black presenters on television were mostly shown in 'safe' areas - that of news and comedy, and I was breaking the mould. Maybe they were right. If we had done a 'feel good' programme with a small element of seriousness, we might have received a more encouraging response. Bruce said he would hold on and wait until the appropriate time to resubmit it. However, he did not live long enough to see that happen.

It is just unfortunate that when you look at magazines and TV shows, there seems to be an absence of black faces, and very few get that large contract to tie them to a particular station. This is not the same if you are white. During my term on TV, Palmer and I were the only black people invited to many celebrity functions, and I was one of the few in the pages of celebrity magazines. I was never to get the opportunity to be a talk show host, but I still longed for the chance.

My next opportunity came when I was on an plane coming down from the North, and sitting next to me was a slim, attractive blonde, Caroline Kingsley. We spoke easily about our work. She was the trade PR person for the McVitie's range of products. So we talked about her job; she had to identify PR opportunities for McVitie's brands. She then mentioned a new product they were about to launch, Go-Ahead, a range of snacks, and I felt I could make a success of its promotion. I knew that if I could get to meet the brand's decision-makers, I could sell my case to them. This young lady seemed sent from heaven.

I asked Caroline to see if the marketing person would accept a proposal from me. We parted at Heathrow, and with a hug, she promised that she would be in touch about a possible meeting.

True to her word, a few days later I got a call saying the team at Go-Ahead would meet with me. I was elated, and even though I didn't have any idea of what to say, I knew the right words would come when it mattered.

I arrived in South London, nice and early for the meeting. I was instantly recognised in reception and got ushered up to the interview room. I had by now got used to public attention, although there were times I wished it were less invasive. On this occasion, though, my popularity would serve to bolster my position at this meeting.

There were quite a few people there, and with all the welcoming out the way, I thanked them for giving me the opportunity to tell them that I was the right person to promote their product.

I told them about the research that showed 95% of the UK public knew Mr Motivator. I also reminded them of two very important facts: I was younger than their other presenter, Jane Asher, and my appeal was across the board from the very young to Baby Boomers.

They listened, and slowly I knew I was winning them over, but they needed something more than the comparisons. Then it came to me: Go-Ahead was new – just like me; it was a fun product – just like me; and it was fat free – one of the messages that I regularly promoted to listeners.

I had proved I was able to hold a roadshow together, and this was how I felt this product should be promoted. We needed to get it in the hands of the consumer across as wide an audience as possible. People at the table were beginning to smile.

Then someone asked the question that made me realise that I got them. "How would you run the roadshow, and how much would it cost?"

Mr Motivator Says: *Let us look at what I did here. I did not wait for the knock at the door, I went out to find people I knew to open the door, and once inside, I was able to provide valuable information to convince marketers that I was a marketable product, a good wholesome image perfect for their brand.*

Always be prepared so that when the opportunity presents itself, you can shine.

This was where I made my exit. I had whetted their appetite; it was now time for my agent to negotiate.

Outside the conference room, Caroline told me I had been good. I nodded in agreement, made my excuses and left.

You know, that saying, 'Don't wait for your ship to come in, swim out to it,' was so apt at that moment, as once again, I proved that if you seize the moment, all you have to do is stop, look and listen. You will know that there is a golden opportunity waiting for all of us.

The proposal was to do a 20-city roadshow. I would have a team of four women working out with me. We would visit shopping centres across the UK, and in each centre, we would get shoppers working out with us and then we would feed the crowd with McVitie's snacks. Complimentary caps and T-shirts were given to anyone who had worked out.

Before I could finish the proposal, there was a call requesting a quote for doing a series of TV ads; they wanted a buyout figure. We asked for £100,000 for the advert and the roadshow would cost on top. They agreed quickly. They wanted to do the adverts immediately; filming would take place in South Africa, and we would fly out that December. I wanted Palmer, Abigail and James with me; they agreed.

Hello! magazine was duly informed that I would be in South Africa and that Abigail's birthday would be celebrated there. They agreed to feature it in the magazine.

Eight days in SA was a wonderful experience. I had been there during the apartheid years, and after the release of Mandela, I had gone with *GMTV* and visited the townships. I noticed a few changes then, but now that time had passed, I was looking forward to seeing how the life of the ordinary South African had been influenced.

It was a good flight on SA Airways and we all flew First Class. We had a lovely room in a hotel in Cape Town. Everyone who has been there says what a wonderful place Cape Town is, and yes, it is beautiful with lovely beaches, but freezing water.

We were to complete three 30-second ads and two ten-second ads, all in eight days, and even though we filmed in quite a few places, we managed the almost impossible.

The most memorable part of the trip was when we were filming on the beach. Picture this. I am on a beach which years before had signs up saying, 'No Blacks Allowed'. Now I am surrounded by many white assistants. How times had changed.

I came back to the UK knowing it would be all over the papers: *Mr Motivator takes the biscuit, Mr Motivator replaces Jane Asher, Mr Motivator takes charge of a £5 million account.*

That year, I was even busier than normal. *GMTV* was upset that I had gone away again and taken a contract with Go-Ahead. They felt that the station was entitled to a percentage of my earnings. I was reminded repeatedly that other presenters could not do adverts and did not enjoy the freedom I had to take on outside contracts. I ignored most of those remarks.

Although I had become more selective, I knew that it was only a question of time before I would no longer be the flavour of the month. I could get replaced so I was prepared to maximise whatever came my way. I moved at lightning speed to capitalise on what good fortune had bestowed on me.

Each week, I went around the country with my team, working in shopping centres and wowing the large crowds.

I am still amazed at the public's fascination with celebrities. Several handed me gifts, dolls they had made of me, lucky coins and personal items.

I was elated by the attention that was given me at every stop. The local press was there, and TV stations often showed up too. McVitie's was very pleased at the numbers who came to participate and sample their products; it worked, and worked very well.

At the end of the campaign, a survey was done, and the public recall of Mr Motivator was extremely high. However, at the end of the year, a contract renewal was denied.

There is an inherent danger in using a celebrity to promote a product. If he is already well-known, it can have the effect of giving more publicity to the celebrity than to the product. That was the case with Go-Ahead; there was all round good recall of me, but not enough of the product.

When I look back at 1997, I realise how busy I had become and Teresa Poole, my PA, was busier than ever. How she coped with all the work is amazing, but I needed her so much. She was able to get me to every appointment and personal appearance on time and calmly. Looking back at the diary, I wonder how I managed each day. There would be hundreds of calls, everyone asking me to open a new shop or to visit a child in need.

But now it was time for a break. I took up an invitation extended to me and my family years before by the Tourism Development Minister from the Seychelles.

As we got on the plane, we were amazed at the beautiful ladies sitting all around us. But then, amongst these strikingly well-dressed ladies, was my very young and chubby Abigail.

Her smile was so infectious and she bore so much resemblance to Palmer, who was a classic beauty and also a beautiful person. You could sense this easily by the way she looked after Abigail and me, and also the way she interacted with other people. Beauty has an effect on people in so many ways.

We had a very good stay in Seychelles, and a number of excursions stood out, such as a helicopter ride which gave us a bird's eye view of this very small island. Most days, we went wandering and meeting the friendly and interesting people, and we were impressed with the simplicity of the island lifestyle.

The Anniversary of The *Windrush*

The year 1998 was the 50th anniversary of the *Windrush*, the ship that took the first boatload of West Indian migrants to Britain to help the country regain its footing after the Second World War. A function was held at the Foreign Office. Tony Blair was Prime Minister, and Robin Cook was the Foreign Secretary.

Palmer and I were invited and as usual, we were outstandingly dressed. We milled around the room, and met many of the original travellers on this first ship to answer the call from Winston Churchill to come and save their mother country. These first West Indians also came for other reasons; it was an opportunity to earn good money quickly and send it to families back home.

From the very mouths of these survivors, we heard that the voyage was neither a wonderful experience, nor one of discovery. They were pioneers who became the backbone of the nursing institutions. They took jobs as bus and train drivers, construction workers and domestics, and they performed many duties that the average English citizen would prefer not to perform.

I had chatted enough and felt it was time to explore. We stepped outside the main reception room and stood at the top of the staircase, admiring the huge, austere paintings that hung from the walls.

As we stood there, I heard a voice say, "Amazing pictures, aren't they?" We looked round and saw Tony Blair coming up the stairs. We exchanged pleasantries. He knew me by sight as well as I knew him.

He said, "Do you know Robin Cook has a bigger office than me?" I said, "Surely not," so he said to come and have a look. We meandered around the corridors of the Foreign Office and stood outside some doors that must have been at least 12 feet tall. He pushed the doors open, and sure enough, it was a massive office. We wandered in, taken in by the splendour and opulence.

We enjoyed some jovial banter for a while before he had to leave to go into the reception. We all laughed and savoured what was a lovely moment in time.

Former Prime Minister John Major and I met each year at the yearly Child of Achievement Awards ceremony, of which he was patron. This special ceremony gave recognition to children who had shown acts of bravery in helping others, or who had survived against the odds. These children were genuine heroes, and every case was a bigger than life story.

The ceremony brought together many celebrities to present awards to the children. The former PM and I would always have some general chit-chat. He had a strong handshake, and I found him a most pleasant person and one who genuinely cared.

Sadly, this charity eventually stopped, which was a shame.

Palmer and I used to take Abigail to most of these events, and were always humbled by these young people, some just past the toddler stage. If Abigail had a cold, we fussed over her as if it was the end of the world.

We would go home with a better knowledge of the lives of others and their suffering, often with a heavy heart, but at the same time with a sense of gratitude for our many blessings.

Chapter 15: Semi-retirement in Jamaica

Our marriage goes from strength to strength. Palmer and I do nothing special to celebrate anniversaries. We made a decision years ago that rather than having arguments about birthdays and anniversaries, we would fill all the days in-between with giving each other cards and presents when necessary. That arrangement has worked because while others argue over the forgetfulness of their partner, we don't have to.

You could say that our relationship does not run the so-called 'normal' course, but what is normal? Surely it's what works for you as a team. We don't take each other for granted, and I believe that we have always pre-empted, then put into place actions that help to avoid what may potentially develop into a powder keg.

We have never had to work at our relationship; confidence once betrayed, the charm is broken. I would never bring home anything that would destroy her trust in me. I am very considerate of her feelings, as she is of mine, teasing notwithstanding, which is in my nature and I cannot help it! We have mutual respect. I can be myself with her; there is nothing that I cannot say in front of her. Therefore, I am an open book. Jealousy does not rear its head either, and that is unusual. I can be out with her and flirt and tease to my heart's content. The recipient is almost always amazed by Palmer's reaction, which is one of happy encouragement. I am always asked, "How do you get away with it?" Simple, she knows her worth. I am a very lucky man, and I know it!

This is a woman who when she was younger, due to her fear of the dentist's needle, would rather suffer the pain without an injection, so with that kind of past, I am sure that she will remain brave. For me, I would rather be a live coward than a dead hero.

You cannot help but notice how we change as the years roll by. I observe the way in which Abigail is changing every day. One noticeable thing is that I have begun to count the years that potentially could be left before my circle of life is complete, so I have started to organise things for those who will follow. Time is precious, and we must make the most of it.

I do look around and I know exactly how I am going to be when I get old, so for now I will continue savouring every moment, and every opportunity to dance one more time.

2005 was the first year in a long while that I felt slightly free. My work and home life became more organised. The business took on its own momentum, and I am slowly getting into a more controlled arena, and that has to be a good thing. After all, part of the reason that I came to Jamaica was to semi-retire.

During November 2005, my mate of 20 years, David French, finally moved in with us. We have a rather strange arrangement, but before I explain, let me take you back.

David has been in my circle of friends for a long time, and a regular companion on my visits to Jamaica. On many such trips, we fantasised about having a bar on the beach, any beach. He has always wanted to move out here, but thought Janice, his wife, would not entertain such a thing. She was in a good position working at a university, and David worked as marketing and promotions manager for Allders.

He mentioned it, but once they started having children, he was sure Jamaica would not happen. First Esme, my god-daughter, came along, and David didn't look forward to years travelling on the road and not seeing much of his family. Janice had gone back to work, and found it stressful combining motherhood and career.

One day in January 2003, Janice came home after a gruesome journey through snow and asked David if he was serious about emigrating to Jamaica.

I had often spoken to them about quality time with their family and extended family. But before they could leave, they had a house and jobs to sort out, and then Janice got pregnant again, and eventually after the arrival of Stefan, they were able to sell their home. Along with the kids, they are now here in Jamaica.

Our arrangement is quite unusual in that they will be building a home on our land. Construction has already started. David is now sales director of H'Evans Scent, my hilltop health retreat. Janice will be teaching yoga and for them, life is going to be great. They are already seeing the benefit of the move. They both have more time for each other and the children, and they are all healthier than ever. The future is looking bright.

Business-wise, we had a number of groups coming in for team building and motivational activities. These are one-day events for large corporations that provide activities such as treasure hunts, 'Climbing the Zip,' and solving puzzles that bind the team together. This side of the business is developing and it is an area that will provide a large portion of our revenue.

The tourist side of business is being worked on, but I had to face a two-year wait to get my operating licence and no matter what I did, it was turned down. After two negative decisions, I called the agencies responsible. I was given no reason for the decision, so I wrote to the then Prime Minister, the Hon. PJ Patterson. In my 12-page dossier, I outlined the catalogue of problems that I had been experiencing. I explained that if tourism in Jamaica was to be developed, then all relevant agencies needed to work together. I told the Prime Minister that it was not a level playing field. Who you knew mattered more than the viability of the tourism entity.

So armed with this document, I went to Kingston. I knew the name of the building where the PM lived. The policewoman on duty said she would ensure that the PM received it.

I decided there and then that if there was not a positive outcome from my letter, I would give up and leave Jamaica behind.

Robbery

As a family, we will never forget the events of the night of 12ᵗʰ February 2005.

It was a Saturday and we had been out shopping. Abigail had spent the morning horseback riding. She came back with glowing praise from her trainer. She was a natural. When her horse bolted, others would have gone over the neck, but not Abigail. She stayed on, and now she was convinced that she was just the best, considering how little time she had been riding.

We had invited over two very good friends of ours, Konrad and Madeline Bayliss, together with their young children, Zack, in the same class as Abigail, and Brianna, who, at five, was small for her age but drop-dead gorgeous.

David and Janice were out for a Valentine's meal, and had brought in babysitters for Esme and Stefan.

The Bayliss family arrived at 6.30 p.m. and I told them there was no need to lock the car as we always felt safe not doing so. Palmer and I showed them to the two rooms we had prepared for them. They are licensed firearm holders, and they took out their guns and put them on top of the bedroom cupboard, out of the children's way.

We went downstairs and sat at the breakfast bar talking, laughing and relaxing. Miguel had gone out to get his hair plaited, Ali was in his room, David and Janice had already gone out, and the babysitters were in the units, away from the main house.

Everything felt peaceful. The balcony door was open.

And then it happened. Out of the corner of my eye, I saw someone run in and I heard Madeline say, "Look." I saw someone wearing a mask, brandishing a gun and followed closely by at least six or seven young men.

The masked man knew where he was going. He knew the layout of the house, because he was using only hand signals to direct his band of robbers. We did not have a chance to move because it all happened very quickly. I had failed to react, I was numb because I was convinced no one would ever dare break in. After all, we had dogs, double fencing and we were safe; but here were intruders!

The masked man walked by me, hit Konrad on the side of his face with the gun, and made his way directly to Ali's room, taking a couple of cohorts with him. Our house is structured so strangers can't see there are rooms behind the utility room. Very few people realise there is an apartment there, that Ali occupied.

They brought Ali out and started to tie him up, face down on the floor. He was gaffer taped, had clothes tied around his head, and was roughed up more than anyone else.

Someone turned off most of the lights. At knife point, we were told to remove our jewellery, money, phones, anything of value. I tried to catch Palmer's hand; what of her large diamond ring? My heart sank when I didn't feel it on her finger.

I took off everything and gave it to the masked man. The other men kept insisting we should not look at them, so we kept our heads down. I trembled out of fear for my family, uncertainty and because my mind kept replaying the news footage we saw of families getting robbed.

Madeline and Konrad were beside themselves, begging for mercy. Their children, feeding off their anguish, became upset. Abigail just asked who these people were; she was inquisitive about everything but she was not afraid. Palmer was calm and, using a very soft voice, kept reassuring Abigail and the others.

Konrad and I were ordered to lie down on our faces, and they gaffer taped our hands behind us. They taped up everyone else's wrists and ankles, then started to ransack the house.

They were concerned about who might come back and they wanted silence, so we obeyed. I prayed David and Janice would not come back early. Through slitted eyes, I could see the men packing videos and electrical appliances into bags.

The masked man came over and, in a muffled voice, demanded the money. I told him it was in a black bag in the office. He went to look, but he couldn't find it, so he came back and warned me not to jeopardise the lives of my wife and family for the sake of money.

I told him I would take them to the bag, but he insisted that my wife showed him where it was.

Palmer went, and a few moments later she returned with it. I continued to tremble as I listened to the sound of Madeline's breathing. She had a history of heart problems and I was concerned that all this was too much for her. Palmer, though, just kept on murmuring softly, saying they would be alright, just co-operate, all will be well, a non-stop litany of assurances, and indeed one of the robbers did try to reassure us, even bringing a cushion for Abigail to rest her head on. But all through this, a suspicion was beginning to form in my mind.

I soon realised they had found the Bayliss' guns. The leader wanted to know where my gun was and if other guns were around. I told him no. He disappeared for a few minutes, and returned holding the lid of our underground safe, with a key in the lock. I knew it! I now had an idea who the masked man was. I could not be sure when he came in, but the way he was directing the others around our house had made me suspicious, and bringing the lid of the safe over to me with a silver key in it confirmed this could only be one of two people.

Four years previously, we had the underground safe installed by the contractor who built the house. He had come from England to do the job, but he was eventually dismissed because of thievery and fraudulently using money assigned for building and workmen's wages. A young man who had worked for him became our caretaker, looking after the house while we were away.

The safe was in a small cupboard buried under the floor and disguised by floor tiles, so quite impossible to see. At the time, it held various papers, as well as travellers' cheques. One day, Palmer had found £500 worth of cheques missing. We reported it to the local police, who did not investigate, and although we had two keys, we couldn't find one of them, so we avoided putting any more money in it.

Our man held the lid down towards my face and wanted to know where the money was now and how to open the other safe.

So he had found the other safe in the bedroom upstairs. He wanted my wife to go, but I told them to take me, as I was the only one who knew the combination.

They untied me and three men escorted me upstairs. As I went up, I tripped on the top step, and that made them even more jittery.

They wanted me to hurry up, but combinations take time. I told them this as one held the gun to the back of my head and the other two kept flicking a knife towards my face. Once the safe was opened, I was forced onto the floor whilst they emptied out the contents. There was JA $450,000 dollars, US $3000, about £450, and a number of pocket watches and gold chains.

Whilst I was on the floor, the masked man asked if a beautiful gold and diamond necklace and matching earrings were 'costume jewellery'. At this point, I was convinced I knew who he was. I couldn't let on, but I knew that a typical Jamaican would ask if "dis ting real?" I had known this robbery had to be by someone in the know. I had suspected the builder of the house or his assistant, but now I knew for sure that it was the builder.

I was taken back downstairs, and this time I was tied up more thoroughly. The term I have heard used was hog-tied, arms and legs behind, and not only did they use gaffer tape, but also rope.

They were using a bit more force and I thought I ought to get a little more vocal, so when they tied my hands, I started to let out a yell, for which I got cuffed around the head. I also kept my hands stretched out which ensured the rope did not tighten too much, allowing me room to undo it.

They kept going into the kitchen. I could hear them opening and closing the fridge door. As they stepped by, I tried to see if there were any distinguishing marks, but all I got was a nostril full of bad-smelling feet.

I was not comfortable; my face was resting on one of the children's bottoms. Palmer kept on talking calmly to everyone, and was having a job keeping Abigail's head down; she was now even more inquisitive about the men.

My emotions overcame me a couple of times and I'd say, "Please, do not hurt my family," but at some stage, a peace came over me. I felt calm about it all. Yes, I could see the reflection on a kitchen unit of a man standing over me with a gun pointing towards my head, but I was no longer afraid.

The lights went out and came back on ten seconds later. The robbers were worried and the boss asked me what had just happened. I told him that the generator had just switched itself off and we were now on the local JPS electricity feed. He asked if that had happened automatically; I said yes.

That was a lie. I knew that Miguel had come home and had switched the generator off to go on local power.

Miguel, who lived with us and did all our cooking, is a multi-talented young man. He also painted and repaired anything mechanical or electrical.

I had been friends with Ali's family for years. They were all over the place and so he had come to live with us as he was left at home with nothing to do.

I prayed he would not come in to watch TV as he sometimes did. I whispered to Palmer and Abigail that I loved them very much.

We breathed easier as we realised he wasn't going to come in. I could now hear further rushing around and uncertainty washed over me again. I had kept my eyes closed for most of it. Now I strained to see something, but all I could make out was more feet stepping over me. Then someone in passing kicked off my glasses and stood on them. I asked them to be careful, but they did not care. I was now unable to see very much.

Throughout all this was the calming dulcet tones of Palmer's voice: keeping the level of fear down, listening out for Madeline's sobbing, reassuring her, and ensuring Abigail did not see or say much. Her calmness kept all our spirits up. I was amazed by her tenacity and that she showed no fear. I could not be more proud of her.

I heard the voice of the 'kind' robber. He kept reassuring the children, much to the annoyance of his colleagues, who cussed him for wasting time on us. Even so, he continued to tell us that no one would be hurt, we would all be OK. I wanted to believe him, and although his was one lonely voice, it gave me hope.

Time seemed to lengthen. I was not aware of how long they had been with us, but I became aware of them trying to open the front door, which they couldn't, so they moved around to the side entrance.

There was a feeling of urgency now, and all but one robber disappeared. This one bent over us and in as menacing a tone as he could muster, told us not to move, we were not to go to the police, and, in true gangster movie style, he said, "We know where you live." With that, he disappeared.

We heard the dogs barking and getting agitated, so Palmer and I knew they were no longer in the house and this meant one of two things: either they were heading toward the units or they were leaving by walking past the dog area. Either way, it was time to get loose.

I managed to untie myself and so did Palmer. She ran to find a knife to free the others while I ran outside to see if the children and babysitters were safe. I sprinted across the driveway to the units, carefully opening the doors. I found everyone asleep. I breathed a sigh of relief as I came outside, hearing the sound of cars rushing away in the distance.

Back inside, although it was as if waking from a sleep, we began to take stock of the situation.

Everyone was freed, but Palmer had a hard time getting Ali out of his bonds. The robbers had hog-tied him so tightly, he had lost circulation to his arms and legs, and they had taped towels around his head. As soon as he revived, he said he knew who the boss was. Ali fought him once, for brutalising a young woman, resulting in him being admitted to hospital; that's why Ali was treated so roughly.

Palmer had managed, miraculously, to keep her mobile phone – Abigail had been instrumental in helping her hide it! I called the police and they said they would notify the local police. I thought we would immediately get a call from Bamboo Police station, but minutes ticked by with no response. I called them and was told the police were on their way.

I held Palmer. They had taken her necklace, a smaller version of mine, and her fingers were now devoid of her wedding and engagement rings.

I felt so sorry they were lost. The diamond was at least three carats, and had been specially designed by a long-lost friend in Hatton

Gardens. For a moment, I forgot that our glass was half-full and not half-empty when, with a little smile, Palmer popped her tongue out. Nestled in her mouth was her ring.

We laughed, and I admired even more her dignity and quick-mindedness through the whole harassing episode.

Palmer took charge of our guests. We felt awful for the Bayliss couple, who for once had put caution to the wind and ended up in their worst nightmare. A conservative couple, they saw criminals everywhere and around every corner.

We looked around the house. Every room had been ransacked; drawers had been overturned and everywhere was the evidence of a robbery. I suddenly started to shiver as the realisation that we were alive hit us.

We surveyed our losses, but thankfully they were all material – nearly all of our electrical items, all our cameras, laptops and jewellery; of course, all the money. My neck and fingers felt naked.

David and Janice arrived home, only to be caught up in the aftermath. The babysitters were awakened, and became so hysterical we were glad they had been asleep through it all.

I was glad David and Janice were not home to share this experience, or they might have reconsidered their decision to remain in Jamaica.

The police eventually arrived. Somehow our emergency message had been relayed as 'robbers on foot' and so they had not hurried to the scene. We gave statements and they left, promising to return by 9.30 a.m. to take fingerprints and full statements.

We finally went to bed, with Abigail in the middle, and we huddled together and thanked God that he had spared our lives; we had been given a second chance. Now we needed to make changes to our security that would make us safer.

For quite a few days, David was stressed. He took it badly and on Janice's advice, we gave him plenty of space to heal and come out of it. Janice, on the other hand, showed no signs of depression or anything; she was very philosophical about the whole thing. Maybe there is something to say for being a Yogi.

Konrad and Madeline became distant, and Palmer and I thought they were focusing on what might have happened, instead of what did. Thinking we could have been killed, or the women sexually assaulted, was a perilous thought. But we understood that they were going through a guilt trip, especially Konrad who was made to feel, not only powerless to defend his family, but also careless, in respect of the loss of his firearm.

Palmer and I talked it through, and then set about doing damage control.

The next day was Sunday, and it became a very uplifting day for us. News travels fast in a small village, and many of our neighbours were gathered at the gate from early in the morning, offering help and comfort. In all, through the day, 95% of the village, and many from the surrounding communities, came to pay their respects.

What truly angered them was the children being duct taped, and everyone focused on who they thought was involved. They also noted certain absences; people who were affiliated or had association with the very person we knew was part of the gang.

The police arrived late on Sunday morning. We gave statements and they went about taking fingerprints. I got in touch with a security firm and arranged for a security guard to be in our home full-time, until I was able to put right all the areas that made us so vulnerable.

On Monday, I had various companies in to give quotations for improving or putting in new fenced areas, particularly behind the units that had given the robbers easy access. Earlier that day, I had surveyed the area outside and noticed that although eight men had come in to rob us, the grass was not trampled down. There was only one line, so they were following one person, someone who knew his way around, providing further confirmation of the leader's identity. They had come across an area of fencing that was not visible from the road, but this section was lower and I had always intended to make this good. To have come across here suggested prior knowledge of the area.

As I got quotations from alarm and fencing companies, I came to the conclusion I had been very lax. I had made the mistake of thinking that, as I had guard dogs, no one in their right mind would try to rob us.

But I had not taken account of the period when the dogs were still in their kennels. In the UK, we take full precautions. We have an alarm fitted in the house with fencing around the property, yet here I was in Jamaica, a place with a reputation for being more crime-ridden, and I had not taken appropriate action to reduce the likelihood of an attack.

By Tuesday, three men had been arrested. They were caught some 60 miles away in Portmore, on the outskirts of the capital, Kingston. They were said to be acting suspiciously, and when they were apprehended, police found a camera and mini-disc player in their possession. We were not able to identify them in a line-up, but one was given 18 months for receiving stolen property.

Police raided the house of the builder, and of course did not find anything in his possession, but it was only a matter of time.

We now know that one other who worked here and was involved has been killed, and the leader of the pack never was apprehended; he has gotten away with the robbery.

We got on with our lives, but it is interesting to note that we were robbed just a week after I was awarded my tourism licence; life is strange.

The Pinks

During our time in Jamaica, we spent a great deal of quality time with two very special people, Con and Patsy Pink. He was 80, she was 72. Palmer had told me about a place on the way up the hill to our home called Sleepy Hollow. She mentioned the view, the ambiance, the peace and tranquillity, and she had been up there many times just to have a look around.

So she took me to see it. As we drove up the stone road, the first building we came to was made of very old traditional wood and concrete, and hanging over the balcony was Mrs Pink. She smiled and invited us in, where we met Mr Pink. Both were small in stature, about five feet two, and they smiled a lot. Immediately, I felt that they were like long-lost friends, and they became our adoptive parents.

We sat and talked for hours. The house is about 120 years old, and the property of several hundred acres had been in Mr Pink's family for well over 50 years. When his father died, the land had been split between him and his brother, and although he got the smaller share, he managed to get the side facing the coast, and a house with a view to die for.

Sleepy Hollow is an eco-tourism business they had developed, right at the top of their land. It is hauntingly beautiful, and in its very naturalistic setting, had a panoramic vista that spread right across a canyon, to nearby Seville, to the North Coast towns of Salem and St. Ann's Bay.

Over the years, with the onset of age, and their own family spread over the globe, the Pinks have found it difficult keeping the business going. They are gradually selling the land acre by acre, but are loath to sell Sleepy Hollow. They wanted it kept in the family, in the hope that one of their children would be able to continue the business. People have seen Sleepy Hollow and want to buy it, but with a view to developing and changing the whole concept. The land had a touch of the real Jamaica about it. There are flowers and plants everywhere which Mr Pink laboriously researched and planted. He knew the origins of each and every one. He had an expansive knowledge of Jamaica's history and lore, and a way of storytelling that we could just sit and listen for hours. I would say he is the most accomplished unofficial historian Jamaica has, and his words should have been recorded for posterity.

Since that first meeting Palmer, Abigail and I have been regular visitors. We met Cherise, their daughter, who is the manager of a spa based in one of Jamaica's five-star hotels. She seemed more like their mother than their child, and I do have to say she had her work cut out for her; they often behaved like mischievous school kids. Mr Pink had a devilish twinkle in his eye and was extremely sharp, his dry humour and subtle wit making for enjoyable and exciting interludes.

It was after one of our many visits that I told the Pinks that they should not sell this land, but instead hold on to it and let it remain in the family.

Mr Pink just said that of all the people he had met, I was the only one who did not want to destroy his legacy. He was in favour of us working with his family to help put Sleepy Hollow on the map again.

At that time, we were just putting into action the concepts of H'Evans Scent, so Sleepy Hollow would form part of my long-term plans and would be a natural progression for us.

Our families became so entwined, hardly a day passed without us seeing each other. We eventually met their other children. Carol lived in Berlin, and Nadine and Johnny lived in the United States. Everyone got on so well, it was as if we had known each other for years.

A few years before, Mr Pink had gone to Germany to visit Carol, and on returning to Jamaica he felt unwell. I took him for a medical check-up. The pain he was in meant it was difficult to manoeuvre him so I had to lift him just like a baby and put him on the X-ray table. It was a recurring prostate problem and he had to undergo surgery to correct it.

He went into surgery November 2003. After that, the house was full of people, friends and family all basically saying goodbye. Palmer and I arrived at one such occasion and promptly left; we refused to be part of this wake of the living.

The next day, we returned, determined to lift his spirits. I had a plan to give him new targets and goals, such as helping me to do our landscaping, something he had a lot of experience in, and also to help me organise a charity cycle ride around the island. This was a trying time for everyone, but he made a good recovery, and so in early 2004, I suggested throwing a 'Celebration of Life' party for him. The Pinks thought it a great idea, and as it was something we wanted to do for them, all we needed was the guest list.

It was H'Evans Scent's maiden voyage, the first event. We laid on food, music and atmosphere. Speeches were made and everyone expressed their love for the man I nicknamed 'Pinkerton.'

For most of 2004, we saw each other every day. Palmer and I dubbed a room at our home the 'Pink's Room' and on most weekends, this is where they would be found. We just wanted to shower them with all our love. And for Abigail, they were the grandparents she never had.

Mr Pink had been on painkillers all year, and that had two effects; it improved his quality of life, and it masked the spread of his cancer.

By the end of 2004, he was starting to slow down. We were all getting concerned as some days he would talk of being in pain, having indigestion, loss of appetite and generally feeling unwell. I would try to get him to go for a walk and sometimes he did, but no great distance. He returned home tired, slept more, and later became more reluctant to go out.

Just before Christmas, we took the Pinks to Kingston and spent a weekend in a hotel. That November, I bought a Pajero, mindful that the pick-up truck was very uncomfortable for Pinkerton to travel in. This pleased him and his laughter returned the more he became pain-free.

Nadine's children, Thalia and Hannah, came to stay with their grandparents for Christmas. They were great, and got on really well with Abigail, to the point where everyone spent Christmas at our home.

Just after the festivities, Mr Pink's condition deteriorated. He ate a little food, but all he wanted to do was sit in his favourite place in the lounge, listening to his music. Although he was being brave, we knew that the pain was getting to him and that he needed to get a full check-up.

One day his legs just gave way, and he was not able to stand or walk. The pain was concentrated in his lower back and he had difficulty sitting and lying down. This time, Mrs Pink insisted on calling the doctor and the next day I took him to the local hospital to get more X-rays done.

I carried Mr Pink into the reception area and found a wheelchair for him. He gritted his teeth against the pain in his back. I deliberately took the wrong turning and ended up in the maternity ward, much to his amusement.

Mrs Pink and I managed to get him into a hospital gown and waited for the porters to take him to X-ray. They came but they didn't know how to handle him and caused excruciating pain when they tried to move him. Mr Pink called for me and I lifted him onto the X-ray table and manoeuvred him into place. I tried to make the nurse laugh, which in turn made him smile, but the pain of every movement was evident. With the X-rays all done, I met Mrs Pink in the changing room and we slowly got him out of the unflattering hospital gown.

Dr 'Poley' Betton helped me get Mr P into the car, but I wanted to delay the going home process. I felt this might be the last time we would all be able to travel together, and I wanted him to take in the wonderful views of St. Ann.

The doctor would call later with the results, so I took a long route home, all along the seafront, through the bay and up into the hills, then on into Ocho Rios. We had some hot fish soup, and Mr Pink enjoyed it. We took our time and only headed home when he reluctantly admitted he was getting tired. I think the same thought went through his head – this was going to be his last outing. Carrying him up the stairs was a job and a half, and I was grateful that I had made arrangements for David to be there.

When the phone call came, Mrs Pink informed us the X-rays had indicated that his bones were paper thin and a broken rib was pushing against the central nervous canal. That was why his legs had given way and why the pain in his back was so acute. What we now needed to do was make him comfortable. Their bedroom was changed to accommodate him better, but he still hankered for his day room, which was light and airy, and at least had a view when the patio doors were open. It was also very cluttered. So Palmer and I took a weekend and cleared it. It got a lick of paint, and Mr Pink moved in, much the happier for seeing the sky.

By May 2005, Mr Pink was even frailer. Palmer and I still visited daily and assisted Mrs Pink, but she later employed a full-time nurse to help her. She also located a motorised hospital bed through a good friend so we set it up and he was much more comfortable, still orchestrating his family's life, still the heartbeat of his little community, and still the elder statesman.

I learned so much from him. His life's experiences were so wonderful to hear and I found his advice invaluable. He had such a grasp of so many matters in life, so I would sit...and talk, listen, and absorb. He was incredibly alert, and there was much that I wanted to know. There was urgency when he spoke, as if he knew how short his time was. Unknown to him, we were told four to eight weeks. So we cherished our time with him.

Before I left for the UK in August, I told him the devil and all his old friends are not ready for him yet. Heaven is a little bit overcrowded and busy after the tsunami, so he should wait until I got back.

Palmer and Abigail were there most days, and I got regular updates.

Mr Motivator says: *Getting older is part of the circle of life and the old saying 'Once a man twice a child' was true for Mr Pink. He was helpless and there is some indignity to having someone doing the very basic of human needs, but in spite of all this, he had a lot to be grateful for.*

So many people die suddenly and never have the time to tell their loved ones what they think or feel about them. Mr Pink was a wise man, and he loved people, so he took the opportunity to say individual goodbyes to his family and his many special friends.

It was a beautiful balmy day on 1ˢᵗ September 2005. From his hilltop ranch, Con requested the doors to his room be left wide open to the flush of the beautiful orchids and that legendary view of the very blue Caribbean Sea. He said he wanted 'natural oxygen.' He said his parents had been waiting on him since early that morning. He said goodbye to his beloved wife Patsy and asked her to leave the room. He thanked his nurse telling her he was feeling no pain. Then he took the last whiff of 'natural oxygen' and peacefully took his exit. Con died as he had lived, in dignity, giving love, and spirited to the end.

I reached his bedside just after he had departed, feeling a great sense of loss, but grateful for having known this wonderful man.

On the home front, 2005 started with the building of David's house. Palmer and I were content, and settled into our daily life. We were so busy, we had no chance to train at Hedonism, so some days we went for a run locally, or trained downstairs in our home gym.

Each week, David and I went to Kingston to see different companies and offer them team building and fun day breaks at H'Evans Scent. We had to take this approach as getting our tourist licence took so long.

My, my, my! Out of the blue on 6th February, I received a call which reaffirmed my faith in fair play and justice. Miss Geri Roye of the Tourism Product Development Company called to say she had some good news. My JTB licence had been granted and would be available for collection soon.

I called Palmer and she laughed fit to burst, then I gave David the news. The cloud that had been over all of us had floated away. We had been very careful how we celebrated so the Sanatogen wine – you know, the wine that fortifies the over-40s – has been our champagne. Two weeks later, I collected my licence and we were ready to start to recoup some of the investments I had made over the years.

In October 2009, an idea I had conceived some three years before came to fruition. For many years, I had wanted to have a Charity Bike Ride around Jamaica, in aid of Marie Curie. I had devised a route and drawn up plans.

They adopted the idea and employed the services of an event company, who joined forces with the Cycle Club of Jamaica, under the guidance of a lady called Jennifer Hilton. The ride was to take place over seven days; 40 people came from the UK, and each had to be sponsored to a minimum of £4,500.

Beginning in Kingston, each day they would ride 60 to 100k, check into a pre-arranged hotel and next morning, back in the saddle again. We were chaperoned by two policemen on bikes and a team of doctors.

What an amazing challenge, but suffice to say that what kept me going was the continual thought that so many would benefit from the efforts of a few. The hills en route saw me gasping for air. I decided very early on that I would go with the leading pack of five riders. You know that feeling when you make a bravado decision and then very quickly you wished you hadn't?

They were burning rubber on the hills. They warned me to get in the right gear and then attack like there's no tomorrow, and whatever I do, don't change gear on the hills, and don't stand up.

As a hill came in sight, everything they said resonated with me but even though I found a way of pedaling forwards, I looked like I was going back even faster. Every hill, and there were many, caused me the same effort, and it was like everything I learnt at the previous hill had no bearing on how I faced the next challenge.

At the finish line, the hugs and the cheers made it so worthwhile, and I was grateful to have been given the strength and tenacity to see it through to the end. Altogether, 40 people had raised over £100,000 for a good cause. Once my groin returned to normal, I would make my decision as to whether I would do this again. It was good, that sense of achievement is always good to have.

But I had so many things to celebrate, so many things to be grateful for. One amazing transformation happened during the year that I must tell you about. It is something that made me so proud.

My son James had been drifting after his degree in Drama; he saw himself as a serious actor in waiting. During that time, he came to Jamaica to learn more about business.

Since 2008, he had been very helpful in the running of H'Evans Scent and he brought an air of originality and youthfulness to my organisation. His first responsibility was to help with the setting up of our paintball operation. I had worked away at getting permission for nearly ten years. Each time, the authorities in Jamaica kept saying no, paintball was a way of glorifying crime and it sent the wrong message. James showed in a report that there was no relationship between paintball and gun crime, and asked, if there was, how would one explain the high level of crime in Jamaica?

We received our permission in the middle of 2008.

James was instrumental in making our paintball operation happen. It is now a wonderful legacy and it provides a good amount of turnover to H'Evans Scent.

But the story I wanted to tell you about is more meaningful and motivational than a lot of other good things in my life.

One day in the middle of 2010, James came in and told Palmer and I the news. He had decided to get fit and healthy. He had looked at himself and did not like what he saw.

I almost fell off my chair. I was sceptical Could this be for real? Was this his light bulb moment, and would it last? I would watch and see.

He started to jog. Moving 247lbs, 17.5 stones, was tough and he was feeling it. From the window, I could see him jogging on the spot, using the mini-trampette, bouncing away. After a while, he would come into the house, out of breath and sweating.

Out came the scales to weigh his portions; meat was the first casualty, and fats, creams, cakes and biscuits followed. My son a vegetarian? Oh, his plan was to be one for six days and celebrate on the seventh. His bedroom wall was covered with a huge chart, weeks across the top, exercises down the side, pictures of well-toned muscles, pictures of good-looking models, fitness trainers, and weight-lifters. This served to chart his progress.

We soon started to see a difference. People were beginning to notice, and more importantly, he noticed. The distance travelled increased: 5k, 10k 20k, all timed so he could show progress. The iPhone became his new brother. He was wearing out his trainers, and new ones became necessary.

All his large clothing was being given away as new clothing was bought. If he got injured, he slowed down for a bit, but as soon as he was about 70% recovered, he was back out there. Continually he modified and changed his routine, to keep motivated.

After one year of training, he was almost at his goal, and he had made himself proud. He started taking pictures of his six-pack and he sent those back to us from the UK. When you lose 80 pounds, you lose a person, but in so doing, you gain yourself.

Mr Motivator says: *No one can force you into making a change in your life. You need to look in the mirror, like what you see, and then decide to make changes or not. That light bulb moment happens for each of us and when it does, all you need to do is make a decision and follow it through.*

Rejuvenation

Love needs a holiday sometime and I have always endorsed Palmer having time away from the family when she could. It was not always possible, but a few years ago, I was invited onto a new reality show where a number of celebrities would be taken to a spa in Thailand and the public would see them going through internal cleansing. I promptly declined, but the write-up made a lot of sense. You go away to a far-flung spa and you drink lots of stuff that cleans you out. Then you avoid solid foods for seven days, and eventually, after drinking this coffee substance, your colon starts to expel different-coloured substances.

After ten days in this memorable location, you leave feeling rejuvenated, and at the same time you lose a lot of weight. They say that for every decade you are alive, your colon holds onto at least one pound of waste matter. So if you are 50, you will have at least five pounds of matter that is of no use.

I read numerous articles and did my research, and everyone who visited this location spoke of light-headedness, headaches, and disorientation - and then, after a week, the great feeling comes and the weight starts to fall off. A loss of some 20lbs seems the norm.

If you ever needed a kick-start to feeling better, to start to lose weight, then this could be the place to visit.

I did not need to lose weight and I could and would not go to any location like this. I just felt that inviting the public into such a personal space did not feel sensible to me. So I told the producers that I could not go. But on evaluating the literature, I wondered about Palmer. After having Abigail, she had put on a lot of weight; it had been difficult for her.

Palmer did not wait for me to finish telling her about it; she wanted to go, and after the first visit, she came back nearly 20lbs lighter. She felt and looked great; I saw the difference when she got home.

I could always tell when the love of herself returned. When her confidence was at its highest, when she knew she was the centre of attention, she would walk into a room as if she owned it. When getting ready, she did not hide in the other room, when showering, she left the door open. When she felt great, her choice of what to wear was the brightest of colours.

She would fall in love with herself all over again, once she felt good. I too would feel the same; I could not resist her.

Mr Motivator Says: *I want to speak to both women and men here, for greater clarity. Men, you must recognise that changes in a woman happens in many forms and she needs your full support and understanding. When she gets pregnant, so many changes go into overdrive: change in shape, hormones, attitude, patience and, most of all, priorities. No longer will you be the focus of her attention; mother-to-be starts to prepare for the impending delivery and she needs continual reassurance that you are still there and that you do still love her. This you must do without being prompted. Surprise her with cards that have great meaning. That meal, breakfast in bed, that anticipation of her likely needs, will pay amazing benefits.*

After delivery, she will not be happy with her shape and she will be taking time to focus on being a mother. You need to rise to the plate with the knowledge that given enough time, she will get back to the person she once was. Notice the changes in her, the way she moves, and those little things will help you to keep annoyances to a minimum.

She may want to argue about the simplest things, but to her these are important. Your understanding and patience hinged with understanding will keep you both being loving until you can fall in love all over again.

She has now been to Koh Samui many times, the last time was in January 2013. She left me looking after Abigail, and I loved these times because it meant I had to do everything that I had done many years before when looking after Carolyne. This bonding was great and my whole time would be focused on looking after Abigail, while Palmer's time was on looking after Palmer. I saw this as a win-win situation.

That February, we had planned to all meet in the UK, Palmer on her way back from Koh Samui, Abigail and I would fly up to the UK and we would visit a number of Sixth Form Colleges with a view to Abigail going there when she graduated from Westwood High School.

It seemed like just yesterday that we were pushing her in a pram. She would be 15 and I hated the thought of her boarding away. But, I needed her out of Jamaica, a place I no longer recognise. Respect for ladies, young children, law and order was at an all-time low. A small island, Jamaica was near the top on the murder league table around the world. Palmer and I could not wait to get her to the UK.

From Glen Prep, her first primary school, to her current school, we have ensured that she was taken to and picked up safely from school. We had seen and heard over the years about many missing girls and teenagers. We were very worried about Abigail's security. Yes, we were going to miss her, but better she was in the UK where we would feel a lot safer. We saw four colleges, but Abigail from all her research had already made up her mind about CATS Canterbury. We still went through the formality of seeing each one, from North to Central and South of England, each one tried to tempt us with the best they had to offer.

It was going to be expensive, because although she was born in the UK and I had spent my whole life paying into the system, Abigail would still be treated as a foreign student. She would pay an arm and a leg to be a psychologist, but that is what she wanted. I am prepared to provide every one of my children with the best legacy that any parent can offer: a good education, which I knew will open many doors and give them a good future.

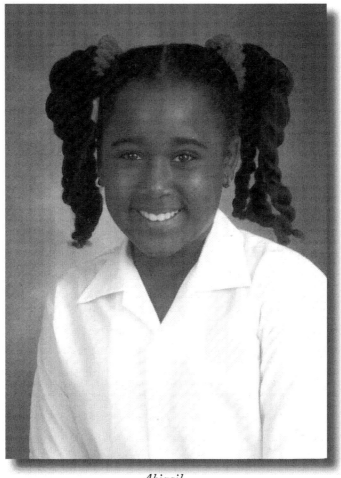

Abigail.

Caring

In April, we got a call from one of Palmer's relatives saying that Valerie, her sister, was ill and in hospital. We went to see her and the diagnosis was not good. This older sister, aged 62, had struggled with myasthenia gravis, an autoimmune condition, for most of her life. Whilst in the UK, she had been given very early retirement and had returned to Jamaica.

The myasthenia gravis was responsible for a number of associated complaints and the rounds of medication had been responsible for bringing on other complaints, which needed further drugs to control the side effects.

How does a medical condition get missed for many years while under doctor supervision? But Valerie had been missed. The news she had just been given – Stage 4 Colon Cancer – was devastating. Cancer, caught early, can be contained for varying times, dependent on the type and where it is.

We visited her a number of times, and on the way back home, I suggested to Palmer that what she now needed was care and attention, that she could not receive if she went back to her home.

We went to visit her and mooted the idea of her coming to live with us. Doctors had not given her much time, but playing God was not clever, and we felt that with a positive atmosphere around her who knows how long she could go on.

Her mind was made up; she was coming home with us. When we got home, Palmer made up her room; this was going to be hers for the foreseeable future. She was quite strong when she walked up the stairs for the first time.

From that day on, all our lives changed. Until you have cared for someone who is terminally ill, you have not cared for anyone. For eight months, we battled with specialists, mood swings, good days and bad days. But Palmer, at the expense of her own health, cared for her sister round the clock. Attending to her every need, sleeping when she could, changing her bedclothes sometimes five times a day. She ballooned with lack of training and pressure; there was no let up. As Valerie got weaker, so our attention to detail became more crucial.

She was afraid of pain, and we prayed silently for relief. When the time came for her to go, she did so with dignity.

She had a good send-off. The funeral was a bringing together, as usual, of a group of people who had waited until death to say how they felt.

It is important that you treat each day as if it your last. Over these years, I have lost so many friends, and you notice as you get older how your circle of friend diminishes. After our family's journey, it was time to pick up the pieces of our lives and get our togetherness back again.

Abigail graduated in June and was in the UK starting her first year of college. She was enjoying the challenge. She was specialising in Biology, Psychology, Sociology, and Maths. It was tough but she was learning to cope. Sharing a room with a stranger, getting to know others from differing nationalities, taking responsibility for timing.

She flew in specially to see her auntie off. There was real upset on her part as they had a special bond. Palmer did her mourning whilst caring for her sister, so there was no need for tears: it was time to move on.

It is not very often that I get the chance to take Palmer on one of my conference appearances, but I had an offer from Diageo who wanted me at the European conference in Barcelona. We made our way there and for one of the first times, she was able to see me in a different setting. Of the 2,500 people there, only 800 were from the UK. But once I arrived onstage. Everyone was on his or her feet from beginning to the very end.

I was a surprise element brought in over the 'death hour' after lunch to wake up all the delegates. It was a roaring success, and we spent 24 hours afterwards soaking up the atmosphere of a lovely city.

That October, 25 people came down from the UK, and once again we did the cycle ride across Jamaica in aid of Marie Curie. Did I find it easier this time? No, in fact it was tougher because since the last occasion, two years earlier, I had not ridden a bike. Where had the past two years gone? Time flies so very fast.

The second bike ride across Jamaica was challenging and rewarding, and it is just a great time to get together with some new people. They come on board, not only to raise funds for Marie Curie but also to chase their own personal demons. I have to thank Him above as I do not seem to have any of those personal problems anymore to deal with. The result is my life seems fairly well-balanced.

But, talking to a number of the participants, many had not bothered to raise the money via sponsorship to take part, but just paid the cost out of their own pockets, just to get away from all that was on their plate back home.

I am not too sure that it worked the way they had hoped, but getting outside the box and looking in does give some relief. Although temporary, it can recharge your battery.

Chapter 16: Tomorrow

So what am I doing now? My life has been charmed, so much has gone well. Although I have sold up in the UK, there is still demand for Mr Motivator there. So I travel there at least every six weeks. Work now is far more varied. I do far more of the spoken word, with less emphasis on the physical.

When I was a regular on television, the focus was on the physical, but now I am able to offer more through the spoken word. I respond happily to requests to deliver motivational speeches on a regular basis in the UK, so I practically live on a plane doing just that.

The crowds warming up to my routine at Bestival.

H'Evans Scent Staff

There is never sameness about any one day or week. Running H'Evans Scent is a continuous challenge. My staff of 22 is made up mainly of young men who, without this job, might have been back on the streets. They have given me such personal satisfaction. Many of them cannot read or write, so I guide and teach them the rudiments of life. I honestly believe that if you are not literate, you will forever be stuck in a time warp. So I pay for a teacher to come in twice a week and teach them to read and write. I firmly believe that more employers need to do exactly that, as the more we empower our employees and give them hope and create opportunity, then the greater the likelihood that they will remain, and if they don't, then at least we will be able to say that we gave them the chance to further themselves.

Most of the guys have taken up adult education programmes, and already I am seeing changes for the better, especially in their work attitude, speech and also in their respect for each other.

I recall, when we started, how it was almost impossible to get anyone to ever say that they were sorry. We worked on it, and slowly I could see the changes in them.

I also made the decision to pay them well, as my business is nothing without their support. H'Evans Scent's advancement is totally dependent on my staff; as they improve, so does the business. Needless to say, I value my staff and we make a terrific team.

Keeping Healthy

I look forward to many years to come. Health is my wealth, and I will continue to train every day.

I have invested in my health and I know that it is important for everyone to do the same. There is an old saying that I have held true over the years, which was used earlier: "Many a man has sacrificed his health in pursuit of wealth and then spent his wealth trying to regain his health. And all that he found was a grave." Therefore, it is important that we get our priorities right.

Our forefathers did not need to focus on exercise as most of their working environment was in the agricultural and manufacturing industry. But today in the Information Age, the computer industry has ensured a more subdued lifestyle, a slowdown in energy consumption.

Obesity has been the slow and silent killer, a problem facing many nations of the world. Countries such as China, that have never had obesity problems, now grapple with this challenge.

Recognising how living patterns have changed is important in trying to address what is a worldwide problem.

Kids were always out playing when the world was far more trusting. Now, with the 'sickos' out there, we ban the children from going outside. We are forced to drive them to school to ensure their safety. I remember walking with my mates for miles to get to school, that was part of our daily routine and that kept us fit.

The result of all this restriction is that exercise needs to be planned, as kids would rather sit in front of any available electronic screen. The same applies to adults who simply eat, sit, drive, and then eat again. We should be advised by this simple equation; energy output needs to be greater than what we are putting in. That is the secret to controlling our weight, and ultimately safeguarding our health.

I am very disciplined. I must exercise every day, and when I miss one session, I feel so guilty, I often wonder sometimes, if this was not my chosen occupation, would I be the same?

Thank God for the opportunity I grabbed, which has now been part of my life for some 32 years. I am warming up for the next 40 years.

Some Important Life Lessons

Here are a few gems that I have lived by:

- Never ever quit. You must keep on going, no matter how hopeless things may seem.

- Life will throw many hurricanes your way, but if you hold everyone closer to you, that will create a barrier against disastrous winds.

- Family is the most important thing we have, and we must never take anyone for granted.

- We must tell each other as often as possible that we care.

- We must share, not just what we materially have, but ourselves, because when we give of ourselves, it is the greatest gift.

- Never take long life for granted. Do all that you can to enjoy today, as this is the only moment we are sure of, and when tomorrow comes, that will be a bonus.

- Take time to share a rewarding experience and an inspiring thought.

- Call each other often, and find time to talk for at least 15 minutes.

- Ask how each person of a family is and be interested in how they are. Some people ask how we are and never wait around long enough to hear the answer.

- Never go to sleep with tension unresolved.

- Obstacles are what you see when you take your eyes off your goals.

- View every mountain as an opportunity to climb to the top, where the view is so much clearer.

- Remember my main motto: 'The Price of Success is Perseverance!'

In closing, follow your heart and do what makes you happy, no matter the consequences. Since moving to Jamaica the opportunities for growth across a number of areas have increased. I now have a number of projects on the go and each has the potential to be great. I realise that Mr Motivator, H'Evans Scent, and Paintsplash Jamaica will all be businesses that will go from strength to strength, and become a legacy for others to receive comfort, enjoyment, employment and training.

Thus H'Evan's Scent shall be an oasis for the community of Free Hill, high in this salubrious countryside, courtesy of me and my family... as we leave our footprints in the sand.

This is the Warm Up, and there is loads more to come. I look forward to sharing it all with you.

Tributes to my family and friends

I must now talk about my relationship with each member of my family and some of my friends.

Carolyne

Carolyne, you and I went through so many things together, from all the struggles that we had, and the tough time that you had with your stepmother. All the abuse that you suffered, I believe, has made you into a fuller person. I am pleased that you are happily married to Johnnie and are raising four wonderful children. Giving your life over to Christ, which surprised me at the time, seems to have given you strength and provided a focus for your life.

I really enjoy visiting with you and the kids when I visit Antigua, and I want you to know that you all have a special place in my heart.

You are so strong, sometimes difficult and argumentative, but these qualities will hold you steadfast and will stop you from being exploited. I know that you will survive, regardless of life's challenges.

James

James, my only son, I love you dearly. I have certainly gained from the struggle to keep you. It was not about winning, it was making sure that you received the best that life could offer.

I am saddened by the fact that things between your mother and I turned sour, but I am sure she would be pleased with the way you have taken control of your life and turned out with such exceptional qualities.

I was so happy to be at your graduation in 2006, where you gained a drama degree. You must never do things just to please me; do what pleases you.

You are warm, sensitive, creative and artful, and somewhat like your old man. This means the only problem you will ever have is choosing which direction to go.

There were times that I think I treated you a bit rougher than Carolyne, but that was because you had it easier than her. But that was because when you came along, I could afford to give you more, financially and emotionally.

In 2008, you have left the UK to be with Palmer, Abigail and me, and for us, this was the happiest that we have been in a long time. I was able to see you, touch you and be with you in a way that I have longed for. You have rekindled some of the missing joy in my life, and I am so glad that you are back in the arms of the family you have always needed, to be closer to the love that you knew existed. Palmer, Abigail and I thank you for your warmth and love.

You have many choices of where you can go, and with so much talent, you will need to sift and choose wisely in what you do.

Keep using that charm, that ability to win people over, the courage to face up to whatever life throws at you. You are a survivor, as your life so far can attest. I am now able to have such glorious repartee with you, and at last I feel more complete.

You have temporarily wandered away from what was your chosen course, and that is not a bad thing. Often we all must go on a sidewards journey to get to our ultimate goal.

Abigail

You will always be the apple of my eye, as you have grown in such a fabulous way. Your reasoning ability is exceptional, and at age 19 to be doing so well in all your studies, showed that you must have your mother's brains, as I still have mine.

You have demonstrated skills in art, singing, dancing, reading, and swimming. Your love for reading will one day pay great dividends, and you will rise to be among the best. Your warmth and smile will open many doors for you.

You will never be an athlete but you will win academically at most things. And the accolades will keep on coming. Keep on working and walking towards your future. Never let anyone's shadow block out your light. As you continue your education at Lancaster University, always remember that I have your back.

Abigail.

Ebony

So far, I have not said much about you. You are my adopted daughter, and my feelings for you are just as if you were my blood.

Choosing between right and wrong is a very important step in one's development, and I hope that you will endeavour to make good all that has gone bad in your life.

Let the past remain in the past, and seek after a good and wholesome life.

You have a wonderful knack of making people do whatever you want, so please channel these energies into a positive way, and then I am sure you will be justly rewarded.

With Ebony.

Palmer

The day that we met was an important day for all of us. You have been there from what seems the beginning, and we have walked, evolved, grown, cried, laughed and dreamed together. I have enjoyed our journey, and it is not a question of would we survive, but I know deep down, it is 'til death do us part.'

Your trust in me is humbling. You have been my most trusted supporter, and you have never leashed me. There has never been a time that I felt pressured to be anything other than who I am.

You are my right arm and I do not wish to ever imagine life without you. I have had many temptations from the world but I know where my heart and home are, and these are important to me.

We have travelled the world together, and then moved to Jamaica together. The decision to return was not as difficult for me as it was for you. But you stuck by me. I value your support and guidance over all these wonderful years.

I am amazed at your coping skills, through difficult and even life threatening situations. You are one tough lady and this has empowered Abigail and myself. The way you are able to impart and share knowledge is exceptional as I see James and Abigail sharing in your consistent love of reading and artistic expression.

I admire you in so many other ways.

I know that our bond is strong, when I realise that we have never had an argument in all our years together - I don't think I have ever had to tell you, "I'm sorry," and that is because we are attuned to each other. It is good that we do not take each other for granted; we anticipate each other's needs and avoid unnecessary confrontations.

It is your uniqueness that puzzles many ladies when they question your unconditional love for me. They will never fully grasp how we make things work. I have never given you an opportunity to mistrust me, and I now treasure the confidence that you have in me.

Enid

Enid, my birth mother, you are always on my mind. There are still some barriers deep in my subconscious, but I just cannot deny the fact that you are my mother. I don't resent you in any way; it is just that it is difficult to reconcile some things at this time.

Time heals many wounds and I know that in time, we will develop a mutual respect for each other. You are getting on now, but I plan to keep in touch and visit whenever possible. It is strange, but I am so grateful for the decision that you made when I was three months old. So I thank you unreservedly.

Meeting my birth mother, Enid.

Cherry

My adopted sister, I have not seen you as regularly as I would have liked. We were never very close, but there was a mutual respect for each other. Cherry, occasionally I think about you and your children, especially the struggle that you went through with bringing them up without a father. You did well by them, and I applaud you.

I wish you well, and may your convictions guide you and keep you. But I wish that you could just occasionally pick up the phone to say hello.

David

I brought you from Jamaica when you were young, and as such, I have always felt responsible for you. Soon enough, you will overcome your challenges, as you carve your place in life. Just keep on working. I know your broken marriage disappointed and hurt you, but every disappointment is a blessing. Sometimes, it is difficult to see how that can be, but it will all come clear in the end.

Reginald

You and I go back to Boys' Brigade. Even though we have not seen each other for a while, we are still inseparable. You are now remarried and I wish you all the very best that life has to offer. You will always be one of my closest mates.

Mercier

You are my closest and most faithful friend, and I cherish our 51 years of sharing. You have been an anchor in my life and such a good example to me. It is clear that God plays a very important part in your life. Your talent is there for all to see and I know that miles have kept us apart, but heartfelt feelings have kept us close.

I love the fact that you have always made me feel comfortable around you and you have never forced your beliefs down my throat. Because of your grace, many can see that you have something very special in your life. I know what it is; that is why I know that you are a special messenger. When I see you and your wonderful family, I know that you have something unique.

Center Parcs Gang

For 13 years, the fitness motivation weekends at Center Parcs was an essential part of my life. It was the meeting place of so many of my fans who became my friends. Religiously, some came to all six weekends. It was just a wonderful experience for so many who became my extended fitness family.

I appreciate the team of golfers who came on the weekend, not to join in my classes, but to make it a meeting place for the team leader and all his mates. I need to make mention of all the main individuals who were part of my weekend.

Lena and Brian, although you never got married, you are an example to most couples. I am happy that you became, and still are, my very close friends.

Roz and Elaine, two of the longest-serving members of my team, who travelled to many countries to teach and film. Thanks for all that you did. I hope you both find joy in whatever you do.

Emma, when you started with me, you were so innocent and green all at the same time, but I admire you as you grew in confidence, and appeared in many of my videos.

Ray and Julianna, two lovely people of varied talents. I wish you well.

Linda, you provided so much, learned information, especially in the field of clinical nutrition. I know that you will continue to look well and continue to be a picture of health and vitality. The close friendship we shared will always remain with me.

Kathy, your knowledge of how the body works was the foundation I needed to succeed. I so appreciate all the things that we shared. You are an inspiration, and I appreciate the guidance that you gave me.

Peter and Lavinia, I am convinced of the value of Tai Chi and the peace it has given you. I see the value of your lesson from the mystic East, and the high level of expertise that you showed, has remained with me.

Jose and Yvonne, your salsa was special, so different and so unique. I loved having you around and I gained so much from your presence.

Louise and Fiona, my two very special friends who shared lunches, dinners, walks and talks, trade shows, and so much. We will always be close, no matter what.

Heather, an old faithful of the Center Parcs movement. You are wise and I cherish the wonderful times we shared.

And to the others, I want to say that you are just as special as the ones that I have mentioned, you made my team complete.

Female Friends

Each of you has had a part in making me who I am. Occasionally you cross my thoughts, and I am happy that we parted as friends. I wish you well.

Boys' Brigade. I'm bottom left.

The Studio.

Kerry from Tumble.

Motivation team.

Bouncefit

Me.